The Prickly Rose

A BIOGRAPHY OF VIOLA FARBER

JEFF SLAYTON

Bloomington, IN Milton Keynes, UK

First published by AuthorHouse 11/16/2006

Printed in the United States of America
Bloomington, Indiana

This book is printed on acid-free paper.

ISBN: 1-4259-6550-4 (sc)

Library of Congress Control Number: 2006908653

Front Cover: Viola Farber in Mildred, *1971. Photographer: Jack Mitchell*

Back Cover: Viola Farber watching company rehearsal, circa 1976. Photographer: Susan Cook

Special Thanks

To Elisabeth Lanzl for her continuous support, encouragement and time that she took to help me revise this book. Without her, none of it would have been finished. I thank her too for the beautiful family photographs and memories.

To Irene Aikin for hanging in there with me for so long, and for all the wonderful family photographs and memories.

To Larry Clark, June Finch, Willi Feuer, Anne Koren, Margaret Jenkins Wax, Remy Charlip, and Sylvain Richard for taking time out from their very busy schedules to be interviewed.

To Karen Levey for all her love, support and hard work throughout a difficult time for us all following Viola's death. I will always be indebted to you.

To the Merce Cunningham Dance Foundation Archives for letting me search through and get copies of photographs, reviews and articles. Special thanks to David Vaughan for all his help.

To Ali Daniels for the many times she read rewrites and helped me find the correct words. Thank you, too, for helping me to keep going.

To Asa Roach for all the good laughs over the telephone, and for being so patient with a first time author.

To Jasper Johns for his love and generosity.

To all the Viola Farber dancers with whom I had many, many years of exciting, fun, and memorable times. You all live in my heart.

And of course, to Viola Farber herself. I cannot imagine where I would be today had I not met her, studied with her, danced with her, fallen in love with her, fought with her, and remained friends with her. I look forward to seeing her again the next time around.

Dedicated to the following people who forever changed my life:
Frances Wessells, Merce Cunningham, Margaret Craske,
and Peter Saul.

Table of Contents

Chapter Nine

Chapter Ten

Foreword

There were many events and people in my life that led me first into dancing and then eventually to meeting Viola Farber. Born in Richmond, Virginia, in 1945, I began dancing at the age of eight, during a time when not many boys knew about dancing, much less studied it. I was born with my right leg turned inwards from the hip, making it impossible for me to walk. Years of wearing a special shoe, sleeping with a bar between my ankles at night, and braces succeeded in straightening the leg, but also left it smaller and weaker than the left leg. The doctor who was treating me suggested to my parents that I be given dancing lessons to help strengthen the leg. He could have suggested sports, but instead he thought that dancing lessons would help heal the leg most quickly.

No one in my family even knew what "dancing lessons" meant, much less where to have me get them. In fact, no one in my family knew anything about the arts, period. My paternal grandmother played the piano, the banjo, and the harmonica by ear, but had never had any formal training in either. She could, however, play a mean boogie-woogie on the piano, and pick out any tune that she heard. Many an evening during my childhood was spent sitting next to that wonderful woman, Sally Slayton, watching the loose fat on her upper arms flapping away as she entertained us all with her music. Perhaps she is the one from whom I get my musicality. I would like to think so, anyway, as I loved her dearly.

At age fourteen, I joined a regional ballet company, Ballet Impromptu, which is now known as the Richmond Ballet, and I also began dancing in musical theater at the now-torn-down Lyric Theatre in Richmond.

After high school, I attended the Richmond Professional Institute, now Virginia Commonwealth University, and majored in Theater Arts. I loved acting, but not getting from it what dancing had given me, I dropped out after one year. At that time, a dance class was not even available there. Now, fortunately, there is a very thriving dance department at VCU.

Not knowing how to continue dancing, I went to work as a draftsman at the Virginia State Highway Department, where both my mother and my brother worked. I stopped studying dance, but taught tap and ballet classes once a week to children in Charles City, Virginia. I hated drafting. I detested wearing a white shirt and tie every day, and spending all day working on the portion of Route 66 that ran through northern Virginia. Whenever someone needed an errand run, my hand was the first to go up. I was ready to do anything to get out of the office.

After two years at the Highway Department, I was working a crossword puzzle one day instead of drawing the little houses, churches, and bushes on the Route 66 plans. Next to the puzzle was an ad announcing an audition for dancers at the Virginia Museum Theatre for the musical *Fanny*. I decided to try out, even though I had not taken a dance class in almost three years. The woman who led the audition was Frances Wessells, who, I was to learn, had worked with Hanya Holm in New York during the 1940s. Somehow I passed the audition and was cast as a dancer in the show. Soon I was spending my evenings after work in class and rehearsals. Frances always gave us a Hanya Holm-based warm-up, which was totally foreign to me. I had never heard of modern dance, much less studied it. I did find, however, that I liked it, and thought it was much more satisfying than ballet. I had been very good at dancing ballet, but considered it too restricting after taking these modern dance classes. I found that I could express my inner emotions more openly in modern dance, whereas with ballet I always had to be character other than myself.

I worked on another show with Frances Wessells, <u>Little Mary Sunshine</u>, at the Barksdale Theatre in Ashland, Virginia. During the run of that show, Frances told me that she thought I had talent, and that I should consider going to college again as a dance major. I had no idea that one could get a degree in dance. Frances told me about Adelphi University in Garden City, New York, that was only a forty-minute train ride away from New York City. If I went there, I could go into the city on weekends to take dance classes and to attend concerts. I was very poor, uneducated in the arts, and scared to death, but with Frances's help I sent in my application to audition. This was in the fall of 1965, and I was twenty years old.

In March of 1966, Frances and I drove to Adelphi University. Thirty or more dancers were there for the audition, which consisted of a dance technique class. We were divided into three groups and told that there would be a ballet barre warm-up and a modern dance movement phrase. I knew that I could do the ballet barre, but still felt insecure about the modern dance. My group was the last one to take the audition class. I noticed that I was the only male attending the audition; this made me very uncomfortable, and I came very close to leaving before the audition began. I had a long time to watch the other dancers warm up, and I did not think that the majority of them looked more trained than I. Once more, I did not relish the idea of being the only male in dance classes again.

What felt like hours later, my group was called in and told to take a place at the barre. As I took my place, I noticed a woman sitting next to the piano wearing a white turtleneck sweater, a dark blue, pinstriped skirt, and beige Hush Puppy shoes. She sat with her legs crossed, and her hair was parted in the middle and pulled back into a bun. It did not look like the type of buns that most female dancers wore. She had tucked her hair under, and at first glance this gave one the illusion that she had short hair. Just by looking at this woman, I knew that she was the person I had to study with. I somehow knew that this woman would lead me to the path that I had been seeking for many years. I felt that I had known her forever.

I finished the audition class, and as I was leaving the room, I asked the chairperson of the dance department, Harry Bernstein, whether I had been accepted into the program. I explained to him that I would need to apply for financial aid and would appreciate if he could tell me. He said that the faculty needed to get together and discuss the entire group, and that we all would be receiving letters in a month or so. This meant that I would not hear until April or May, and, if I was selected, it would only give me a few months to find the money to pay for the tuition. Back in Richmond, I had a job, but I had few or no savings. I was living with my lover, Chuck, who never seemed to be able to hold down a job. I was paying off a car loan and had a lease on an apartment. If accepted, I would have to give notice to my boss, split up with my partner, and sell my car, all in a very short period.

The woman whom I had seen sitting next to the piano was standing next to Harry Bernstein, and she had overheard my request. Flashing a huge smile, and waving her hand in the air, she said, "Of course he can come!" Mr. Bernstein turned bright red and stomped out of the studio. The woman smiled at me again and strolled out after him.

I returned to Richmond; gave notice to the Highway Department;

broke up with my lover, who threw a knife at me when I told him my plans; sold my car, and made plans to leave Richmond. Frances and I celebrated my good luck weeks before the official letter arrived stating that I had been accepted into the dance department at Adelphi University. I relied totally on the words of that one teacher, which gave me enough encouragement to begin making plans.

In September of 1966, at age twenty-one, I checked into a dormitory at Adelphi, registered for classes, and went to purchase my textbooks. I had been placed into the intermediate modern dance and ballet levels. On the first day of modern technique class, I found out that I was indeed the only male, not only in my class, but also in the entire dance department. As we were getting to know each other, I saw the woman who had given me the smile and encouraging words, walk into the studio and to the front of the class.

"Good morning, dancers." She said. "My name is Viola Farber and I will be teaching you once a week during this semester."

The next year changed my life completely. I never moved back to Virginia, and meeting Viola led me into a lifetime career in dance.

Viola Farber and I were friends for just over thirty-two years. For nine of those years we were married. Viola was warm, loving, intelligent, humorous, stern, and sometimes unforgiving. She was strong and stubborn, yet vulnerable. She had masculine traits, yet she was one of the most feminine creatures whom I have ever met. She had a wonderful sense of humor, and yet her dark moods sometimes sent her into the depths of depression. Her dancing was magical to behold. She had a presence, an "it", onstage that defies explanation. She was a master teacher, and, for this author and for many who saw her work, a choreographic genius. She loved dancing and it loved her back.

My hope is that this book will help those who did not have the pleasure of meeting Viola, seeing her perform, seeing her work, or studying dance with her to understand why so many of us respected, admired, and loved her. Viola did not keep very good notes on her work. She was terrible at dealing with paperwork and was not the least bit interested in becoming good at it. She had bad luck finding good managers. The good ones whom she did find did not stay with her very long because there was never enough money for salaries. She loved that dance left no debris behind, and was not all that interested in having her work survive after she had stopped choreographing. Upon her death, no videotapes of her company's repertory were found in her apartment. The only videotapes I found there were those of dances that she had choreographed for companies other than her own. She was never interested in reviving old works, only in choreographing new ones.

Viola's company materials were spread over three cities in two continents, the United States and Europe. Much of what I could find was not in very good order, but I have the former members of her company to thank for a somewhat complete list of composers and costume designers for many of Viola's dances.

Viola Farber disbanded her company in 1983, and she died in 1998. At present, there are no dance companies that have a work by Viola Farber in their repertory, with the exception of the Repertory Dance Theatre in Salt Lake City, Utah. Anyone interested in viewing a limited number of videotapes and films of her work may do so by going to the Dance Video section of the New York Public Library for the Performing Arts in New York City. Also, that library has a copy of the oral history of Viola Farber, compiled by Rose Anne Thom.

Besides, the legacy of Viola Farber lives on in the muscles of the dancers who were fortunate enough to have studied with her, and in the choreographers who were influenced by her work. Adjectives like mysterious, unique, astonishing, amazing, vulnerable, strong, and powerful constantly show up in articles, reviews, and statements by dance critics and people who knew Viola. Phrases like "blonde lovely," "possessing a body where the top half seems to move independently of the lower half," and "she has managed to create a new form of movement style all her own" appear more than once in descriptions of her dancing and her choreography. Critics could not seem to agree as to whether her work was violent, lyrical, or hard-edged. Perhaps it was all of those things. What everyone agreed on was that Viola Farber was definitely someone to be reckoned with, and to be admired. Many also agreed that she was a legend during her own lifetime.

Was Viola a mystery to those who knew her? Yes, but mostly, I think, she was a far larger mystery to herself. Never really happy, never really content, Viola was someone who will be remembered by many, and who will be placed among the greats in any serious book on dance history.

Viola was at the core of my being from the fall of 1966 until her death in the winter of 1998. I met her when I was twenty-one, and I was fifty-three when she died. She taught me more than just dancing. She taught me how to love and how to keep going even when that seemed impossible. Viola taught me about life. She is still very important in my life, and I hope that I will never forget the reason why. I hope that I never forget all the things that she taught me, and all the joy she brought to my life. If I had not met Viola, I would probably be living a very different life today.

In the following text, I have tried to describe not only Viola Farber the artist, but also Viola Farber the woman. My profession was not that of a writer, but I was Viola's closest friend, her husband for nine years, and her dancing partner for over twenty years. I hope that the dancers of the future will find the information included here to be helpful both to their studies of Dance History, and to give them an insight into what it took to survive in New York City during Viola's generation. I have also tried to convey the sacrifices that Viola made for her art. Dance was her passion and her life.

Chapter One

The Early Years

IN 1931, GERMANY WAS IN the midst of a depression, and it was the time when Adolf Hitler was rapidly climbing to power. The Expressionist Movement, led by the extraordinary dancer and choreographer Mary Wigman, had just appeared on the art scene in Germany, and in the United States, one of her students, Hanya Holm, had opened the first Mary Wigman School of Dance in New York City. Martha Graham, inspired by this new form of expressionist dance, began to choreograph in a way that was totally foreign to dance audiences in America. During this turbulent, but inspiring time, Anna Viola Farber was born on February 25, 1931, in Heidelberg, Germany. She was the youngest of three girls born to Eduard and Dora Farber.

Her father was born on April 17, 1892, in Brody, Galicia (Austria-Hungary, now in Russia), where his parents had traveled from their home in Leipzig, Germany. Although of Jewish decent, as an adult Eduard Farber never practiced that religion. He and his family rarely Attended church of any kind. When they did go, it was to a Protestant church. By 1931, Eduard Farber had obtained a Doctor of Philosophy degree in chemistry at the University of Leipzig. He had wanted to study philosophy, but his parents insisted that he select a more practical field. The couple settled in the old, picturesque university town of Heidelberg.

Eduard Farber was a tall, lean, but sturdy looking man. He wore glasses, and looked very much the intellectual that he was. At home he enjoyed playing chamber music with his wife Dora and their many friends.

During his life, Eduard Farber published several books related to chemistry, and the history of that science. The first was published in Germany and titled Die Geschichtliche Entwicklung der Chemie (1921), Berlin, Julius Springer. Others were published in the United States after he moved his family there in 1938. They included The Evolution of Chemistry (1952) New York, Ronald Press; Nobel Prize Winners in Chemistry (1953) New York, Schuman; Great Chemists (1961), New York, Interscience; Nobel Prize Winners in Chemistry 1901-1961 (1963), New York, Abelard-Schuman; Oxygen and Oxidation (1967), Washington, D.C., Washington Academy of Science; and The Evolution of Chemistry (1969), New York, Ronald Press. He received an Honor Award from the Washington Chapter of the American Institute of Chemists in 1954, and in 1964 the Dexter Award of the Division of the History of Chemistry of the American Chemical Society. In 1931, the year Viola was born, Eduard Farber held the position of Chief Chemist and Director of Chemical Research at the Deutsche Bergin and Holzhydrolyse A.G. in Mannheim-Rheinau.

Dora Schmidt was born on October 4, 1892, in Berlin. She was short and somewhat stocky in stature and wore her jet-black hair parted in the middle. With a strong interest in foreign languages, she had hoped to become an interpreter, but at the time that was not considered an appropriate field for a young lady. She therefore became a school teacher, but she never really enjoyed teaching. Dora and Eduard met at the home of friends in Düsseldorf, where both were working. Shortly before she and Eduard were married, she left her teaching job and never took on another, instead becoming a mother and housekeeper. Her interest in languages led her to study Italian and English. She also taught herself a considerable amount of Russian. Along with these talents, she loved music and played the piano quite well.

During the first twelve years of their marriage, Dora and Eduard became the parents of three girls, whom they named Elisabeth, Irene, and Anna Viola. Elisabeth had her mother's looks, but Irene and Viola had more of their father's features. What they all shared were beautiful large, straight teeth that flashed at one when they smiled.

Dora was a very loving mother, who was affectionately called Mutti by her three daughters. She had a very active social life in Heidelberg, and their upper middle class status allowed the Farbers, as was common at the time, to hire nannies to take care of the three girls, and maids to take care of the household chores.

A nervous person, Dora suffered with chronic stomach problems and insomnia. She was very aware and apprehensive of the Nazi movement in Germany, all too understandable considering the later events that took place there.

Eduard left the care of the house and children to his wife, but always took an active and stern role in the children's recreation and mainly their academic training and performance. He played the violin, but when his second daughter, Irene, became proficient at it, he gave up the instrument, and the violin became hers

Heidelberg is located north of the Black Forest, in a beautiful area in the southwestern part of Germany. Viola was much too young to understand what was going on politically around her. By all accounts, Viola was a very happy, talented child. She often spoke later of wonderful vacations with her family in Switzerland, lying in her bed at night in

Heidelberg listening to her parents and relatives play chamber music, and dancing, often falling asleep at night to this beautiful music. Later, Viola became a very accomplished pianist, and her love and knowledge of music influenced the way she used or did not use music in her choreography.

The Farbers usually went on long walks on Sundays. Sometimes these walks took them to the small village of Ziegelhausen, just outside Heidelberg, along the Neckar River, which flows through both Heidelberg and Ziegelhausen. Eduard Farber helped make these rigorous walks more enjoyable for his daughters by cleverly crafting stories. Their names appeared in each story, with specific inversions of letters. Elisabeth said that "…I am sure that there was always a specific moral that we were supposed to have conveyed to us in these stories, which we dearly loved. I wish we had records of some of them."

"He was a lovely, lovely man." Viola said.

There was an atmosphere of war in the air in Germany during the mid 1930s. Soldiers paraded on the streets, families had to practice blackout drills, and when the SA or the SS held parades near their schools, all of the children were required to go and stand on the sidewalks to watch. Elisabeth remembers that the inscription above the entrance to the main university building in Heidelberg was changed from "To the Free Spirit" to read "To the German Spirit." This was only one of the many alterations that illustrate the changing climate within Germany during that time.

On a hilltop behind the family's apartment building, the Nazis built a large amphitheater where they held festivities of which the young Farber girls were quite aware, although they had more important childhood things to think about at the time.

Viola and her sisters were baptized Protestant. There were already ministers who fought against the Nazis, and it was extremely dangerous to oppose the Nazis. This made it difficult to attend church without its becoming a political statement. "I guess that the church in Heidelberg where we would have gone was already polluted, so we didn't go," Viola related during one of our interviews.

Eduard Farber was very intent on his family doing things that were physically healthy. The girls had weekly gymnastics classes. Viola attended a private kindergarten and then the first grade in Heidelberg. At age six, she began taking ballet lessons. She was gifted at dancing and loved it very much. Her teacher, who was Russian, taught in the ballet school of Heidelberg's city theater, where at Christmas time the children danced in the productions of popular fairy tales.

Her teacher often gave the children sweets when they accomplished certain dance movements. "I got candy for doing the splits," Viola related. "And I was put on pointe immediately. I remember that my toes would bleed. There was some form of lamb's wool that one used at that time. This must have been 1937. I would take my pointe shoes off and undo whatever lamb's wool there was, and it was always full of blood. I don't remember that it hurt; I just remember that the pain was part of it, and it was fine. I loved doing it. It is probably fortunate that I didn't continue, because I had just started class. There's no way that my feet could have been strong enough to manage that, but I did."

Viola was extremely talented. The teacher asked Viola's parents whether the three daughters could perform in "Hansel and Gretel," but her parents refused because they feared that it would be discovered that the girls were half Jewish. In Germany at that time there was a law that no one with any Jewish blood could appear on stage. Because of the danger involved, Viola's mother did not like the idea of her daughters dancing, and so she was taken out of the school. Viola did not find out the real reason why she was taken out of dance classes until she was in her teens, but thought that the reason was that she was not good enough to dance. Therefore, she concentrated her energies on studying the piano.

On the long family outings, the Farber family sang songs, customary on such hikes. At the time of this writing, Irene still had a collection of these German "Wanderlieder" (hiking songs), and could sing them whenever she was asked. The family drove out into the country and hiked in beautiful meadows and forests. The girls made little wreaths for their hair from the wild flowers that they picked along the way. Elisabeth did not join in very often, but Irene and Viola knew how to do handstands and cartwheels. They would flip over, do back bends, or simply dance around as the hikes progressed. At home, Viola and Irene danced around the living room to their parents' musical accompaniment.

Viola once told me a wonderful story about how, as a girl of five years or so, her mother found her sitting in the middle of their living room crying. When asked why she was crying, Viola told her mother that she was upset because she did not have a beautiful tail like her cat. Her mother went into the attic and found an old boa. She tied it around Viola's waist, which let it drag along behind her. Viola said that she went around the house for days with that tail, and how much she loved Mutti for making one for her.

In 1933, Hitler and the Nazi party took power in Germany, and Eduard Farber decided that it was time to leave Germany, and to immigrate with his family to the United States. He was concerned not only for himself, but also because his wife was never discreet about expressing her hatred of the Nazis. One day, Dora noticed one of the maids acting strange and seemingly being ecstatic. When asked what was wrong, the maid said that she had just seen Hitler speak. Dora spat back, "Oh! So that's why you look so sick!" This was not a time when saying such things was safe. At any time, anybody could have reported her and she would have been arrested, or worse, would simply have disappeared without any explanation from the Nazis. Dora said these kinds of things anyway and then regretted them later. She would become terrified and sit and wait for the doorbell to ring.

From 1933 to 1937, the family's requests to leave Germany were denied. The Nazis knew of Eduard's accomplishments in wood chemistry and wanted him to continue his work on making sugar from wood products. He also was a consultant to firms interested in trying to find a commercial process for producing glycerin from carbohydrates. He was certain that these were the only reasons that he had not been singled out.

Eduard had no intentions of helping Hitler in any way. Finally, in 1938, he received permission to take his family to America. The condition of his acceptance, however, was that he would not be allowed to take very much money with him, and that he had to return to Germany in a few months. His German employer was a prominent industrialist, who felt strongly that the situation in Germany could not last, and that the Nazi party would be overthrown in a few months, or in a year at the latest. He was finally able to help provide the Farber family with the necessary papers to leave Germany, and round-trip tickets to and from America were purchased so that it appeared that the family would be returning to Germany. Dr. Farber, however, never planned on returning. He had left his life's savings with relatives in New Jersey, so that he could begin a new life once the family had safely left Germany. On July 19, 1938, the Farber family boarded the liner *Europa* in Bremerhaven, Germany. They did not realize it at the time, but the *Europa* was one of the last passenger ships that were allowed to sail from Germany before the start of World War II.

Viola vaguely remembered the train ride to the boat dock and the voyage across the Atlantic to New York. "It was a very strange thing.

Mutti tried to make it seem very exciting, because some members of her father's family had lived in Texas for many years. She'd say, 'Oh, I am so glad that we're going to America; that's where my relatives are.' She tried to sound upbeat and cheerful, while in reality she was terrified."

Viola had always been intrigued by nuns. She had a memory of seeing monks walking in a garden on her way to school in Heidelberg. Years later, she asked her eldest sister about it, but Elisabeth didn't know quite where that could have been. However, Elisabeth can remember monks walking near a monastery outside the city, reading their prayer books and chanting. Viola was fascinated by nuns because of the way they dressed. There were two nuns on the liner *Europa*, she recalled, "And they used to sit and read. I remember this very clearly." Irene added that Viola sometimes sat with the nuns on the ship and sang songs.

When Dr. Farber and his family arrived in the United States, he called his relatives in New Jersey to tell them that they had arrived. To his horror and dismay, Dr. Farber was told that his relatives were so certain that he would not be able to get out of Germany alive that they had spent all of the money that had been left with them. The money had been sufficient to see the family through a period of settling in the U.S., and now Dr. Farber was suddenly faced with the problem of completely starting over again in a foreign country. He had very little money, no home to take his family to and no employment, in spite of contracts he had established during several previous trips to the U.S.

At first, the Farber family lived in a small Methodist town, Ocean Grove, in New Jersey, and it was here that Viola and her sisters went to their first American schools. Viola was put into the second grade. Her mother having been a teacher had helped her daughters to learn some English. The girls had also had a tutor for English before leaving Germany.

Although they were a curiosity in this small community, the family members were treated well by the people of Ocean Grove. One of Viola's teachers, Mrs. Wilgus, was of German descent. She knew some German and helped the girls adjust. Viola turned out to be very gifted with languages, and at the age of seven picked up more English very quickly.

Besides having traveled extensively in the United States, Dr. Farber had letters of introduction which gained him entrance to a number of industrial laboratories, but none of these had openings for a chemist in his field. His talent and knowledge of wood chemistry, however, soon helped him obtain the position of director of research in a small laboratory of the Polyxor Chemical Company in New Haven, Connecticut.

In New Haven, Viola resumed piano lessons with an excellent teacher named Stanley Need. The family Attended the Plymouth Congregational Church, where Elisabeth learned to play the organ and sang in a high school girls' choir. Viola and her family became naturalized citizens of the United States late in 1944, when Viola was thirteen years old. It was during this year that Eduard Farber Americanized his last name, changing it from Färber simply to Farber, to make it easier for their new friends in America.

When Viola was in junior high school, her father's work caused them to move from New Haven to Washington, D.C., where he became the chief chemist at the Timber Engineering Company. He remained in that position until his retirement in 1957.

Viola studied French in high school, and because she already spoke German and English, the language came easily to her. She admitted to me much later, however, that although she had a very good accent when reading French aloud in class, if she was asked to translate what she had read, she had a very difficult time doing so.

According to her sister Irene, it was during her high school years that Viola developed a habit of not eating well, a habit that continued throughout her life. She was not overweight, nor was she anorexic or bulimic, but she clearly did not enjoy the process of eating. It was something that had to be done to stay alive, but not something that interested her very much. Viola hated to eat anything that had to be cut with a knife. She much preferred ground round to steak or, better yet, soups, salads, and fish. The latter, however, were never her first choice. A quick hamburger was far more appealing, and it took less time to eat. She preferred to spend time on other activities like reading or practicing the piano. Her mother was upset over this, and did not know how to handle the situation. Viola had a mind of her own and did things her own way.

Although Viola had not had any formal dance training since the age of six, she continued to dance on her own. She knew that it was her passion. However, having been told at the age of six, "No, you cannot do this anymore," left her with the feeling that she should not be dancing. "Perhaps it was this that made me want to stay away from it [dancing]. I don't know how traumatic it was. Maybe it was like having to blow your nose and not having a tissue." Viola had always thought that her parents had taken her out of the Christmas play back in Germany because she was not good enough. It was not until she was in her mid teens that she discovered the real reason they had taken her out. Even having had the truth finally explained to her, she was left with a deep-rooted insecurity about her talent as a dancer. Viola had focused her energies on the piano, and therefore, when it came time for her to go to college, she decided that music would be her vocation, and the piano her instrument. She applied to and was accepted at the University of Illinois at Champaign-Urbana. She only stayed there for one year, however, and never declared a major, but simply took courses in music. It was here that she stumbled across modern dance classes being taught by Margaret Erlanger, one of the pioneers of dance in American universities. Ms. Erlanger was the chair of the dance program at the University of Illinois, and she was responsible for the first dance artist in residence program in the country. The first dance artist whom she had hired was Merce Cunningham.

Some time during this first year of college, Viola took up smoking cigarettes. She said that it was while taking a swimming class for physical education that she had her first cigarette. Other women were smoking before and after the class, and for some reason it appealed to her, and by the end of that semester she was smoking up to a pack a day. Smoking affected Viola later on in her life. First, it must be said that it was not known then just how dangerous smoking was to one's health. Like most dancers of her generation, and others later for that matter, Viola smoked for several reasons. As many before her, she lit the first cigarette to "fit in" with her peers, and then it became a means for going longer without eating. Then it became an addictive habit, a stress reliever. She also had been experiencing increasingly severe migraine headaches, and she found that smoking temporarily eased the pain. Viola never used drugs, and she never had a huge weight problem, but it was not long before she was smoking close to two packs a day. Her family was horrified, but nothing they said or did changed Viola's habits. Besides, her father was a heavy smoker. She was independent and determined to make her own way, and her own mistakes.

Viola did not enjoy the Midwest and decided that for her second year of college she would return to Washington, D.C., and attend George Washington University. Her courses there included piano and dance. Her dance instructor was Erica Thimey, who recognized Viola's talent right away. She invited Viola to join her dance company, which performed primarily for children.

Viola's piano teacher, Emerson Meyers, once said to her that "Beethoven wrote music to keep the amateurs out!" Because she never found Beethoven easy to play, she feared that she might not live up to her teacher's expectations. Emerson Meyers also told Viola that she was a musical snob because she would sneer at practicing certain composers' works. "And I was!" She said. "There were some works that I really wasn't interested in learning. But I had to. It wasn't all wonderful music, you know. And I had a very good teacher by the name of Mr. Smith for music theory. We went through a book by [Paul] Hindemith, the German composer, who assigned 18ᵗʰ century harmony exercises. We had to do our assignments from this book. We'd go through them as soon as we could, and then he'd say, 'Now that was the rule at the time. Listen to this. This breaks all those rules!' I thought that was a wonderful way to learn. And he would encourage us to compose. He played music for us, Debussy, Ravel, and all those people, but he also played Cage. That was the first time I'd ever heard music by John Cage."

During this time, Viola played chamber music on Sundays at home with her father and two of his scientist friends. She continued to take courses in both music and dance, and although she was very intelligent, she was far from being academically absorbed. Beginning to enjoy dancing much more than piano, she concentrated on her modern and ballet classes rather than on practicing the piano.

With Mr. Smith's encouragement, however, Viola wrote songs, both the lyrics and the music. Mr. Smith was very sorry to learn that she wanted to dance. He recognized her potential as a musician and as a composer. Viola excelled in both piano and dancing, which made her choice of careers very difficult.

After one year, Emerson Meyers, Viola's favorite professor, left George Washington University to teach at a Catholic university which had a wonderful music department. Viola was considering following him there when she came across an advertisement in the <u>Saturday Review of Literature</u> for Black Mountain College in North Carolina. The ad made it sound like a place where she could study both dance and music. She did not know at the time that choosing to go to this small, but very progressive college in the Smoky Mountains would change her life forever.

*Dora Farber,
family photograph,
Germany,
April 1919.*

*Left to right:
Viola's sister
Irene, Viola
at age 6
months,
Dora Farber,
Elisabeth;*

*Left to right: Eduard Farber, Dora Farber, Anna (Nanny),
Elisabeth, Viola, and Irene on a family walk, Germany, 1934.*

*Viola at age 2 (center) with her sisters Elisabeth and Irene;
family photograph, Heidelberg, Germany, 1933.*

Left to right: Elisabeth, Viola, Irene; family photograph, Heidelberg, Germany, circa 1935.

Left to right: Irene, Elisabeth, Viola at age 4, Eduard Farber; family photograph, Ziegelhausen, Germany, Spring 1935.

Left to right: Elisabeth, Eduard, Viola, Irene; family photograph, Heidelberg, Germany, 1937.

Farber family boarding the ship Europa to sail to America. Left to right: unknown Woman, Irene, Elisabeth, Eduard, Viola, Dora; family photograph, Brennerhaven, Germany, July 19, 1938.

Farber family at dinner aboard the passenger ship Europa *while sailing to America; family photograph, July 24, 1938.*

*Viola at age 12;
family photograph,
New Haven, Conn., 1943.*

*Viola at age 20;
family photograph,
Washington,
D.C., 1951.*

Viola in Washington, D.C.;
family photograph, 1952.

Heidelberg, Germany; family photograph.

Chapter Two

The Cunningham Years

VIOLA ENROLLED AT BLACK MOUNTAIN College in 1951, at age twenty. The first person she met when she arrived on campus was the musician and composer Nick Cernovich. Modern dancer and choreographer Katherine Litz taught there at the time, as did the poet Charles Olsen. But it was the resident dancer and choreographer Merce Cunningham, along with musician and composer John Cage, who would most influence Viola's life at this time.

"When I first arrived at Black Mountain College, we drove up in a cab to this rather dilapidated building, and Nick Cernovich came out of the dining hall, dancing away, and he took my suitcase and said, 'I'll take those!' He took me to another dilapidated building which was my dormitory, where the boiler used to break down and we'd have to move to other buildings."

During the year that Viola was there, the curriculum at Black Mountain College was very open and somewhat disorganized. Students could create their own class schedule. Part of the duties for each student included taking turns cooking meals, serving in the dining room, or cleaning up in the cafeteria. I heard Viola mention many times to people interviewing her about Black Mountain College that her main job there was cutting up the okra that they ate for dinner.

"...everyone was supposed to spend, I think, three afternoons a week, doing what work needed to be done to maintain the college. There'd be a list on the wall in the dining hall about what you were to do, and with whom," she told me.

I asked what part of her experience at Black Mountain most affected her work later on. I expected a long and detailed answer. Instead, Viola simply gave a humorous questioning response followed by a huge smile and laughter. "Well...the lack of any kind of apparent organization?" Although Viola's later choreography often appeared chaotic, her work was extremely organized, but perhaps this is what she was referring to.

In describing her classes with Katie Litz, Viola told me that Katie would come into the studio, sit down in front of the class, and instruct the students to improvise movements for a while. Later, Katie would say that she was going to leave for a few minutes, and when she got back that they would improvise! Viola felt that the classes were extremely loose in structure, and that what the students mainly did was improvise. Viola added, however, that watching Katie Litz dance was an extraordinary learning experience. It inspired Viola to observe this incredible woman move about the dance studio, running at full speed only to "stop on a dime" at will without a quiver. From Litz, Viola learned to take a simple movement, improvise on it, and come up with longer and more complex movement phrases. Katie Litz was a unique dancer, a description that Viola would later be given by other dancers, choreographers, and critics.

During her year at Black Mountain College, Viola took piano lessons with composer Lou Harrison. "They were torture for both of us," she said. "We would do anything to get out of it, like I'd say that I had a sore throat and he'd say that he had to go into town. But he would encourage me to give little piano concerts, and I was a competent amateur. I was very musical, but I didn't play the piano that well. The whole college would come to listen to me play Mozart and Chopin badly."

Viola continued. "Then there was Charles Olson's class, one of the first days I was there. I was terrified when I first went there because here were all these guys with beards and they all seemed terribly....not just bright, I somehow had the impression that everybody knew about everything, things I'd never heard of....I just didn't even know there were such things, never mind knowing anything about them. And I was very impressed. Then I realized that what they knew a lot about was only this one little thing (their own subject) maybe."

One day it was announced that Merce Cunningham was coming to Black Mountain College to teach. Viola knew of Cunningham from a very small photograph of Cunningham in the Borzoi Book of Modern Dance by Margaret Lloyd.

"I decided for some reason that I had to study with Merce Cunningham." Viola told interviewer Donna Faye Burchfield. I had no idea what that was, but I decided that that was what I wanted to do, and I took class with Merce."

Once he arrived, Viola sneaked into the studio at Black Mountain College and watched Merce Cunningham rehearse. She had never seen anyone move like this man did, nor had she ever seen a dance movement that did not appear to have a storyline. His work looked to her like random movements thrown together haphazardly.

"I was just fascinated by Merce and what he did. I didn't like it very much, but I thought that it was amazing, and that I would like to learn to do it." She thought that he was one of the most incredible dancers whom she had ever seen, and she never could guess where he was going next. His technique was exquisite, but not always visible, meaning that the movement he danced did not always look like it required a strong technique, when, as any dancer knew, it really did. He used his technique as every dancer should; to let the expression of the art of dance come before that of one's technical abilities.

Viola also often sneaked into the music hall to listen to David Tudor practice the piano. "He practiced the piano and instead of playing scales, to warm up his fingers, he would play late Beethoven, which is extremely difficult music to play. We used to sneak into the dining hall, lie under something, and just listen. It was beautiful," Viola said, looking as if she could still hear David Tudor playing.

Viola also had her first affair while at Black Mountain. She fell in love with a jazz musician by the name of Jay Watt. The relationship was not too heated at first, but by the end of the year they were considering living together. The one thing that bothered Viola about Jay, however, was his drinking.

Viola said that some of the old buildings at Black Mountain College seemed to be haunted. She never actually saw any spirits, but repeated several stories of hearing loud banging and crashing when she knew that she was alone in the dormitory where she was staying. Once during spring break, when most of the campus population was away, she and her room mate locked themselves in their dormitory all night because the sounds coming from downstairs were so awful. When they went downstairs the next morning to see what damage had been done, there was absolutely nothing out of place and no sign of what could have been making all the noise. If it had been wild animals in the building, there would at least have been signs of things having been turned over, or cabinet contents spilled on the floor. There was nothing.

Other artists at Black Mountain College at the time included painters, poets, potters, composers, choreographers, and writers. Some of the now famous people who were there the year Viola attended were

Robert Rauschenberg, Cy Twombly, Max Dehn, Charles deKooning, M.C. Richards, Franz Kline, Hilda Morley, Hazel Larsen, Flora Shephard, and Johanna Yalowitz.

The lack of structure at Black Mountain College both intrigued and frightened Viola. She had been raised in a German family, with everything having a strict form and many rules that had to be obeyed. However, she soon began to enjoy this new way of looking at life and at art.

By the end of her year at Black Mountain College she decided to move to New York City to continue studying with Merce Cunningham. This had been her third attempt at completing college, and her third time leaving the world of academia without finishing work for a degree. Viola's parents were not too happy about her decision, but they were always supportive of whatever decisions she made regarding her career goals. Shortly after classes ended at Black Mountain College and after a short visit to her parents in Washington, D.C., Viola packed her bags once again and headed off for New York City. Jay Watt followed her to New York; however, because of his drinking, their relationship did not last.

Viola's sister, Irene, remembers that her family had mixed feelings about the move, and about Viola's career choice. "If I had an attitude about it at all, it was that Viola would and should do what she wanted. I regretted that our paths would diverge even more, but by then we were all used to a great degree of independence from each other.

"I knew how much it meant to Viola to be doing what she was doing, from a conversation between her and my friend, Trude, during a visit to my family, near San Francisco: We were driving to the ocean, a half hour from my house, Viola marveling at the scenery and lack of traffic, when Trude suggested she should consider moving to San Francisco, where there was great interest in modern dance, and in the arts in general. Without hesitation Viola answered, 'I wasn't cut out to be a pioneer.'" At this time, there was not a great deal of dance going on in San Francisco, or at least that was the impression New York dancers had of dance on the west coast.

Irene does remember that their father was not very pleased Viola going to New York to become a dancer, but that their mother was very proud of her. Viola told Irene that she felt that her father viewed her as a sort of clown. This feeling haunted her for many years. Irene put it this way:

"In my experience, as we became adults, our parents gave us their views and opinions about our various plans, but did not demand our compliance. They were remarkably accepting of our pursuing different paths.

"Knowing of the more lax sexual mores in the New York artists' culture, they were concerned about Viola's possible lifestyle. Years later I heard from Viola that our mother had already thought of the problem of, perhaps, a child "out of wedlock." Her solution: 'Bob and Irene can adopt it.' To this I would happily have agreed."

Viola's father was apprehensive about Viola living in New York without sufficient money. He worried that she might live in an unsafe neighborhood where she could possibly get mugged, raped, or murdered. He felt that a more lucrative career, such as one in science, was the more acceptable and obvious choice, and that she would then meet a nice man, marry, and settle down to a more "normal" life of raising a family.

"Our mother, who resented for the rest of her life that her parents had forced her to become a school teacher, much against her own wishes, must have been more ready to give in to Viola's wishes." Irene said. "Besides, our mother was well aware that this daughter had a will and determination stronger than her own. Our father, I imagine, would have agreed that she should follow her chosen path, but with misgivings and a lack of enthusiasm."

The fact that New York was not too far from Washington, D.C., eased Viola's parent's minds somewhat. She went home often for visits, and, as Irene pointed out, she could visit her parents much more often than could she or Elisabeth. Elisabeth was married, with two children, and was living in Chicago. Irene was living in Woodside, California, with her husband and family. Viola was especially good about visiting her parents during the traditional holidays.

"Another bond between them was that our mother continued to sew and knit for Viola. Apparently, help with clothing was acceptable, but help with feeding was not." Irene added, "Our parents were greatly concerned about Viola's health: the smoking, excessive physical strain, irregular hours, and poor nutrition. I don't know if our parents knew that for a long time, as she told me, she subsisted mainly on honey, nuts, and yogurt. They were upset at Viola's refusal to let them help her; she had a need to prove to them that she could make it on her own.

"Ever since high school we were concerned about Viola's health, but our mother felt defeated, saying that she was unable to prevail against her stubborn will. Yet in other contexts theirs was a relationship of great mutual love and respect," according to Irene.

Once in New York, Viola had to find a way of earning a living, which was not easy. Like many other dancers before her, she waited on tables, worked at temporary jobs for insurance companies, and even had a job as a "Stage Coach Lovely" in a bar in New Jersey, where she had to perform and then sit in the bar with the customers between shows. Viola had a very womanly physique. Her hair was dark blond, and her eyes were hazel, often appearing quite green. She had full, sensual lips and, in the photos of that time, an often sad expression on her face and in her eyes. For whatever reason, Viola was not comfortable with her beauty, and she often hid it by not wearing makeup, parting her hair down the middle, and pulling it tightly back into a bun. She did not have a typical dancer's body; she was tall, with full breasts and shapely hips. Long-legged, Viola's physique would have turned many heads, had she not hidden her body underneath loose dresses or, more often than not, old denim jeans and sweaters.

All of this caused her to look somewhat severe and unapproachable, but it worked to her advantage at the bar to keep the customers from pawing her. The bar owner, however, was not pleased. Part of Viola's job was to mix with the customers and to get them to spend money on drinks and tips. She was not about to prostitute herself for anyone, and because the customers were not spending money on her for drinks, the "Stage Coach Lovely" job did not last long.

A big financial problem was that of paying rent. Viola managed to find a very small apartment on East 1st Street between 1st and 2nd Avenues. In the early 1950s, this was far from being a good area for a young single woman to be living in, and coming home alone from work late at night. Most of the money Viola earned went toward rent and dance classes, and when she had to choose between eating a meal and taking a dance class, dance always won. She lived in a cold-water flat, meaning that there was no hot running water in the apartment, and also often that she had to share a bathroom down the hall with all the other tenants on her floor. Bath water had to be heated on the stove. Her apartment was on the top floor of a six- walk-up. Thus, after taking a dance class and working on her feet all day, often without eating, she had to walk home and up six flights of stairs to an apartment where she couldn't even soak her aching body in a hot bath.

There was one awful experience that took place during the time that Viola lived in this apartment. Every night, she saw another young woman in the apartment that was directly across the street from hers.

She did not know the woman, but they sometimes waved to each other. Viola thought that the woman lived alone because she rarely saw anyone else moving around in the apartment with her. One day, some months later, the woman did not appear at her window and Viola assumed that she had moved. A few days later, Viola read in the newspaper that a young woman had been found murdered in her apartment. The address was given, and Viola knew that it was the woman who used to wave to her. Knowing that a murder had taken place close by, and to someone to whom she had a connection, frightened Viola a great deal, and she was terrified to go home alone.

Luckily, Viola soon met other dancers at Merce Cunningham's studio and was able to move to a somewhat nicer apartment with a roommate. That roommate was Susan Capland, later Susan Rossin, a woman who would become Viola's closest and dearest friends for more than 40 years.

Soon Viola found a better way to pay for her dance classes than doing a lot of temporary jobs or dancing in bars. Because she was a very good pianist, she made an arrangement with Merce Cunningham to play for some of his classes in payment for some of the classes that she took. She also played for Anthony Tudor's ballet classes at the old Metropolitan Opera House, along with those of Margaret Craske. Anthony Tudor told Viola that he enjoyed her music for ballet classes, as she "played like a man!" What he heard in her music was Viola's passion for movement and the power in that passion. She wanted to be taking the classes, not sitting down to playing for them, and so her great love and talent for dancing was coming through her music. Margaret Craske soon became Viola's main ballet teacher, and influential in even more ways than just dancing.

A story that Viola often told regarded her classes with Merce Cunningham. She did not play very often for him, and one day she asked how much she owed him for taking class. Cunningham took out a black notebook, looked inside, and told her that she didn't owe him any money. Several weeks passed, and Viola saw that same black notebook lying on a table in Cunningham's studio. When she looked inside to check what she owed, she discovered that it wasn't his accounts book. "There was absolutely nothing written in it!" Viola laughed.

Viola also played for dance classes at the New Dance Group on Forty-Seventh Street. These were classes taught by Bertran Ross, one of the lead male dancers in the Martha Graham Dance Company, and Sophie Maslow, another member of the company. Because Viola had never seen a Graham technique class, she arrived early and waited to talk to Bertran Ross about the type of music he wanted for his class.

She waited and waited for Mr. Ross to arrive. The dancers who were taking the class began to fill the room, stretching out on the floor and chatting with each other. They seemed totally unaware that Viola existed; much less that she was the new dance musician. As the time for the class to begin approached, Viola became more and more nervous because she knew that there would not be time to talk to Mr. Ross beforehand. Finally, at the exact time that the class was scheduled to begin, Mr. Ross walked into the studio wearing a pair of dark sunglasses and carrying a cup of coffee. He walked right past the piano without acknowledging Viola, and sat down in a chair at the front of the class. He then placed his head in one hand, and said, "And."

She didn't even have time to think, "And, what?" Viola had to begin playing. All that she could do was to watch the dancers on the floor and follow them. She had no idea what kind of music she was expected to play, or in what meter or at what tempo. Although it was agony for her, she got the job, and with this new income, Viola could continue to pay for her classes with Merce Cunningham.

During Viola's first year in New York, Cunningham formed his first formal company of dancers. He had worked previously as a soloist, collaborating with his life partner, John Cage, and working with different dancers on specific projects. Viola was asked to be part of the original company. Just as she was fascinated with Cunningham's dancing; he was very much intrigued with hers; he had not seen anyone like her.

"It was in the early 1950s that I first encountered Viola," Cunningham said. "It must have been in class, she a student, and I her teacher. There was this amazing looking young girl. The angular way that she had of moving, one part arriving after another. You were never quite sure, watching her, if they would make it, but it was difficult to take one's eyes off her. She could only be described in old fashioned terms as a 'loose-limbed lovely.' Coupled with this odd distortion was an acute rhythmic sense."

She was not technically strong at that time, but possessed a way of moving that was totally unique. Her body was extremely flexible, her leg extensions high. She also had a sensual feminine body, rather than the often rail-like stereotype of the female dancer. Her body did not have any excess weight, but she had soft curves. She had feet that all dancers would envy: Her unusually high arches were dubbed "Golden Arches" by dancer and choreographer Gus Solomons, Jr. When Viola stood on full releve, she often appeared to be on pointe. Her ballet classes with Margaret Craske not only allowed her feet to look beautiful, but they helped to strengthen them and support the work that was required for Cunningham's strenuous choreography.

One day, Miss Craske taught a very fast allegro phrase across the floor. Before letting the class begin, Miss Craske said to Viola, "Now, Viola," in her high-pitched English accent, "I know that this phrase will be extremely difficult for you, not only because you are a modern [dancer], but because your feet are quite large!" Although close to tears from the remark, Viola decided to do her best. One can only guess that, if she felt, and even appeared, somewhat awkward, it would have been an amazing experience to watch Viola dance that movement phrase. It may not have been pure classical ballet, but one can bet that it was beautiful dancing.

By the summer of 1953, after several years of working alone, Merce Cunningham asked Viola to join his newly formed company. He took a teaching position at Black Mountain College that summer with the understanding that he would bring his small company of dancers, and that he could use studio time to choreograph and rehearse. The first group of dancers in his company included such dance legends as Carolyn Brown, Remy Charlip, Viola Farber, Paul Taylor, Anita Dencks, and Marianne Preger (later, Marianne Simon). Other dancers who performed with the company that first year included Joanne Melsher, Deborah Moscowitz, Timothy La Farge, and Ethel Brodsky.

The dancers received no salary. This monetary situation was something to which Viola was to become accustomed while working with the Cunningham company in its early years. They did not dance for money, but for the love and joy of being able to work with Cunningham. During a light, joking moment, the women in the company agreed that in order to dance with Cunningham they had to swear nun-like vows of Poverty, Chastity, and Obedience.

Carolyn Brown remembers those early days, meeting Viola first in New York and later on the trip to Black Mountain College.

"I think that I first met Viola in Merce's classes in New York in 1952. And it was in this funny studio that wasn't his, but which he rented from Stuart Hodes. It was the first year that I was in New York. At that time, Marianne Preger Simon was there and Joanne Melsher and Remy Charlip, and me. It was at this time that we all met and when that little nucleus of dancers formed.

"I was going to Julliard at the same time that I was studying with

Merce." Carolyn added. "Two of the people there, Paul Taylor and Anita Dencks, were at Julliard too, and they were curious about him. Paul had heard all these rumors about him, and so they came down and took a class with Merce. At the end of that year, in the spring of 1953, Merce asked a number of us if we would like to go to Black Mountain College. Paul, Anita, and Viola went for the whole summer as students and Joanne, Marianne, Remy, and I went for the last three weeks as sort of Merce's fledgling company. Anyway, the four of us were not paid. We paid our own way down there, and Merce took no salary so that we could go. He taught for nothing for the whole summer.

"Viola had a scholarship," Carolyn continued. "She never knew I think, who gave it to her, but suddenly her whole tuition and board were paid. Paul [Taylor] thought he had a scholarship, but at the end of the summer they gave him a bill. He couldn't afford to pay, so in essence he did get a scholarship. I think the only person who was actually paid to be at Black Mountain was Anita."

The first performance of the Merce Cunningham Dance Company took place at Black Mountain College. All of the choreography was by Cunningham, and the program for that first performance was:

Banjo
Music: Louis Moreau Gottschalk
Costumes: Remy Charlip
Dancers: Merce Cunningham, Carolyn Brown, Viola Farber, Joanne Melsher, Remy Charlip, and Paul Taylor

Dime A Dance
Music: *The Whole World*, 19th century piano music, selected by David Tudor

33

Costumes: Remy Charlip

Dancers: The company

Septet

Music: *Trois bordeaux en forme de poire* by Erik Satie

Costumes: Remy Charlip

Dancers: Merce Cunningham, Carolyn Brown, Viola Farber, Anita
Dencks, Joanne Melsher, Remy Charlip, and Paul Taylor

Back in New York, Viola again went about searching out odd jobs so
that she could pay her bills. The Cunningham company only paid her
for performances, and in the first years of its existence, those were few
and far between. The company rehearsed all year for one performance
in New York, which was then canceled at the last minute. The dancers
received no pay. Luckily, Viola had Susan as a roommate with whom
to share the rent. Together they scraped up enough money to eat, even
if the food wasn't always nutritious or plentiful. The friends that Viola
made during those early years in New York remained her friends for life.
Outside the Cunningham company, her closest friends included Susan
Capland (Rossin), Peter Saul, Loren (Tex) Hightower, Paul Taylor,
Bunty Kelly, Marie Adair, Sally Wilson, and Donald Mahler. They all
studied ballet with Miss Craske, and they often lived within blocks of
each other.

Margaret Craske was a master ballet teacher who taught at the Old
Met along with Antony Tudor, and with whom many of the Cunningham
dancers studied in New York. Miss Craske had grown up in England,
and had had a long career as a ballerina with the Ballets Russes during
the time of Diaghilev and Cecchetti. She had once owned a flourishing
school of ballet in London, and taught for the Sadler's Wells Ballet
Company (later the Royal Ballet). Miss Craske choreographed for the

Carl Rosa Opera as well. She moved to America in 1946. In New York, Miss Craske taught for American Ballet Theatre, and then for many years she was assistant director of the Metropolitan Opera School of Ballet. Finally, she taught for the Manhattan School of Ballet.

Other artists that became life long friends with Viola were the painters Jasper Johns and Robert Rauschenberg. Rauschenberg was at Black Mountain College for a while and later became the art director for the Cunningham company.

When one friend went on tour, another took care of watering plants or feeding pets. Viola had a solid-black female cat, which she named Miss Kitty. Susan or one of her other friends cared for the cat while Viola toured. Miss Kitty soon became very jealous of Viola's time, and did not like it at all when she traveled. Viola told me that whenever she took her suitcase out to pack for a tour, she had to keep the top closed, or else Miss Kitty would jump into the suitcase and urinate on her clothes. Viola took this as a form of punishment from her cat for leaving her.

When asked whether she was proud of Viola's being in the Merce Cunningham Dance Company, her sister Irene said, "I had been proud of Viola from the time she was born. Our mother was proud of her success. Our father had his usual reservations."

Elisabeth said that she was very "impressed that my sister would enter the Mecca of the arts in the United States. However, it was a world that I knew little about, so all I could do was to wish her well. I had not heard of Merce Cunningham before Viola joined the company, but I certainly, and I am sure to her family members as well, became extremely proud of her for being in such a prominent and innovative company.

"I know that our parents were extremely concerned over Viola's health. I wonder whether they did enough to help her out during her several illnesses and frequent periods of unwell. I myself didn't know until you interviewed me for this book what frightening episodes of sickness she had in New York."

Elisabeth's last statement shows again how independent Viola was, even at a very young age. She was a single woman living in New York alone during a time when not many parents would have allowed their daughters even to consider such a lifestyle. It also causes one to wonder whether Viola even told her family how poor she was and how often she was getting sick from not eating properly, or living in cold water flats with little or no heat during the winters.

Viola also worked with other well known choreographers during those first years with the Cunningham company. One was Paul Taylor, whom she had first met in 1952 during her first year in New York. Viola spoke of only one dance in which she performed with Taylor, and that was before his talent as a choreographer was well known. The dance was titled *Jack And The Beanstalk*, and its performance turned out to be the very first one of the newly formed Paul Taylor Dance Company.

"It was in the fall or winter in New York after our return from Black Mountain, and the piece had begun as a composition class assignment. Merce taught composition classes at Black Mountain, because it wasn't just the company there, but there were other dance students as well. It was a chance dance that each of us made that we had put together," Viola said of the performance with Taylor.

A chance dance is one in which the movement is randomly put together. There are many methods of going about that process. Merce Cunningham uses I-Ching to help him select the order in which movements are put together, which section of a dance is to follow which, or who will perform certain movements. Other choreographers may write movements down and toss them into a hat, and the order of the movements is determined by randomly selecting these pieces of paper.

In *Jack And The Beanstalk*, Viola danced the role of Jack's mother, with Paul Taylor dancing the role of Jack. She wore a pair of under drawers and a sleeveless T-shirt. Diagonally across her chest she wore a sash, like the ones worn by beauty pageant contestants, with letters spelling out the word MOTHER. The piece was performed at the Masters Institute on the upper west side of Manhattan. She told me that she had pictures of *Jack And The Beanstalk* somewhere among her belongings, but did not know just where they were. Although extremely organized, Viola often forgot just where a lot of her highly organized items were stored. The photos were never found.

Another dance in which she performed, and one which she remembered fondly, was called *Dracula*, choreographed by Katherine (Katie) Litz.

"I had been in Merce's company for several years, I think, when I danced in *Dracula*. I remember because I once found a telegram from Merce wishing Remy [Charlip] and me 'good luck.' We performed it at Hunter College or at the YMHA," she said. Viola danced the role of one of the vampires and Remy Charlip the role of the doctor. She found it an extraordinary experience to work with Katie Litz after working with Merce Cunningham. She commented,

"When working with Merce one came into rehearsal and he said, 'Do this, do this, do that,' and you did this, this, and that. And if you didn't do it quite right, Merce would say, 'Oh! OK. then try this.' The implication was always that if you couldn't do it the first time that you would never be able to do it.

"With Katie, we would go into rehearsal and she would think for hours and hours about what was the best foot to step on to do such and such, and I would think, 'Oh, my gosh, Katie, just decide which foot and we'll all try to do it and we might even succeed.'

"And there was that wonderful thing that Remy always use to quote that she used to say as we were rehearsing a kind of crowd scene. Which was, 'Now? During the performance we will improvise this section, but for now let's just improvise.'"

Viola laughed after telling this story.

"I remember David Tudor would come into rehearsals because the music was a Charles Ives piano sonata," she continued. "We spent a lot of time sitting around drinking tea, and then we would rehearse. What was also a very nice change [from working with Cunningham] was, if a dancer could come up with something, she would talk about it and then we would sort of play. If you had an idea about what you wanted to do for that section, one would say let's do this or that, and Katie might see it and say, 'Oh, yes. Do that.' So, in a way we had more to do with making our own roles."

Viola had a wonderful solo in the Cunningham work titled *Antic Meet* (1958), in which she was required to carry a set piece designed by Robert Rauschenberg. David Vaughan wrote in his book titled <u>Merce Cunningham: Fifty Years</u> (Aperture, 1998):

> A solo for Farber, no. 3 in the original scheme (for Antic Meet). Instead of providing the "bundles" that Cunningham had envisaged, Rauschenberg gave her an open umbrella with Christmas tree lights inside it - a fantastic, beautiful object. The dance was much as Cunningham described it, a gradual crossing of the space with sudden changes of direction and many small movements of the feet - something Farber was superbly equipped to perform.

Viola said that the umbrella was extremely top-heavy because of the battery attached to power the lights, and that it was difficult to perform with, but no one who saw the solo was aware of her having any problem.

The period was an extraordinary time in the history of the Merce Cunningham Dance Company. Some say that these were the best years artistically for the company. Financially, however, it was the most difficult time. Often the company was subsidized through the selling of paintings by Rauschenberg. The collaboration of Cunningham and Rauschenberg was always a brilliant one, but often a rocky one as well. Cunningham enjoyed the work of Rauschenberg and depended on him for financial support. What sometimes came with that support was that Rauschenberg got more praise and press coverage than did Cunningham. This conflict of visibility, rather than any artistic differences, caused the two artists to go their separate ways, although Rauschenberg continued to work on specific projects with Cunningham throughout the years.

During the 1950s and the early 1960s, the company often traveled in a VW bus. Cunningham was once asked why his company was the size it was, a total of nine people including Cage and Rauschenberg. Cunningham answered that it was how many people that could fit into the VW bus.

Viola often told me of the fun that the company had in that VW. She and Rauschenberg entertained the group by making up funny stories. They invented names and situations, and soon everyone on the bus was laughing. Perhaps Viola acquired this gift from her walks in Germany with her father.

Touring was difficult in part because of the close quarters on the VW bus, and the many hours of driving that the company had to endure going from performance to performance or, in many cases, from state to state.

"Bob [Robert Rauschenberg] once asked me when we were in the VW bus, driving to some city in the U.S. to perform, why dancers got paid so little for doing their art." Viola said. "I answered back, 'I don't know, Bob,' and he then said to me with laughter, 'Look at what people pay me for my paintings, and all I do is make furniture! [Rauschenberg referring to his paintings as furniture]" People can hang paintings on their walls, or put sculptures in their homes, but they cannot pay to bring dancers home to live with them, or to perform a dance that can be viewed by their guests or friends whenever they want.

In an interview, I asked Carolyn Brown about Viola's dancing in those early years with the company. Viola always told me that the twitching for which she became famous onstage was actually a result of her trying to stay in her balances, and that her technique was very weak at the time.

"Well, that was true of all of us!" Carolyn remembers. "We all tried to stand up in his [Cunningham's] classes, because in those early classes we'd spend so much time on one leg that the tears would be burning in my eyes and they'd sometimes run down my checks. I looked miserable, and my body was screaming in pain.

"I remember that Paul [Taylor] and Viola did this amazing duet that I believe Paul had made for her." Carolyn said. "Even then that extraordinary quality of hers was visible. Even though she may not have thought she was technically able to handle Merce's work, the uniqueness of the way her body was put together made the quality of her dancing extremely interesting. And Paul used that quality. Viola was extraordinarily beautiful, but she didn't want <u>anyone</u> to know it!

"She would hide her beauty all the time," Carolyn said. "And Remy would say sometimes [to Viola], 'All right, I'm going to do your hair. And I'm going to do this and that.' But within minutes after he had left, she would put her hair back the way it had been. She didn't seem to want to be beautiful, but she was extraordinarily beautiful. And her body was very beautiful in a very unique way. She's a unique dancer!"

Viola disguised her good looks throughout her life. When I met her at Adelphi University, she was thirty-five years old. In 1967, during my second semester there, I went to visit Viola at her New York Apartment on Jones Street in Greenwich Village. I arrived early and caught her unprepared. When she opened the door, she was dressed only in a bathrobe, and her hair was hanging loosely around her face and shoulders. I literally gasped because of the change. There before me stood an amazing beauty. No make-up still, but the transformation was incredible. Ten minutes later, when she emerged from her bathroom, she was back in her spinster-like costume, her hair pulled back into a tight bun, glasses, and a very unbecoming, colorless dress.

"At Connecticut College one summer, " Carolyn remarked, "I remember that she had a very prim kind of hair style where she had her hair long, pulled back in a bun and everything, and Remy put in one of those comb things that lifted it off one's face, and fixed her hair. Apparently all the way across campus, on her way to rehearsal, everybody kept saying, 'My God, Viola, what have you done? You're so gorgeous! You look so beautiful!' The next day, it was gone!"

Those early years were difficult for all the dancers in the Cunningham company. Viola, as I mentioned earlier, had to take on several jobs in order to pay the bills and to continue to work with the company. As a result, she was often in poor health. Throughout her illnesses, however, she continued to work, take classes, and rehearse.

"She got sick a lot and working with her was sometimes difficult." Brown added. "She did all these jobs, and so sometimes she would come to the studio and she would be so black, so scary, miserable, and I remember once Marianne Preger Simon said, 'I will not let this bother me. I will not let her get to me. I will not!' Viola would come in and suddenly everyone would be quiet, because she was so unhappy. It was very intimidating when Viola was in a bad mood." On the other side of the coin, Carolyn remembers that Viola also had an amazing sense of humor, especially when she was around people like Robert Rauschenberg. She confirmed the stories about Viola and Rauschenberg in the VW bus: "They would tell stories while we were riding in the VW bus, pretending to be different people, and they would have us screaming with laughter. They had such fun together. They'd get us all involved in it, but they had a wonderful rapport, the two of them."

Viola sometimes, however, had a kind of Puritanical aura about dancing and performing. She once said to me that she used to feel that performing onstage was almost obscene or unworthy. Perhaps this was because she had grown up with such intellectual parents and felt that the work her father had done was much more 'important' to the rest of the world. She could sometimes make people around her in the Cunningham company feel that what they all were doing was narcissistic and stupid. Fortunately for all, this did not happen very often. Viola was intelligent and resourceful, and if she had truly believed that the work was unworthy, she would not nearly have killed herself working so hard to continue dancing and performing with the company. As the years passed, Viola grew more and more comfortable with dancing as a profession, but never really felt that she had lived up to her father's expectations of what she could have done with her intelligence.

"I was fortunate," Carolyn commented. "I had a husband (musician and composer Earl Brown) who supported me. Life was very, very difficult for Viola, there's no question about it."

A frightening story about Viola's early years in the company is the time that she had a telephone stalker. It is commonplace now to hear about women being stalked, but in the 1950s it was rarely discussed openly. Viola said that one night she was packing to go on tour when her telephone rang. It was a man caller who wished her a safe trip and good luck for the company's tour. She asked who it was, but the man only said, "See you when you get back," and then hung up.

Viola did not think too much of this until he called again five minutes after she got home from the tour. The man said, "Welcome home! I hope that the tour went well," and then hung up. These calls continued for weeks. The man knew when she left the apartment, when she got home, and when she was going away on tour. Again Viola was afraid to go home and terrified to leave. She thought that the caller was someone connected to the company, but did not recognize his voice, and no one she asked knew anything about the calls. Just when she was about to contact the police, the calls stopped. Viola never found out who the caller was.

During her early years in New York, Viola began searching for some kind of spiritual path to follow. She was still affected by her German upbringing and a strong sense of morality. Perhaps it was the influence of being around liberal minded artists, or simply from being "out in the real world," that made her begin to question the religious and moral teachings of her childhood. The search led her from one form of religion to another. An avid reader, she read book after book on religions around the world, and even for a short time in the mid 1950s, she attended services at a Catholic and at an Episcopal church. Although she was a very spiritual person, none of these organized religions satisfied her, and she did not stay with them. Finally her best friend, Susan, introduced Viola to the teachings of an Indian master who changed Viola's entire direction and outlook on life, art, mankind, and God. That master was the Avatar Meher Baba, the Beloved, and the God Man. Meher Baba was from India, and had a very large Indian following. He was also known as the Silent Teacher, as he had not spoken since his mid forties;

communicating through the use of an alphabet board. At this time, too, he had a growing following in England and in the United States.

Viola put it this way during one of our interviews in April of 1995 in her apartment in Bronxville, New York.

"Susan and I met my second year in New York. I saw her at Merce's classes. Merce's classes were then at Sheridan Square, in an upstairs studio. I don't know what they do there now. Some kind of body-building thing.

"Susan was there in class. Not very regularly. And she was also at the Met (Metropolitan Opera Ballet School). We went home together one night, and it turned out that we lived very close to each other. She lived on East 3rd Street, between 1st and 2nd Avenues, and I lived on East 4th Street, between 2nd and 3rd in an apartment that had been David Tudor's and M.C. Richard's. So we'd start, after class, going up to each other's apartments. She would come up and often bring me wine and beer.

"It was Susan who saw, in my apartment, when I got sort of manic about finding some kind of spiritual path, that I had all kinds of books about saints and God only knows what else.

"She said, 'What is all this?' And I told her that I was trying to find something for myself, and that's when she told me about Miss Craske. And that's a very strong relationship with someone, the person who leads one to Baba. I later heard about Baba from Miss Craske, but first I'd heard about Him from Susan."

Through Susan, Viola arranged a meeting with Miss Craske to learn more about Meher Baba. Miss Craske had left England during World War II to live at Meherabad, Baba's home and ashram in India, for seven years. After the war, Meher Baba told Miss Craske that she was to leave India and move to America to teach ballet and to spread the word about him. She would become one of his Western disciples.

Viola met with Miss Craske and began reading many books about and written by Meher Baba, including a very difficult book titled *God to Man and Man to God: The Discourses of Meher Baba*, written by Meher Baba and edited by C.B. Purdom. Viola admitted that she understood only about a third of the discourses, but found the book *The God Man* by C.B. Purdom much more understandable and meaningful. It was not until she, and other dancers who studied with Miss Craske, was able finally to meet Meher Baba in New York City in 1956 at the Hotel Delmonico, where he was staying. It was a direct result of this meeting that Viola became a true Baba follower. She took one look at this incredible man and believed that he was God.

Unlike many Indian gurus who become well known in the United States and Europe, Meher Baba asked for nothing but one's love. No money was asked of anyone, and this was made clear to all: following Baba meant that one was putting oneself through a lifetime of devotion, inner search, and perhaps even hardship. Baba lovers or followers believe that Baba was the reincarnation of Buddha, Krishna, Jesus, and other "God men." Baba was often quoted as saying that we would never be able to understand or truly comprehend him, but that all he asked was our undeniable love and trust in him.

Baba was a strong connection between Viola and several of her friends.

"Peter [Saul] was a student at the Met." Viola said. "That's how I met him. I had seen him, but I didn't know him until I got involved with Baba. There were times when all of us would get together. All of us meaning Bunty [Kelly], Tex [Hightower], Donald [Mahler], Peter, Susan, and Naomi Westerfelt." That group was to grow over the years.

In 1956, Viola traveled with Miss Craske, and with other dancer friends who followed Meher Baba, to the Meher Spiritual Center in

Myrtle Beach, South Carolina, on a property of approximately 500 acres, which was owned and run by an extraordinary woman and disciple of Meher Baba, Elizabeth Patterson. That this kind of religious retreat existed in the South was extraordinary in itself. The South was full of, and run by, the Southern Baptist and Jehovah's Witness religions. This center still exists, however, and now has followers living and visiting all year round. It has its own bookstore and newsletter, and a strong connection with the Sheriar Press, Inc.

In addition to the above-mentioned Meher Baba friends, other dancers who went on that same trip to Myrtle Beach were Harry Bernstein, Cathryn Damon, Marie Adair, and a French dancer, Jean Cebron, among others. Some of these dancers were honored by having the opportunity to perform for Meher Baba in what was called the Barn.

They were all experienced dancers, and among them was a young French dancer, Jean Cebron, who had a gift of artistry which enabled him to allow the meaning of anything he might be dancing to come from the depths of his being. He gave Baba his all, and immediately Baba stopped the program and made Jean sat cross-legged on the ground close to, but with his back to, Baba and for about three minutes there was a deep and pregnant silence in the Barn.

The well-known choreographer Paul Taylor, although not one of Baba's followers, announced that he would like to

create something for Baba and he arranged
a beautiful small pas de deux for Viola
Farber (who now runs her own company)
and Peter Saul (now teaching).

    Perhaps for one moment in time,
these young dancers came close to being
the dance rather than just dancing. Only
Baba's presence could have worked that
miracle."

Margaret Craske
The Dance of Love: My Life With
Meher Baba
Sheriar Press, Inc., 1980

Viola met Baba at other times, once in America and again in 1962, when she traveled with the Western followers to Poona, India, on what was known as the East-West Gathering. Another East-West Gathering was scheduled for the spring of 1969, but it was canceled when Meher Baba became very ill and died on February 7, 1969, just eighteen days before his seventy-fifth birthday. He was born on February 25, 1894. Viola was born on February 25, 1931.

During this time, from the late 1950s and into the early 1960s, many of Viola's friends and colleagues found Viola's belief in Meher Baba strange; however, no one really questioned her belief or stopped loving her because of it. They respected Viola and knew that she was a highly intelligent woman; still, some found it difficult to associate her intelligence, her open-mindedness, and her liberal thinking with her belief in Meher Baba. Her own family found it odd, but over the years came to accept it. Viola's sister, Irene, even came close to also becoming a Baba follower, and she still speaks of him.

Meanwhile, Viola's work with the Cunningham company continued. The company was still not being paid for rehearsal time in New York, and she still had to take on several part-time jobs to pay her bills. All of this was taking a huge toll on her health, as she often did not have enough money to buy food. When she did have some money, she would sometimes spend it on food for her cat, Miss Kitty. Nevertheless, Viola loved what she was doing and thought that dancing was worth the sacrifice she was making.

In 1957, when she was twenty-six and had been in New York for five years, Viola's finances improved a little because she was asked to teach part-time at Adelphi University. This required only a forty minute train ride from Manhattan, and the pay was better than working several temporary jobs. It wasn't enough money, however, so that she could give them all up. The dance chairperson at Adelphi, Harry Bernstein, was the husband of Viola's good friend Bunty Kelly, who was also on the faculty. Viola had taught very little up to this point and only at Cunningham's studio when he was not available. She was very nervous about teaching, but desperately needed the income. The job also meant that, for the first time since she had moved to New York, Viola would have medical insurance, something she truly needed. It was soon apparent that Viola was a very talented teacher, and her classes were very popular with the students.

Around this time Viola moved into a small, railroad-type apartment on Jones Street in Greenwich Village. She had been sharing an apartment with Susan on the East side, but Susan had met and married Alfred Rossin and moved to Riverdale, New York, a wealthy suburb north of New York City. Viola and Miss Kitty took up life together in New York's "Bohemian" neighborhood.

Cunningham continued to choreograph new works, and the company's popularity spread in New York, and throughout the rest of the United States. A few university dance departments hired the company to perform, and yet they continuously struggled to stay afloat. Merce was, however, quickly becoming well-known for his collaborations with other artists. Viola was suddenly being surrounded by painters, composers and other artists attracted to Cunningham's work.

Between 1953 and 1960 Viola danced in the premieres of eight Cunningham dance works. They were *Septet* (1953), *Minutiae* (1954), *Suite For Five* (1956), *Nocturnes* (1956), *Summerspace* (1958), *Antic Meet* (1958), *Rune* (1959) and *Crises* (1960). She often said that *Rune* was her favorite of that period, but it was her role in *Crises* for which she was often singled out. She did things that looked physically impossible. She balanced on one leg while the rest of her body went in many different directions, or one part twitched in total isolation from the rest.

Part of Viola's costume in *Crises* was a large rubber band around one wrist and around her waist. During a brief duet in *Crises*, Cunningham slid one hand through the rubber band on her wrist, and his other hand in the one around her waist. The pair then did a series of movements that pulled them apart and around each other. During rehearsals for *Crises*, Viola developed a burn from the thick rubber band on her wrist from this duet, and she had to wear a large bandage around it. She said that some of her friends, who knew how depressed and overworked she could sometimes get, asked her whether she had tried to commit suicide. She thought that this was funny until she realized that they were serious.

Merce Cunningham told a nice story about Viola in the performance of *Crises* in 1960.

"We were presenting the first performance of *Crises*, the dance with the player piano music by Conlon Nancarrow, at the summer dance festival in Connecticut College. *Crises* began with Viola on stage right and I on stage left. Our movements were separate from each other. I was trying to do my part of this duet, but at the same time wanted to watch Viola in that extraordinary way that she had of putting together several movements in a given amount of time. One knew everything would get there at the end, and during the time that it took, the process of watching her pull it all together was fascinating. ....Once when we were performing together she said, 'Don't worry, I'll get there.' I said, 'Viola, I never worry. You always do.'"

At the first performance of *Crises*, Cunningham's friend M.C. Richards, who was in the audience, told him later what a woman sitting behind her had said: "If that blond girl were my daughter, I'd snatch her right off the stage."

Dance critic, Clive Barnes, wrote the following:

> "...of the four girls, Viola Farber shines in this dance (*Crises*), her body giving like pliable putty, then sharpening to steel in a series of intricate, individual movements accompanied by a striking focus.
> Merce Cunningham's greatness as a dancer is projected with a penetrating intensity particular to himself, although his characteristic quick, intense style has been captured most closely by Viola Farber."

In September of 1963, Viola was one of twelve pianists to play a work titled *Vexations* by Eric Satie in an event organized by John Cage. The piece was played over and over for 18 hours and 40 minutes, with each musician playing for twenty minutes. Viola was the first to begin the performance at 6 PM that evening, and the last to sit down the following day to complete the playing. The other pianists were John Cage, David Tudor, Christian Wolff, Philip Corner, Robert Wood, MacRae Cook, John Cale, David Del Tredici, James Tenney, Howard Klein, and Joshua Rifkin. Each performer was on the stage for a short period before he or she played a given number of repetitions, and then he or she stayed to count the repetitions for the next pianist. This must have been a wonderful time to be in New York when the "avant-garde" movement was just beginning, except that no one knew to call it that. These artists did not think of themselves as the "avant-garde" artists: they simply did what they did. That label was given them later.

In the spring of 1964, the Cunningham company embarked on a very ambitious world tour. Rauschenberg again helped to finance the tour by selling some of his paintings, and with the help of the Foundation for Contemporary Performance Arts and the John D. Rockefeller Foundation; the 3rd Fund gave its support by covering the travel expenses to the Far East. (It was at this time that the Merce Cunningham Dance Foundation was first formed). The tour lasted six months and included performances in France, England, Finland, Sweden, Poland, Germany, Italy, India, and Japan. The dancers in the company received $165 a week, without a per diem stipend. Somehow, most of the dancers still managed to save some of their salaries during this long and exhausting tour.

Here are excerpts from three reviews that singled out Viola while she was performing on that world tour.

> Dancers like Carolyn Brown and Viola
> Farber could be soloists in the most important
> companies in the world, under any label."
> Le Combat, Paris, France, June 18, 1964.

51

"I would go a long way to see Viola
Farber dance - and not merely again, but
again and again. This blonde dancer is
poetry in motion."
The Times of India, Bombay,
October 16, 1964, author unknown.

"Merce Cunningham, Carolyn Brown
and Viola Farber again dominated the
evening. Each member of the company
gave ample evidence of the discipline
that goes to make fine dancing and,
as on Thursday, Viola Farber attracted
much favorable comment, despite the
fact that there were fewer openings for
display of individual talent."
The Times of India, Bombay, October
17, 1964, author unknown.

During a rehearsal in Helsinki, a stage light gel frame fell and struck
her on the head. "Oh, no! Not again!" Viola was heard to exclaim as
she fell to the floor. The company rushed to help Viola lie down on
the stage. One of the dancers in the company, Steve Paxton, took a
fur coat, a prop in Cunningham's *Antic Meet*, and draped it over Viola.
Cunningham himself dashed off to find a telephone to call a doctor.
When he got back, Paxton told him that he did not think the injury
was too serious, but that she was losing a lot of blood from a large gash
in her scalp.

Cunningham told this story many times in my presence. He said that Carolyn sat down next to Viola to comfort her. Viola was awake and alert throughout all of this. When an ambulance arrived, two men came into the theater carrying a stretcher, and picked up Carolyn instead of Viola, who was nowhere to be seen. While everyone was waiting and dealing with other things, Viola had gotten up and gone back to her dressing room. When they asked her where she had gone, Viola very calmly replied, "I went to get my purse."

Viola then lay down on the stretcher, and the men took her off to a hospital. Cunningham's story has her returning with about six stitches in her scalp, but Viola said that it was more like fourteen stitches that were required. She said that she did perform that night, but that she had a horrible, pounding headache the entire time. She said that the most difficult thing she had to do was to execute a dance movement that required her to bend forward.

Viola often told me that the world tour was very difficult for her because everywhere they went, the audiences and critics raved about Cunningham and Carolyn Brown. Her calf, which she had injured before the world tour began, was giving her problems, and she was not enjoying all the traveling. The one city that fell in love with her was Paris. The French audiences and critics adored her and could not get enough of her and her dancing. She said that her dressing room was filled with flowers every night, and after each performance it was filled with audience members waiting to see her. This was a huge boost for her ego, and the French loved the fact that she could speak their language. Everything took a 180 degree turn, however, when the company next performed in London and once again the attention went to Merce and Carolyn.

Another humorous story, although not funny at the time, that Cunningham enjoyed telling involved Viola and Carolyn Brown. The company was in India, and many of the dancers were stricken with diarrhea. On one particular night, Carolyn was so ill that she couldn't get up from the floor of her dressing room. Cunningham came into the room to see how she was doing. When Viola explained the situation to him and said that Carolyn would not be performing that night, Cunningham exclaimed, "Shit!" to which Viola replied, "Exactly!"

Following the world tour in 1964, several of the dancers decided to leave the company. It had been a long and grueling tour, and they felt that it was time for them to move on. Viola was one of those dancers. She had been in the company for eleven years and felt tired and somewhat beaten down. Her body hurt, and she was broke and exhausted. She was seriously considering a complete career change.

Cunningham was, of course, devastated by the great exodus from his company. He thought of the dancers as family, not to mention all the work that lay ahead for him to replace them. He had a special love for Viola, and her desire to leave the company upset him the most.

Cunningham finally asked Viola to reconsider leaving the company, and she agreed to stay on for one more year. This was in 1964. She stayed to help him teach other dancers the parts of those who had left: also, he promised to make a duet for the two of them. He did choreograph that duet, titled *Paired*. Viola loved performing this duet with Cunningham; it was the only time she was on stage alone with him for an entire dance. However, she said sadly, "Merce didn't seem to put it on the program very often."

I never saw that dance performed, and to my knowledge there is no videotape or film of *Paired*. Too bad, it must have been extraordinary to witness these two unique dancers, both of them incredible performers and strong personalities, dancing together on the stage. I found only one picture taken during that dance, and it is not a very good one. Cunningham described *Paired* as a dance that was made up of nine sections or events, and the sequence of how those nine sections was determined during the performance. Each section was given a color, and a cue sheet was located off stage. In David Vaughan's book, *Merce Cunningham, Fifty Years* (Aperture, New York), Cunningham states, "There were preparatory running steps in between events during which either of us could go off stage, dip paint, [re-enter] and smear it on the other as a cue to the next movement."

Cunningham described *Paired* as a "violent" dance. He told me that once Viola kicked him in the forehead and that he once dropped her on her head. In another performance, it seems, they hit their heads together. Viola told me that Cunningham was always dropping her on her head during rehearsal and/or performance. I have no way of knowing whether this is true or not, but I also have no reason to doubt her.

Like her work in *Crises*, Viola was said to have excelled in *Paired*, and that the dance movement fit her extremely well. It was the kind of movement that only Viola could do and make it look exciting. Consider these reviews:

Jill Johnston wrote in The Village Voice:
> "*Paired* is a high-spirited gambol for any season of mind or body blooming to burst. Cunningham matched himself with Viola Farber. Miss Farber is an accomplished technician, but she has never been a tightly screwed together dancer. Her body moves more in segments than in one piece, and she gives many people the pleasant sensation that she might just not make it. She does always make it, but there

is also the feeling of weight and effort and a slight uncertainty in the shifts from one balance to another. Coupled with warmth in her dancing, this quality approaches what I believe some person of letters has called a divine awkwardness. In *Paired*, Cunningham exploited the quality toward its potential for abandonment, and the result was an astonishing series of encounters in which Cunningham assisted Miss Farber (by lifts and propulsion) in some exquisitely loose-jointed flops and flings. Cunningham himself has a rough-edged freedom to his dancing that makes the duet a fine match. And the dance is a funny kind of game. They occasionally smear a handful of paint on each other. Then you could see him walk into the wings and wipe his hands on a black cloth. The he walks back and stalks his side of the stage with light anticipation, cocking his head toward the empty side, waiting for his "prey" to come back."

In contrast, Marcia Marks wrote in <u>Dancemagazine</u>:

> "Paired was not an entirely successful romp for Mr. Cunningham and Viola Farber (whose excessively heavy breathing was a jarring note throughout both evenings). To John Cage's grinding, clanking, amplified static, the dancers sparred, daubing paint on each other, testing each other, delighting in their discoveries of each other, and enjoying each other hugely - obviously meant for each other."

The heavy breathing that Marks writes about was mostly due to the energy required in the dance. One cannot deny, however, that it also had to do with the fact that when she was not dancing, Viola chain-smoked. This was at a time when it was still accepted to smoke indoors, and she lit up a cigarette whenever and wherever she could. She never smoked during class or when she was teaching, but the minute that there was a break, she headed for her purse and her cigarettes.

Carolyn Brown remembers *Paired* as aggressive and almost hostile. "I don't know if that was his original intention, but that's what it ended up being. Because they were slapping each other with paint, and just that act, of slapping a woman with paint -- I mean, it wasn't caressing her or stroking, and the movement that they would then do was so aggressive."

Viola would be the first to say after reading the three different versions of how people saw *Paired* that one person's idea of aggressiveness is another's idea of high energy. A dance that appears ugly to one person may look beautiful to another.

Viola's presence was just as powerful, just as electric as Merce Cunningham's. Some think that it was for this reason that he more often chose to use Carolyn Brown as his partner instead of Viola. Carolyn was a strong presence herself, but in many ways she was Merce's opposite. She was an amazing dancer, and it was mainly her perfect technique that drew attention, not the animal-like quality that both Merce and Viola possessed.

Viola had an unexplainable presence that drew the audience's eye and that separated her from the rest of the dancers without her trying. It came from within herself, and probably not even Viola could explain what it was. It was that rare element which the most brilliant performers, in any of the performing arts, possess. They are born with it; it is not taught to them, but is nurtured by life, by the teaching of their mentors, and by experience in performance.

During my time with the Cunningham "family circle" (1967-1970), dancers often labeled Viola Farber and Carolyn Brown as "fire" and "ice," With Viola the one who possessed the "fire". Carolyn's exquisite technique, but somewhat aloof manner onstage earned her the designation of "ice."

Comparing Viola and Carolyn, Clive Barnes wrote the following in 1964.

> "You are also helped if you have Viola
> Farber, looking like a tennis champion
> and smiling her Giaconda smile with a
> neatly shocking heartiness. The contrast
> between Farber and Brown (the exquisite,
> faultless, flame-like Brown) was one of

the season's delights. If Cunningham had
not got them in his company he would
have to have invented them; more than
once during the season I found myself
wondering, to some purpose, whether or
not he could have done so."

The competition between Carolyn and Viola was obvious to
everyone, if not to themselves. Carolyn remembered that Cunningham
sometimes fostered such competitiveness in his company, not just
between her and Viola, to evoke certain qualities in his dancers. She
said that she did feel, however, that Viola often needed to pick a fight
with somebody before going onstage in order to get herself motivated.
Carolyn confessed being somewhat envious of Viola because so many
of Carolyn's friends seemed truly to love Viola.

"They adored her personally, and they adored her dancing. And
that was Bob [Robert Rauschenberg] and Jap [Jasper Johns]. It was
because I felt conventional in the sense that my training was classical
ballet basically. Although I was a Denishawn dancer, I always felt that
people identified me as a ballet dancer, a classically trained ballet dancer.
Viola, like Merce, was unique! She was a <u>real</u> modern dancer. That
made me feel less because the people whose work, art work I respected
so highly really adored her, or seemed to think so highly of her. I could
not be jealous of Viola or her dancing because there's no way I could
compete. I mean, my body's not put together like that.

"I think that the first word that would come out [about Viola's
dancing] is passion. Passion and commitment and a peculiar pent-up
energy, and a disregard for 'correctness.'"

Carolyn remembers watching Viola in Merce's *Nocturnes* and
thinking, "There was a kind of romantic mysteriousness about her. You

didn't know what was going on, or what that aura was, but that it was very special. She was just a unique dancer, unlike any other dancer."

One funny story about Viola during my interview with Carolyn Brown included the pianist and composer David Tudor.

"He was another one of those people that I respected incredibly who absolutely adored Viola, and at some point David and M.C. Richards weren't getting along very well, and David was very involved in his spiritual quest. M.C. decided that David and Viola should get together as a romantic pair, because she said, 'All we're doing is contemplating our navels, and maybe Viola and David could contemplate their navels together!'

"And I said, 'I don't think that Viola would be interested in just contemplating navels."

All through these years, the constant companion to Viola was her cat Miss Kitty. Boyfriends came and went, but Miss Kitty stayed and loved Viola very much.

Miss Kitty, who lived to be 18 years old, had some particular habits. In the morning, when she wanted to be fed, she jumped on the bed and tried to wake Viola. If Viola did not get up, she first took one claw and very gently scratched Viola's nose, taking care not to break the skin. If this didn't work, Miss Kitty would jump up onto Viola's dresser and, one by one, pull tissues out of a Kleenex box until Viola finally got up to feed her.

Miss Kitty was quite a lucky cat. One hot summer night while Viola was sleeping, Miss Kitty was sleeping on the windowsill. At the time, Viola was living on the fourth floor. There was no screen on the window, and Miss Kitty fell off. She used up one of her nine lives that night as she managed to claw her way down the brick wall of the building's exterior and landed on the second-story window ledge below. Viola was awakened by Miss Kitty's cries and had to go downstairs at

2 a.m., wake her neighbor, and retrieve the cat. Miss Kitty's paws were bloody, and she was missing several claws, but otherwise she was all right.

As mentioned earlier, sometimes Viola did not have enough money even to buy groceries for herself, but she went to a small grocery store on Greenwich Avenue to buy cat food for Miss Kitty. This little store was owned by a pair of sisters named Rose and Mary. The sisters became aware that Viola was buying food for her cat, but not herself. They soon figured out that Viola was unable to buy food for herself, and without making a large to-do about it, gave her a small bag of groceries free of charge. Who says that New Yorkers are not nice?

Viola and Steve Paxton, the father of Contact Improvisation, danced together for a few years in the Cunningham company. He knew Miss Kitty and wrote a poem for Viola. The poem is not dated; I asked Steve whether he could remember what year he wrote it, but he could not, so I will just place it here:

ODE 4 VIOLA
BY
STEVE PAXTON

Viola, in the city, lives with Kitty,
who's her cat.
They live together, happy, in a neatly
furnished flat.
For dulcet temps le ve's Vi, a dancer,
world renown,
her eyes down cast, her head held high,
fleet feet petitely proud.

The Prickly Rose

Kitty did not dance. At home no pas de chat
for her. She'd
languorously glide from room to other
room immersed
in the housework and light mouse work which 5D
but seldom needed
awaiting Vi return, whose love for her
was not exceeded.

But caution! Should the hour be late when firm
upon the stair,
Vi's step precedes the key-in-lock. Inquiring
head of hair,
and ears and face & throat peek in to see if
what portends
is Kitty inimical, a kitty who will not be
wooed, or loved, or even be friends.

For Kitty loved Vi jealously, and Vi could have no others.
So often that's the case with Kitty Cats
who have no mothers.

No, Viola had a duty; she was due
to dance in Denver.
and she thought that Kitty's visiting a
friend would be no sin.
Perhaps vacationing would be a treat-especially if Vi,
to ease the Strain of parting, Baked a luscious
meat loaf pie.

The Cunningham Years

Departure time did come too soon;
Viola, although harried,
hurried quickly to the store, but they (alas)
no chopped carried.
And she had no time to chop some,
but Kitty, understanding,
when she left at last, warm smile she gave, and
wished a happy landing.

Viola wept a gentle tear from friend so good
and true.
And remorse for unbaked meat loaf pie filled
travel day with rue.
She gratefully acknowledged luck in her
feline relations;
for no meat loaf repercussions, for no Kitty
complications.

For Kitty loved Vi only, such that she
would have no others.
As so often is the case with kitty cats
who have no mothers.

Septet *(1953). Left to right: Merce Cunningham, Viola Farber, Steve Paxton. Photographer unknown. Copyright: Cunningham Dance Foundation.*

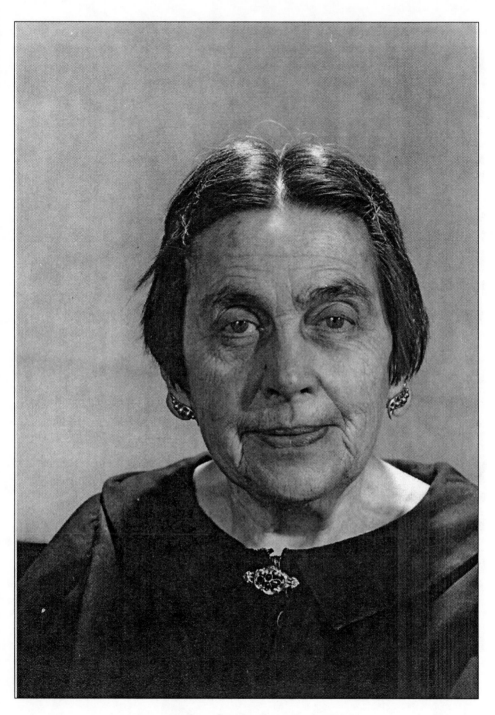

Dora Farber; family photograph, 1955.

Eduard Farber at work; photographer unknown. Washington, D.C., circa 1955.

Nocturnes *(1956), Left to right: Viola Farber, Bruce King, Remy Charlip, Carolyn Brown, Merce Cunningham. Photographer: Louis A. Stevenson, Jr.*

Viola with her father, Washington, D.C., 1957, family photograph.

Nocturnes *(1956), Merce Cunningham and Viola Farber*
Photographer: Louis A. Stevenson, Jr.

Nocturnes *(1956), Merce Cunningham and Viola Farber*
Photographer: Richard Rutledge.

Viola Farber in Merce Cunningham's Summerspace *(1958),*
Photographer: Richard Rutledge.

Viola and Susan Rossin horseback riding in Helmville, Montana on the Rossin's ranch. Photograph by Alfred Rossin, circa 1958.

Viola with dancer friends at the Meher Baba Center in Myrtle Beach, South Carolina, 1959.

Photograph property of the Viola Farber Archives.

Viola Farber and Merce Cunningham in Crises, *1960. Photographer: Harry Shunk.*

Viola Farber and Merce Cunningham in Crises, *1960.*
Photographer: John Wulp

Aeon, *Merce Cunningham Dance Company. Left to right: Steve Paxton, Carolyn Brown, Judith Dunn, Marilyn Wood, Viola Farber, Shareen Blair (on floor). Photographer: Robert Rauschenberg*

Left to right: Viola Farber, Merce Cunningham, Carolyn Brown in Story, *1963, Photographer: Marvin Silver*

Painting by Jasper Johns titled Portrait – Viola Farber *(1961-1962), with window closed. Photograph by Rudolph Burckhardt.*
Art © Jasper Johns/Licensed by VAGA, New York, NY

Painting by Jasper Johns titled Portrait – Viola Farber *(1961-1962), with window open. Photograph by Rudolph Burckhardt. Art © Jasper Johns/Licensed by VAGA, New York, NY*

Viola at the American Dance Festival, Connecticut College,
New Haven, CT., 1964, Photographer: Remy Charlip

Barbara Lloyd and Viola in Tokyo, Japan during the World Tour with the Cunningham company, 1964. Photographer unknown.

Viola and Merce Cunningham in Paired, *1964. Photographer: Sig T. Karlsson.*

Meher Baba; photograph curiosity of the Meher Spiritual Center, Inc.

Chapter Three

The formation of the Viola Farber Dance Company

IN 1965, AT AGE THIRTY-FOUR, Viola finally gave her notice to
the Cunningham company. It was a year after the world tour. She had
kept her bargain with Cunningham, and now was ready to move on.
He had made the duet, *Paired*, for her, but on tour the duet was rarely
on the program. Her departure was a huge loss for the company, but
she had given it thirteen years of her life. She was not certain that she
wanted to continue dancing, or that she wanted to keep living in New
York. She still had her part time job at Adelphi University, and she
would let some time go by before making up her mind what to do and
where to go next.

Her friend Susan and Susan's husband, Alfred Rossin, had purchased
a beautiful new home in New City, New York, a drive of about an hour
and a half up the Palisades Parkway from Manhattan. They now had
two sons, Mark and Eric, who had become Viola's God sons. The
Rossins had several acres around their mountainside home, and they
built a small guest house especially for Viola just yards from their main
house. They wanted to give the little house to Viola, but she insisted
that the only way that she could feel comfortable having the house was

if the Rossins willed it to their two sons. They accepted, but it was unofficially Viola's.

The little house was lovely. The outside was cinder block, painted white. On the ground floor there were a cozy living room with a wood-burning fireplace, a small, but well equipped kitchen, and a small dance studio. The studio was just the size for Viola to plan her classes or to work on choreography. She hardly had time to be there except on weekends, but did so whenever possible. The upstairs of the house had a good-sized bedroom and bath, which were only above the living room and kitchen, so that the studio could have a high ceiling.

Viola loved going to that house. It was in the middle of dogwoods and other kinds of trees, and the wild animals often came around during the early evening. Viola often saw woodchucks, deer, rabbits, foxes, and skunks. Birds, too, were plentiful. She was quite aware that she would not be able to have that house without the generosity of her friends, and she was very grateful.

She had begun dating a musician, and the two of them had great times at the little house, and having meals with the Rossins. Viola was good with children, and Mark and Eric loved her.

During this period, Viola had thought that she was quietly going to bow out of the dancing profession, but instead began making a solo for herself and being asked to be a guest artist at several dance departments throughout the country, where she began to enjoy making dances.

"When I quit Merce I wanted to become an actress," she said. "I still wanted to go to dance classes, but I didn't want to perform. However, I had to earn a living, and dancing was all I was trained to do."

The first solo that Viola choreographed for herself in New York was performed at The Bridge Theater on 14th Street in Manhattan. She said that she agreed to dance there because she was bored with just teaching.

"I had, in any case, in the last few years with Merce, when I had time in the wings, which seemed frequent to me, begun hopping about doing stuff. So I made a dance of scraps that I had worked on that had interested me then. I also danced about my present situation in life. I remember I had hurt my foot, my Achilles tendon, on the world tour. In the dance there was a big thing where I raced around the stage with a limp, and I just did things that I wanted to do. I felt so easy about doing these things because I thought that nobody would care, nobody, so I just did them. I did movements that were left over that I wanted to get out. And I enjoyed doing it," Viola said with a large smile. It was 1965, and the title of the dance was *Seconds*.

In the fall of 1966 Harry Bernstein, the chairperson of the dance department at Adelphi University, asked Viola to choreograph a new work for the 1967 spring faculty dance concert. Viola had not choreographed very much at this point and the idea frightened her, but she agreed to do it. It was at this time that I was a student there and had auditioned for Viola. I was taking one class with her that met twice a week, and she let me sneak into her advanced technique class when it fit my schedule. She made me promise that if Mr. Bernstein came into the room that I would not tell him that she had allowed me to take the class. I agreed.

The day after Viola's audition, the results were posted in one of the studios. I was shocked and horribly disappointed that my name was not on the list. At the time there were only two men in the dance department, and the other one had not even auditioned. I did not know whether I was good enough to be in the piece, but I had somehow assumed that I would get in. When I next saw Viola, I asked her why she had not taken me.

"Jeff!" She said. "Please don't think that it is because of your dancing. I wanted to do a piece with twelve dancers, and I just didn't know how I could work with eleven women and just one man."

I accepted her explanation, but needed to be around this incredible woman. I asked whether I could attend rehearsals and help take notes and/or take care of cuing up the music for her. She smiled, took a drag on her cigarette, and with the smoke trailing out of her mouth as she spoke, said, "Sure!" After the second rehearsal, Viola couldn't bear seeing me sit there and put me into her dance called *Here They Come Now*.

At the end of that semester, Viola gave her notice to the dance department at Adelphi. She had accepted a part-time job teaching technique and choreography at Bennington College in Vermont. She had also begun to teach on a fairly regular basis at the Cunningham studio, which at that time, 1967, was located on Third Avenue just south of 33rd Street. I could not imagine not studying with Viola, and in June of 1967 I wrote her a letter asking for advice about leaving school and trying to make dancing my profession. At the time, I was apartment sitting for her while she was doing a teaching residency at the University of Michigan. Here is what she wrote back to me. It is a great letter trying to explain to a very young and very naïve dancer the realities of being a modern dancer in the United States. It is a very long letter, but it gives, in her own words, a picture of what her life was like, her thoughts and a good sense of what she was doing while in residence. The name of the solo that Viola mentions was *Seconds*.

Friday, 1967

Dear Jeff,

It is very difficult for me to advise you about quitting or staying in school. I guess the main reason I'm not all for leaving and just dancing is the practical problem of earning a living with which you'll be faced even if you do dance with a company. It's probably easier to get better jobs if you have a college degree. On the other hand, I suppose it's possible that if you stay at college, by the time you get through you may only have a "good job" and not much dancing ahead of you. There is also the consideration that you may, after ten or fifteen years, become tired of dancing and your chances of doing anything else will be more limited if you haven't gotten a degree. If you do get scholarships (this is if you leave school) to study dance, and I certainly think you could, you would still need money for food and rent, etc.

I really don't mean to make it all sound so terrible; it's just that I feel you should know more or less the kind of things you are facing, although in a way you can never know that because, fortunately, one can't foresee the future! Things are getting easier for dancers, I think. There are more performances everywhere so people are paid more for dancing. You might also be able to get T.V. or Broadway musical jobs which pay more per hour than filing. Also, it's not so awful to be poor if you are doing something you love to do. As for learning and knowledge I think you can probably get that in or out of college.

This is all a sort of rambling list of pros and cons as I think of them. The thing is that you have to make the final decision yourself. And perhaps what it amounts to is deciding whether to do what you want very badly to do now and take chances on insecurity, failure, etc. or whether to play it safer and think about the future and all that kind of thing.

Sorry I can't be of more help.

Thanks for forwarding mail and sending phone and Con Ed checks. Kitty's purr is usually inaudible but you can feel it if you touch her throat, so she's probably purring more than you think.

Don Redlich is arriving Sunday evening and we, mainly he, are performing on Tuesday! It will be my first performance in more than 1 ½ years, so should be an interesting experience for me. I have a large studio at my disposal whenever I'm not teaching, so have been working there for hours every day. I have made a ridiculously difficult solo. Also unfortunately did something to my left leg, and hope it doesn't get worse. Checked into the university health center (faculty are not supposed to go there unless they're on their last gasp evidently) today for a heat treatment. The physiotherapist said it was just a muscle spasm – nothing torn.

I visited my oldest sister and her family near Chicago last weekend. They've gone off for a year in Vienna this week and I wanted to see them before they left. Next weekend the dance woman from the University of Illinois is coming here and then driving me to Urbana to stay in her new house and to see the glorious university. She wants me to come and teach there, and I've told her quite a few times that I won't but I think she's still trying.

I am really enjoying my time here now after the first shock of heat and very inept students wore off. People are very pleasant, the trees and grass smell good, there are lots of birds and squirrels to watch, and I have so much time to work by myself. Even the students look a little better.

Susan has called twice. They're evidently having a very good time at their ranch.

Love,

Viola

After reading this letter, I decided to enroll in a two-week workshop at the Cunningham studio. After that, I returned to Adelphi University for a three-week summer workshop, but knew that I would not be returning there in the fall. Viola and Dan Wagoner, a former member of the Paul Taylor Dance Company who was also on the faculty of the summer workshop, took me along to see the Cunningham company perform at the American Dance Festival at Connecticut College, and after seeing this performance I had my sights set on New York and studying with Viola at the Cunningham studio. I was twenty-one, and it was the second time I had dropped out of college, but I knew now what I wanted to do. A few months later, I was performing with the Merce Cunningham Dance Company.

In the fall of 1967, while driving home one night from Bennington College, Viola was involved in a one-car accident with her VW Bug that she had purchased a little over a year before. It was dark by the time Viola reached the New York State line, and a strong wind was blowing. Driving through a wooded area, as she rounded a sharp curve, her little car was hit by a very strong gust of wind and she lost control. Viola remembers the car rolling over at least once and ending up on its side in the ditch with the door on the driver's side open. She managed to crawl out of the car, but couldn't tell where she was, or just how badly she was injured. She decided to stay where she was and hope that help would arrive soon.

Fortunately for Viola, a man driving a semi truck in the opposite direction noticed a pair of headlights facing him at a very strange angle. He stopped his truck and ran across the highway to investigate. He found Viola sitting next to her car badly bruised, but with no bones broken. The truck driver then looked inside the car and told Viola the front windshield was broken and lying in the back seat. Viola realized that she was very lucky that she had not been decapitated. As it was, she had been thrown to the floor of the car as it rolled over into the ditch, and the windshield had missed her.

The truck driver radioed the nearest towing company, which towed her car into a repair shop. She was very lucky to be alive and, thanks to the owner of the repair shop, she got a ride to the nearest train station and returned home.

In September of 1967, Viola had also taken on a new part-time job at Sarah Lawrence College in Bronxville, New York. Instead of staying home and nursing her bruises and sore muscles, Viola took a train the next morning to Bronxville and taught her classes. Knowing Viola, I would guess that she never told her students about the accident or that her body was covered with bruises, cuts, and scratches.

Viola had car insurance, but had the repair shop owner sell her car for scrap. When I asked her why, she confessed to me that this had been her second car accident in just a few months. A truck driver had forced hers and another car off the road, and although nothing had happened to her car, the man in the other car had been killed. It was more than a year later that the trial for that first accident took place. Luckily for Viola, the lawyer for the trucking company settled out of court, stating that it had been the driver of their truck who had been at fault. Viola was so shaken by these two accidents that she never owned another car and, although she did keep renewing her driver's license, she rarely drove again.

Also in 1967, Viola was invited by the Ohio State University dance faculty to be an artist in residence. It was here that she made a dance titled *Pop. 18.*, because there were eighteen dancers in the piece and the "Pop." stood for population. Dancer Larry Clark was a student there at the time, and he recalls Viola's visit.

"I was a junior and she came in to set a piece for us. We had this lady coming in from New York and I wasn't a very good dancer, not technically anyway. I had just started to find my legs and that sort of thing.

"I was selected to dance in the piece, and I was really blown away that I was selected, number one; number two, my training was basically [José] Limón and [Martha] Graham, so I had never really experienced Cunningham technique. I was just absolutely enthralled with what she was doing, but I would get so frustrated and, of course, Viola was in the whole New York way of teaching, and crowds and fast-moving pace. We were from Ohio, a little slower and a little bit more maternal in our teaching."

Larry Clark found Viola's work extremely challenging, and when Viola would ask the class to repeat a dance phrase beginning on the left side, Larry said that he thought to himself, "Holy shit! I can't do it on the right side, much less the left side!

"And I learned so much from her that first time. Then she did this piece called *Pop.18*, which I just loved. It was funny because when she arrived, she had extremely short hair and that shocked everybody."

What really impressed Larry Clark was how Viola loved the individuality of each dancer. She wanted everyone to be him or herself in her dance classes as well as in her choreography. He had not come across such an experience with the majority of his other dance teachers.

"Basically (at the university) we would learn pieces, repertory pieces of [José] Limón or whomever that were originally choreographed for other dancers many years before. You had to fit a body mold and then when our teachers were choreographing, of course, they worked with concepts and so forth. But Viola really worked with individual body differences and that to me was phenomenal. She gave you a lot of room for experimentation and she loved it when you'd fall down and throw your body around. To me that was a whole opening. Not just in the dance world. It was a whole opening psychologically for me."

Viola allowed the dancers to feel that each was not only different physically from everyone else, but also different in every way. She didn't want them to hide that difference, but to bring it out in their dancing. It was not just how long they could balance, or how high they could jump, but it was all the other things in their physiologic and emotional make-up that made each one's dancing unique. Although not alone in this teaching style, Viola was one of the best able to bring out that uniqueness in her dancers.

"That really turned me on, and it kept me going for a long time," added Larry Clark.

Viola returned to Ohio State in 1968, but her residency was cut short by the Kent State riots and the Ohio State riot which took place at the same time. The administration decided to shut down the campus, and Viola's classes were moved a few miles away to a local dance studio. The situation at the university did not improve, and eventually she had to give up the idea of choreographing a second work for the students. She returned to New York.

That year, Viola performed a new solo of her own in New York in a dance series at St. Luke's Church on the West Side. She had mentioned to Remy Charlip, a friend and fellow artist, that she was not sure whether she wanted to do this, but that she needed to take some time off for herself. He said, "Well, do! Take it for yourself and make a solo." She did, and from this discussion with Remy came the title of the dance, *Time Out*.

In the spring of 1968, Viola and her good friend, Peter Saul, were asked to perform at the Billy Rose Theatre in a concert put together by John Cage, David Tudor, and Gordon Mumma, all of them composers and musicians working with Merce Cunningham. The performance was to be a matinee during the same week that the Cunningham company was performing there. At this time, I was both dancing with the Cunningham company, and living with Peter Saul, and so I was with both of them a lot. Peter would tell me how difficult things were going for him, and later Viola would tell me how difficult rehearsals were with Peter. Peter Saul had been a soloist with the American Ballet Theatre, and later changed to modern dance. He joined the Cunningham company, performing with that company for just under three years, 1965-1967. He was the man I replaced in the Cunningham company in the fall of 1967. The Billy Rose performance would be his debut as a choreographer, and he was very nervous about the entire project.

According to Viola, Peter could not make up his mind what he wanted to do, and kept changing the choreography from rehearsal to rehearsal. She did not really know until their dress rehearsal exactly what Peter was going to do. The audience never realized this, however, because both looked as if they had been performing the piece for years.

The event was a collaboration of Viola, Peter, and the three composers, and was titled *The Music of Conlon Nancarrow*. Viola and Peter were choreographing only one duet to one piece by Nancarrow. The rest of the performance consisted of works by Nancarrow as performed by Cage, Tudor, and Mumma. As well as doing some wonderful and serious choreography, Viola and Peter pulled out all the stops for this one-time performance. Viola appeared briefly at the beginning in a long, slinky red dress and a long black wig. It is said that even Merce Cunningham did not know until he was told later that the beautiful "creature" who made the brief, but unforgettable crossing in the dance was Viola. This crossing took place as Peter was performing a solo. Viola finished her crossing, and quickly removed the wig and dress, and joined Peter on stage for a beautiful and technically difficult duet.

For this performance, Viola and Peter had rigged up a wheel chair so that it looked like a big, mobile easy chair. Near the end of the dance, Peter was again dancing alone when Viola entered from stage left and crossed the stage sitting in this chair. As she neared him, Peter began running on and off stage bestowing huge bouquets of flowers on Viola's lap each time he came back. He repeated this until Viola was totally covered with flowers. At this point, Viola pulled out a pistol from underneath her dress and shot Peter. As he hit the floor and the lights were fading, Viola turned her face toward the audience and gave them a huge villainous grin. It was a remarkable evening of dance, music, and comedy.

Viola was busy teaching part time at Bennington College and doing teaching residencies when she could. This unfinished letter written to her sister, Irene Aikin, was found in an old notebook with no date. It must have been written around 1968 or 1969, and it demonstrates how, even in her early years of teaching, she really did not enjoy teaching dance in an academic setting.

Dear Irene -

I am sitting in my office at Bennington waiting to

"counsel" someone.

After trying very hard for a month to love it here, have decided that I don't and that it's all right of me not to. As faculty member one is supposed to be very involved with the community and all sorts of things other than teaching one's subjects, which with my part-timeness is rather impossible. Also, it seems to me that everyone is so involved with the mechanics of being a free individual that the actual work - like learning how to dance - gets rather left out. As I wrote you several years ago, I think, I am getting to be more and more a prune like pill.

Around this time, Viola's father was diagnosed with lung cancer. This was a huge blow to Viola. Even though she had never quite lived up to her father's expectations academically, they remained very close. She flew back and forth between New York and Washington, D.C., as often as she could to help her mother take care of her father before his death in 1969. Her mother was also showing signs of failing health, but the family did not recognize it at the time. Viola recalls Mutti once saying to her, "Viola, your father is going to be furious when he comes home from work and finds that sick man in his bed upstairs!" The man upstairs was, of course, her husband. Viola and her sisters, Irene and Elisabeth, attributed this to their mother being tired and overwhelmed by her husband's illness. Elisabeth remembers how wonderful Viola was in looking after their father during his illness:

"I knew how to take care of the regular duties of calling the doctors or going to get prescriptions filled, but Viola knew how to make Poppi comfortable. Her touch was beautiful, and she seemed to know how to ease his pain temporarily."

During her father's illness, Viola began work on a new solo and, although not based directly on him, the piece was about trying to go on living in spite of some hideous illness or other deformity. She wore a long pale green shift dress over a gray leotard and tights, and a baseball mitt on her left hand. The baseball mitt represented her father's cancer. The solo was titled *Legacy*, and she performed it at the Judson Church on Washington Square in New York.

The concert that started Viola thinking about forming her own company was held at the Judson Church in 1968. Works included on the program were choreographed for a group of students who were studying with her at the Cunningham studio while Merce's company was on tour in South America in the summer of 1968. Also included were two well known dancers, Margaret Jenkins and Dan Wagoner. The dance was titled *Notebook* and also included June Finch and Cathy Powers. Powers had studied with Viola at Adelphi University. There was a duet for Margaret Jenkins and Dan Wagoner that was part of *Notebook* and that was later lifted from the dance and reworked as a duet titled *Excerpt*. (When Margaret Jenkins left the company a short while later, Anne Koren took over her role.) The evening was shared by Peter Saul who premiered two dances which he had choreographed.

June Finch had first seen Viola dance with the Cunningham company in New London, Connecticut, and then studied with her at the Cunningham studio after Viola had left the company. Margaret Jenkins, who was a friend, came in one day and said that Viola had asked her to do a duet, and June asked her to find out whether Viola would need other dancers, and to tell Viola that she was interested.

"The next day Viola asked me if I wanted to work with her." June said. "The exciting thing was working with somebody who was just starting out; the work was being choreographed for us. There was no learning somebody's old parts, and there was never any question one was in the presence of a genius at work. It was a totally extraordinary challenge. Every day we were asked to risk almost our lives and limbs," June Finch said.

Notebook was performed in 1968 at the Judson Church along with Viola's solo *Legacy*. June remembers that following the concert a dancer named Sara Rudner, who later became one of Twyla Tharp's leading dancers, came back-stage and said of the concert, "Merce Cunningham, eat your heart out!"

Also after that concert, Merce Cunningham came backstage to see Viola, and he asked her how she got the dancers to dance that way.

"I just asked them to," Viola responded.

Since leaving the Cunningham company in 1965, she had not performed on a regular basis, but she had not become an actress as she had once hoped. She had not even taken a single acting class. Here she was, at age thirty-eight, still living in a run-down apartment on Jones Street in New York, teaching modern dance part-time in three different places, and traveling all over the U.S. doing residencies in university dance departments. She was always sick with colds or worse disorders, and she was always on the brink of being broke. She wasn't even dating at this time, as her relationship with a musician she had met at Adelphi University had ended badly. She began to believe that she would never marry and would remain childless. Secretly Viola began to wonder whether she would be able to have children. She had never used contraceptives while having affairs, and she had never gotten pregnant. All this only helped to worsen Viola's already dark mood swings. On top of all this, her father died, and although she knew it was inevitable, she took his death very hard.

But things were just beginning to change for her. In the summer of 1969, she collaborated with dancer/choreographer Don Redlich on a dance titled *Tristan and Iseult*. Both had been hired to teach for several weeks in a dance workshop at the University of Wisconsin. They started the dance wearing clothes made of paper, and as the dance progressed the clothes were torn off, revealing bright-colored tights and leotards. Don Redlich later set this same dance for him and Gladys Balin, but unfortunately, for whatever reason, failed to mention in the program that the dance had originally been choreographed by both him and Viola Farber. Viola never forgot this and never forgave Don for the omission. According to her, it was she who had come up with the concept for the dance. Only she and Don knew the real story.

There are a few letters from Viola, kept by her sister Elisabeth, that were written to their mother right after the death of their father. The family home in Washington, D.C., was being sold and Mutti was getting ready to move to Chicago to live near Elisabeth. Her health was growing progressively worse, and she had been diagnosed with Alzheimer's disease.

October 12, 1969

Dear Mutti,

Happy Columbus Day. That's what today is, evidently.

Tomorrow the final closing of the house sale takes place. Elisabeth says she wrote you about what has been done with everything. The books go to a dealer in New York, recommended by Multhauf, who will give us a fair price for them.

I have been feeling rather blah with some kind of mild virus - everyone in New York seems to have bad colds, headaches, or something else uncomfortable.

Have been inquiring about apartments and looking in newspapers, but rents in New York are so incredibly high that I haven't found anything yet. Have gotten really tired of my peeling walls and ceilings and cockroaches in every cupboard and drawer.

Have been asked to teach in France for a few weeks - will have to figure out how to fit it in with everything else.

How are you?

Love -

Viola

The books that Viola mentions were books owned by her father, related to chemistry. At the time of this letter, Viola was living on Jones Street in the Greenwich Village area of Manhattan. She was traveling back and forth between New York and Washington, D.C., to see her mother and to help with the packing up of the family's belongings. I am certain that she could not afford to move at this time, as whatever small amount of money she had managed to save was being spent on air and train fares. Viola's mother finally moved to a small apartment outside Chicago in the fall of 1969.

December 5, 1969

Dear Mutti -

It was so nice to see you and be with you again. How does it feel to be back in your own tranquil apartment again?

I am, as usual, busy teaching and rehearsing and taking ballet classes with Miss Craske. She and Buddy

[Alfred Rossin] are flying to India this Sunday for a week, mainly so that she can be with the Indian disciples of Baba for a while.

What would you like for Christmas?

Love - Viola

Also in 1969, Viola began rehearsing with a small, core group of dancers in New York. She had decided to give a concert in New York in a small non-theater setting on the upper west side. That first group of dancers included herself, Mirjam Berns, June Finch, Rosalind Newman, Andé Peck (who had met Viola at Bennington College), Dan Wagoner, and me. I was, at this time, a member of the Cunningham company, and Mirjam Berns was a member of the Dan Wagoner Dance Company which had recently been formed.

Dan and Viola had decided to rent a studio space together on East 17th Street between Fifth Avenue and Broadway, off Union Square. Both had become popular teachers as well as emerging New York choreographers, but neither could afford a space on his or her own. Each had a small nucleus of dancers who studied with them on a daily basis, and both needed a space to rehearse their budding companies. Neither was making a lot of money from teaching, as their students included dancers in their companies who were taking class every day free of charge in lieu of a salary for rehearsals.

Although Viola had not officially announced the formation of her company, she was beginning to work with the same dancers on a regular basis. Those dancers included Margaret Jenkins, Dan Wagoner, June Finch, Andé Peck, Rosalind Newman and me. Larry Clark and Ann Koren would soon be added to this list.

It was in this studio that Viola began a long-lasting working relationship with two remarkable dance musicians, Pat Richter and Moshe Goldberg. Both had played for her classes at the Cunningham studio, and they would continue playing in her own dance studios for a number of years. Although very different in playing styles, the two are among the best musicians for dance classes in New York. I must take a moment to explain why I use the word musician instead of accompanist when writing about those who play for dance classes. It was a pet peeve of Viola's, who hated the word accompanist. She said that it made the musician appear less important to the classes. It is for this reason that I honor Viola's belief in this matter.

In January of 1970, Viola agreed to make a guest appearance with the Cunningham company at the Brooklyn Academy of Music. She was asked to revive her role in Cunningham's *Crises*, a dance that had been a favorite of her fans. She was worried that she would not be able to remember the dance, but found that, once rehearsals began, the movements came back quite easily. I was performing with the company at that time, and although I was not in *Crises*, I remember standing in the wings during performances and being in awe of what I witnessed. Viola was amazing; some who had seen her in earlier days said that she danced even better than she had originally. I do not know whether there are video tapes of this revival of *Crises*, but I do know that the Cunningham Dance Foundation has video tapes of the company performing this dance. It is quite extraordinary to see the original cast performing.

Here is a letter that Viola wrote to her mother and to her sister and her husband right after finishing that performance at the BAM. An injury to her wrist was caused, as in earlier years, by the rubber bands worn on the wrist in *Crises*. The students whom she mentions were in the University of Utah's Department of Dance, and members of the Repertory Dance Theatre (RDT). The dance that she made there was for RDT and was titled *Passengers*.

January 19, 1970

Dear Mutti, dear Lanzls,

There's no rest for the wicked. Finished last performance with Merce Friday night, taught Saturday morning, and flew to Salt Lake City Saturday evening. Of course the plane left two hours late, but to soothe any irate passengers they gave out free drinks on the flight. I contented myself with a modest glass of champagne. (My wrist is wounded so I can't lean it on the pad, which is why my handwriting is odder than usual - nothing serious, though, and it's healing.)

Spent Sunday afternoon auditioning hordes of students for the piece I'm supposed to make and having meetings about schedule. Today I gave myself class in a huge empty gym, then taught class and started rehearsing afternoon and evening. The students are lovely - friendly, bright, hardworking. This younger generation can't be all bad. At least four offered me rides, invited me to dinner, etc. And they learn quickly and with a minimum of fuss.

The weather is almost spring-like - I had expected to be knee deep in snow. The air is clear and refreshing, although they say they recently had an "inversion" when pollution absolutely enshrouded the city.
How are you?

> Love -
>
> Vi

The formation of the Viola Farber Dance Company

A performance in New York was the first concert Viola advertised as presented by the Viola Farber Dance Company, held in a building that housed the WBAI radio station. The building had previously been a church, and the company performed in a very small space that had once been the church sanctuary. A small portable stage was built, with one wall used as the back of the performance space. Because it was a room, not a theater, the audience was on three sides of the stage and very close to the performers. The space had not been used in years and was extremely dusty and dirty. The walls were peeling, and the place was devoid of any theater lighting or sound equipment.

Viola had hired a talented lighting designer by the name of Beverly Emmons. After the company had finished its first spacing rehearsal for the performance, Beverly told Viola not to despair, that all would be fine. Indeed, when Viola returned the next day Beverly, her small stage crew and a few friends of Viola's had totally transformed the space so that it would present the company well. She had draped cloth over much of the wall space, set up light trees, and scrubbed the floors clean. Viola was moved to tears at this show of love and devotion. Everyone had worked very hard to make her company's New York debut look as good and as professional as possible.

The performances at the WBAI radio station proceeded without a hitch. The small space was crammed to capacity (it sat approximately 100 people) and then some, by dancers and critics who came to see this new dance company. The program consisted of *Excerpt, Duet for Mirjam and Jeff, Legacy* and *Quota*. Although these included a solo, two duets, and a trio, the audiences' response, as well as that of the critics, was as if a very large company with a huge repertory had appeared on the New York dance scene. Viola decided at that moment that perhaps she wanted to stay in this dance profession after all, and that just maybe she had something worthwhile to add to the art of dance.

Viola officially named her company the Viola Farber Dance Company shortly after the WBAI concert by incorporating the company and filing for not-for-profit status with the IRS. She also hired managers from an umbrella management group called Artservices, which was run by Mimi Johnson and Margaret Wood. Two of the other dance artists, among many, managed by Artservices at the time were Lucinda Childs and Trisha Brown.

In August of 1970, I decided to leave the Cunningham company in the hopes that Viola asked me to join her company as a full-time member. Fortunately, for me, she did so within a couple of months.

Viola's early work was often filled with sections where the dancers were allowed to rearrange, or improvise on, a very set movement phrase. She established very definite rules or limits for the dancers so that they were not free to do just anything that they wanted. After a while, we were given a set of rules as to what to do with this phrase. Sometimes we were told to change the tempo of the phrase, but to keep it in the original order. Then Viola would add another possibility such as allowing us to change the directions of the phrase, taking it anywhere in the space that we chose. Then she might ask us to jump a movement that was not originally choreographed as a jump, or to do the movement on the floor when it was first meant to be executed standing up. We might then be allowed to rearrange the phrase, while still being told to do "only" the movement within the phrase. Then Viola would sit back and watch all of us "play" with the phrase. Sometimes she let us go on for five or ten minutes before stopping us to allow us to search for all the available possibilities. She seemed to enjoy watching this type of rehearsal and often was heard to say that she could sit for hours and observe the dancers experiment with one phrase.

She choreographed many sections in which our movements were set and where we had no freedoms whatsoever. For going from one section to the next, a cue would be given; a visual cue, a movement cue, or a sound cue. In one dance, June Finch ran around from dancer to dancer quietly saying "ready," and when she had reached us all, we went into the next part of the dance. Often the cue to change sections would be a movement cue taken from one of the dancers onstage, or a dancer that had not been onstage during a particular section entering the space. If the dance had internal or set musical cues, we changed with the music. The term often given to Viola's way of choreographing is "indeterminacy." It is doubtful that Viola ever thought of this particular characterization while she was choreographing. She did what she did, and it was the critics and dance historians who later attached the labels.

After about a year, Dan Wagoner left Viola's company to spend full time working with his own. Margaret Jenkins left shortly thereafter to move to San Francisco with her husband, and to form her own dance company. Dan was replaced by Larry Clark, and Margaret by Anne Koren. I was now a full time member of the company as well. We were a small group of dedicated dancers, working for nothing but love and the chance to work with Viola. We were never paid for rehearsals, but we did get to take class each and every day free of charge. Viola always paid us for performances, even if it sometimes was only a token amount. She gave us jobs teaching at her studio, and she helped to find us other teaching jobs in and around New York. When on tour, however, we were paid a weekly salary plus a per diem allowance. We lived on love, hard work, unemployment benefits, and hope.

Larry Clark remembers how, in 1970, he was asked by Viola to dance with her company.

"I remember I started taking class with Dan and also with Viola, primarily with Viola. One day, she asked me if I would work with her, and I thought she meant she needed another male and that I was going to do one piece in a concert that she had coming up.

"Someone said to me a couple of days later, 'Congratulations. You got in Viola's company.' I said, 'No. I'm not in Viola's company. I'm just doing a piece that she needed an extra guy for.' So I went to Viola and said, 'Viola, you want me just to do this concert with you, right?' I didn't know how to say it. And she said, 'No, I want you to join my company.' And I said, 'Holy shit!' I was so happy." Larry stayed with the company for ten years.

The dancers in Viola's company had to make choices onstage in front of the audiences, and she entrusted them with the making of those choices. This was very different from what she had experienced working with Merce Cunningham. His work was, of course, beautiful and technically very challenging, to say the least, but she never felt included in the making of his work. Nor did he give the dancers the artistic freedom onstage that Viola did. She felt that Cunningham often "pigeonholed" his dancers, giving them the same kind of movements much of the time.

Viola constantly forced her dancers to grow in all areas of their dancing. She helped them to discover that their dancing involved not only their physical technique, but also their spirit, soul, emotions, and musicality. She mentored them in the truest sense of the word. They grew as artists, as performers, as teachers, and as human beings while working in her company.

Merce Cunningham rarely spoke directly to his dancers, and he rehearsed them with a stopwatch. For example, he would walk into rehearsal, sit down, and say that he wanted to see the dance *Crises*. When they came to the end of the dance, he clicked his stop watch, looked at it, and told the dancers whether they had been too fast or too slow. He rarely said why they were too fast or too slow, or in what section of the dance, or how they should go about remedying this. He only said, "Do it again!" The company would usually rehearsed three pieces each day, and when they were finished, Cunningham, more often than not, simply said "thank you" and got up and left.

Viola was the opposite. She talked to her dancers. She directly involved them in the making of her dances, and she told them what each needed to work on and why. If a dancer couldn't accomplish a certain movement in rehearsal, she gave that dancer the time to learn how to do it. She also usually gave an exercise in her technique class the next day that aided the dancer in becoming stronger at what she wanted her or him to do. Starting in the early years, Viola made her company members feel that she was not only their employer, but also their friend. Rehearsals were difficult and exhausting, but often also great fun.

Viola did not discuss with her company what a new dance was about while she was choreographing it, but she was more communicative to the dancers than was her mentor, Merce Cunningham. She gave the dancers hints by asking them to give her more passion or fire in this or that movement phrase. Also, the dancers could tell what quality she wanted by the way she demonstrated the movement. All a dancer had to do was to stay alert and use her or his eyes and senses, and the meaning or direction of the work took shape as she choreographed it.

However, giving her dancers artistic liberties did not always work out the way that Viola had envisioned. Such was the case with the ill-fated dance called *Co-Op*, choreographed in 1970. This was Viola's first, and perhaps last, attempt at making a dance built totally on movements choreographed by the dancers in the company. The title came from the cooperative manner in which it was choreographed.

Six dancers performed *Co-Op*. Each dancer made up two one-minute phrases, and we all learned each other's phrases, making a total of twelve minutes of dancing. Each dancer was also allowed two minutes of free time to do anything that he or she chose to do. Then Viola instructed them to eliminate one of the two minutes of movement; each dancer could choose which phrase to discard. This left eighteen minutes of dance. She then had them put the eighteen minutes together in any order in which they chose. During the performance of *Co-Op*, Viola sat on the edge of the performance space and called out the passage of time at the half-minute and minute points.

For the free minutes, one dancer, Anne Koren, chose to dance while doing vocal warm-up exercises that she had learned in college while she studied acting. I chose to tap-dance, and to stand leaning against a wall looking like a sinister southern redneck leaning against a gas station doorway. One movement or activity phrase by Rosalind Newman was to crawl across the floor while putting on shoes and tying the laces. Other dance phrases were packed with highly skilled dancing.

Co-Op went well in rehearsals and through the first two performances, which took place at the Dance Theatre Workshop on 18th Street in New York City. However, Viola soon noticed that the dancers were taking more and more liberties and getting sillier and sillier as the audience responded with laughter. She got so angry during one performance that she did not speak to us afterwards, and instead of rehearsing us and telling us how to change what we were doing, she pulled the dance from the repertory the next day. *Co-Op* lasted in the company's repertory for only one performance season. This was, however, the only work that Viola removed from her repertory because she was dissatisfied with the dancers' performance.

John Percival wrote this about *Co-Op* in his January, 1972 review for <u>Dance and Dancers</u>:

> "Some of what the dancers did was very interesting, some of it less so. The more straightforward dance passages, developing a particular theme in an individual

way, seemed to me preferable to those where they played about."

Many of the reviewers of *Co-Op* had similar things to say, so therefore Viola was probably correct in following her instincts to drop the dance from the company's repertory as quickly as she did. I never found out if Viola was really angry at how we had performed *Co-Op* or whether she simply did not like the dance. She never mentioned the dance again, and she never apologized for her action.

Viola was a woman of the world, and not much escaped her attention. This ability to see more than most people also led Viola to have her dark moments. Her mood swings were sometimes brought on by overwork and poor health, but often they seemed to appear from nowhere, and caused many dancers to claim that Viola had a mean streak that made them afraid of her. It was, according to Margaret Jenkins, this mean streak that led her to quit the company. Like many choreographers, Viola seemed to need a scapegoat, a dancer whom she used to vent her frustrations. For Viola, it was always a woman in the company who became this scapegoat. The first was Rosalind Newman. After her, it was June Finch, then Susan Matheke, and finally Anne Koren. June said that she had danced with Viola's company many years before she became the target of Viola's wrath. She added that it was extremely difficult when Viola went on one of her rampages against her, and that she was, during those events, tempted to run out of the rehearsal, never to return. But, June was quick to add, "All the rehearsals were not like that. Most of the time they were exhilarating and wonderful." I agree that Viola was, for the most part, exciting to work with and for, yet she did not intend to make the dancers fear her, they felt that at any moment Viola might lash out at one of them.

Many of Viola's early dances were performed in silence. She said that the main reason for this was that her concern that her work was not strong enough to stand up to most composers for whom she had great respect. This is an excellent example of Viola's low self-esteem. From the start, her choreography was strong and very well crafted. She did, however, choreograph one piece in 1969 to music played by a wonderful bluegrass group named the *Iron Mountain String Band*. One member of this group, Caleb "Tuck" Finch, was the husband of company member June Finch. The other members were Peggy Haine, Eric Davidson, and Paul Newman (not to be confused with the actor). The dance was a trio for three women titled *Quota*.

The next New York performance of the company took place in 1970 in the gymnasium on the campus of Barnard College. The evening was shared with choreographer James Cunningham. The first dance that Viola choreographed for the two of us after I left the Cunningham company was a duet titled *Tendency*. This was my official debut as a full time member of her company. Viola's half of the program included *Quota*, *Excerpt,* and *Tendency*. I remember Viola standing on the sidelines once we had finished our half of the program, and watching James Cunningham's group perform. She loved him and his work, but I remember her turning to me and saying, "What an odd mix of dancing this audience is getting tonight!"

As I mentioned earlier, during the four years before 1971, I had been in a relationship with one of Viola's best friends, Peter Saul. The three of us had, over the years, spent a great deal of time together. During the making of *Tendency*, I broke up with Peter, and began to spend more and more time with Viola. We often went out to dinner after rehearsals, stopped off somewhere for coffee, or I helped Viola with errands like food shopping. We even went to a movie together, which neither of us had done in a long time, mainly because we could not afford it. After a few weeks, I began to stay at Viola's apartment longer and longer. We seemed never to run out of things to talk about, and each made the other laugh. I had rarely seen Viola laugh, although I was to find out that she had a wonderful sense of humor, and that she loved to laugh. I very often found myself walking from her apartment in the West Village, all the way across town to the apartment I was subletting on East 10th Street, at two o'clock in the morning. I remember thinking about the first time I saw Viola at Adelphi University, and how I felt that I had known her forever. I felt that I would be with her, in some capacity or other, forever as well.

I remember seeing Viola walking toward me during those days, in late 1970, when we had planned to meet on some particular corner. Before she saw me, I had a good opportunity to observe her as she walked through the crowds of New York. It was probably due to living alone for so many years in Manhattan, but Viola always walked with her purse or dance bag clutched tightly to her chest, never letting it hang loose from her shoulder. She always avoided making eye contact with people, but one could sense that she was on a keen lookout for anyone who might think of harassing her. I know that there were a couple of homeless men who "hung out" in her neighborhood whom Viola would cross the street to avoid. She once admitted that she had on several occasions passed by her apartment and walked around the block so that these men would not know where she lived. I think, but am not certain, that Viola was never mugged on the streets of New York. The entire time I knew her, she always seemed extremely nervous while walking in any city, whether or not she was alone.

The first tour that the Farber company took was a brief, one-performance and teaching residency at Cornell University in Ithaca, NY, in 1971. The company drove there in two vehicles, a car and a very old VW van owned by Dan Wagoner; the same van that Dan used when touring with his own company. It was winter and very cold, and the van's heater was not working. It was so cold that ice formed on the inside of the windows, and Dan entertained the dancers who were with him by carving out a television set on one of the windows and pretending that the view outside was a TV show. Viola was in the van, along with June Finch, me, and the lighting designer, Molly*, and her dog. We all laughed a great deal in spite of the discomfort we felt from the cold.

The Cornell residency, which included a performance on February 4, 1971, in the Alice Statler Auditorium, went very well. The program included five works, *Passage, Tendency, Excerpt, Curriculum,* and *Co-Op,* the latter two being the newest works in the repertory. After the performance, there was a reception with tons of food for the dancers, all of which had been prepared by the student dancers in the Cornell dance program, directed by Peggy Lawlor.

The trip back to New York was even colder in the van because we traveled during the night. Molly's dog spent the entire trip on the floor at Viola's feet until we were almost at home. We were traveling along the West Side Highway when the animal jumped into Viola's lap and proceeded to throw up. We were astonished when, instead of getting upset; Viola simply chuckled and proceeded to comfort the poor carsick dog.

Viola rarely took a day off from work. When the company was not rehearsing, performing, or on tour, she went alone on teaching residencies or to choreograph new works for other small dance companies throughout the United States, France, Germany and England. The income went toward supporting the company and its employees.

In most small dance companies, the last person to get paid is the choreographer, if indeed she or he gets paid at all. As for Viola,

---

* I have contacted everyone on that first tour, and searched the Farber Archives. I can not find Molly's last name.

during much of the time she had her company, the money that paid her own rent, food, etc. came from doing other teaching or choreographic jobs separate from, and in addition to, the company work.

Sharing the studio on 17th Street with Dan Wagoner was becoming complicated for both artists. Both taught classes, and both had dance companies that needed time and space to rehearse. There simply were not enough hours in the week to accommodate both companies in the tiny studio. The two were competing for the same dance students, trying to coordinate the rehearsal times, and rapidly becoming less and less friendly toward each other. Viola knew that something had to change, and since Dan had been the one to find the studio on 17th Street, she and the company set out to find their own studio elsewhere.

During this extremely busy time, Viola and I fell in love. We were working on the duet titled *Tendency*, which we would later nickname our courting dance. Karen Levey, who performed with the Paul Taylor and Dan Wagoner companies, and later Viola's company, often said that she knew whether or not Viola and I were getting along by the way we performed the duet. If things were going well between us, we were playful on stage. If not, we rarely looked at each other. The dance was built in such a way that we were supposed to react to each other in a similar way as jazz musicians do musically while jamming together.

During our dating period, if Viola spotted someone we knew while we were walking in the street holding hands, she jerked her hand away. There were several reasons for this. One was the complex situation that marriage would put me in as a company member. Up until then I was just another dancer in the company, who also taught classes at the studio. Another reason was much more complicated. Viola was my senior by fifteen years, and I am gay. She did not want to tell anyone about our plans until she was certain that our relationship was truly serious. I was willing to go along with this secrecy because I was just as surprised at our relationship as Viola was.

Six months after our first date, on June 14, 1971 we shocked ourselves, the company, and the entire dance community by getting married. The marriage took place in the Garden Room of the Judson Church on Washington Square in New York. Viola had just turned forty and I was twenty-five. We had managed to keep our courting and our plans for getting married a secret. The only people who knew beforehand of our marriage plans, and who attended the wedding, were Peter Saul, Margaret Craske, Donald Mahler, and the minister who performed the wedding ceremony. Viola had informed only one company member, June Finch, the day before because June had invited Viola to dinner on the 14th, and so Viola asked whether I could join them as we would be married by that time. June agreed to keep the secret, because Viola wanted to tell the other company members herself.

The ceremony was very short, and the only wording that we changed within the vows was that we took out the phrase about promising to obey. I mention this fact with great love and respect for Viola only because I was soon to find out that she was not about to obey anyone, but she often expected everyone to obey her.

Upon leaving the church, we ran into Judith Dunn, a wonderful dancer and choreographer, and a former member of the Cunningham company during the time that Viola was there. She asked us what we were up to, and when we told her that we had just gotten married, Judith replied, "Oh, no! Why?"

The "wedding party" then went to lunch on Sixth Avenue in the West Village, after which Viola and I went to the studio as usual for rehearsal. It was only then that Viola broke the news to the company. One dancer fell to the floor, one cried, and after a very long silence the dancers voiced their congratulations and surprise. We had really succeeded in keeping our romance and marriage a secret. This was not an easy task in the dance community, which is very small and, as the choreographer Murray Louis is quoted as having said, "crowded." Another once said that the dance community was so small that a dancer could stand alone in an elevator and think about some personal event, and soon everyone in the dance world would know about it.

After rehearsal that day, Viola was scheduled to teach a beginning dance class. June Finch insisted, however, that someone else in the company teach the class, because we had already rehearsed on our wedding day and we deserved to begin our life as husband and wife. To my amazement, Viola agreed, and we left to go to June's place for dinner. It was one of the few times during our marriage that we came first and the company second. That night after dinner, I moved into Viola's small, railroad style apartment on Jones Street.

Viola always appeared strong and in control in public. She ran her company with great authority, and she was in total control while teaching, dancing, and choreographing a new work. The woman at home was often a totally different person. She still enjoyed being in control, but she was often insecure and constantly needed reassurance that her work was good, and that her dancing was still strong enough to be seen on stage. She was always asking me whether she was too old to perform, or whether I thought that her work was boring. She complained to me about having to work so hard, and after all that work that her company still was not touring as much as she felt it should.

She disliked large social gatherings. She made up any excuse not to attend parties that she should have gone to in order to promote herself and the company. I tried my best to get her to go to these functions, and I did manage literally to drag her to a few of them, but usually she refused.

Now that she was older, and with all her success, Viola was still insecure about her looks. Long before blue jeans were fashionable, Viola wore them. She rarely wore a dress or a skirt, and she now wore her hair cut very short. This was the early 1970s, and short hair was not yet fashionable for women. I thought that the cut was perfect for her, but even though she wanted it that way, she seemed very much affected by the way many people in the street stared at her. She felt that people stared at us because of our age difference, and many people whom we met for the first time often assumed that we were siblings or, worse, mother and son.

Many people have often said that Viola's dancing was unique and mysterious. I quite agree. Having been married to her, I think that part of that uniqueness and mystery came from her insecurity, vulnerability, and her shyness about her looks. She was also very uncomfortable about performing, but, at the same time, loved doing so. Part of her felt that performing was not doing enough to help make the world a better place in which to live. Dancing was in her blood, however, and she did it like no one else.

Viola and I did not go on a honeymoon trip after the wedding. The company had just found a small loft on White Street, in the area of Manhattan now called Soho, and Viola was scheduled to go to Salt Lake City to work. White Street is located in lower Manhattan, just south of Canal Street. The loft was on the second floor of a four-story building that had once belonged to the telephone company. Each of the top three floors were occupied by artists, and the ground floor was used for storage by a business firm. The walls of the loft were in horrible shape, but it had a fairly good wood floor and a space that was just large enough for a dance studio.

The company took over the lease of the loft in the summer of 1971, a few days after Viola and I were married. Viola had a commitment with the Repertory Dance Theatre to choreograph a new work, and so she flew off to Salt Lake City for three weeks. Meanwhile, several members of the company set out to turn the dark and dingy loft into a new home for the company, and they were determined to get the job finished before Viola returned to New York. They ripped out the old telephone cables from the walls, sanded and refinished the floors, painted the walls and ceilings, and built partitions to make dressing room areas. Anyone who has spent time in New York City during July and August knows how hot and humid it can be. The studio had windows in the front and back of the building. The back windows, however, looked onto the back of another building, so that there was very little cross ventilation in that loft. The dancers put in many long, hot and sweaty hours, and they finished in just under three weeks. When Viola returned from Utah and walked into the studio for the first time, seeing the look of joy and surprise on her face was worth all their hard work. The Viola Farber Dance Studio was ready to open for business.

The size of the entire loft was approximately twenty-five by eighty feet. The dancing space was approximately thirty-five feet long and twenty-five feet deep, not very large for a dance studio. The only heat was provided by a small gas heater in the front where the teacher stood. The studio was so cold in the winter that a wet towel which Larry Clark used to help him not slip during rehearsals froze and became totally unusable. There was a tiny office area as one walked into the studio, and two dressing rooms were located at the front of the loft. Although both rooms were quite small, the women's dressing area was twice as large as the men's. The loft was small, but it was a home for the company. Because the company could not afford a new piano for the studio, Viola donated her own upright piano from our small apartment on Jones Street. This was a true sacrifice for Viola as she thought of that piano as much more than just a musical instrument.

During the first month or so that the studio was open, the class

115

consisted mainly of the company members, plus a few loyal students. Viola's classes had been packed on 17th Street, and she thought that perhaps it was going to take a while for the dancers to get used to the new location. When, after two months, however, the classes were still not being attended by more dancers. Viola confided in me that she was worried that the company was going to lose the studio; the money for the rent simply was not there.

I do not know how I thought of this, but I suggested to Viola that we raise the fee for the classes. I guess I was thinking of the old saying, "You get what you pay for." It worked: We advertised that the cost of each class had gone up by two dollars. I believe that dancers saw this and believed that business must be good and that, if they wanted to be where the action was, they had best hustle on down to White Street. Within two weeks, Viola's classes were once again packed to overflowing.

Viola's management company, Artservices, suggested that she rent the studio out whenever the company was away on tour. That way, the loft would not be sitting there empty and losing money during such times. Viola agreed, and for a while everything went smoothly. Money was coming in from dancers renting the space to rehearse, and in some cases, to teach their own classes.

Then the company went on a small tour of upstate New York, being out of town from Friday through Sunday for two consecutive weekends. The studio was rented to a small theater group. The first Monday that the company was back, Viola went into the studio to prepare to teach class. Minutes later she called me into the studio.

"Jeff. Am I crazy or is the piano gone?" She asked.

"No, Viola." I answered. "The piano is gone all right!"

Sure enough, someone had come into the studio and stolen the piano and its bench. The door had been locked when we came in, the windows were all locked, and the freight elevator door was locked as well. Viola was of course upset over the loss of her piano, but the loss of the sheet music that had belonged to her mother and that was inside the piano bench made her sit down on the floor and weep. Money could somehow be found to replace the piano, but the sheet music was irreplaceable. The two policemen who answered the call said that it was the first time that they had ever heard of a piano being reported as stolen. For the rest of the week, Viola clapped and snapped her fingers to keep the beat for class.

One week later Viola and I again arrived at the studio before anyone else. Viola walked into the space and screamed. I ran into the studio to find her standing in front of a bare wall that was covered with mirrors when we had left a few days ago. Whoever stole the piano the week before had returned for the mirrors. The theft was done very professionally; there was not a splinter of glass or wood anywhere on the floor. This time when we called the police, we reported to them that we had found one of the front windows next to the fire escape unlocked. What the police concluded, and they were probably correct, is that someone from the theater group had purposefully left the windows unlocked and returned later. The thieves had then slipped in through the unlocked window and let their accomplices in through the front door. They reversed the process when they departed.

The minimalist composer Philip Glass was living in the building next door at the time and later told Viola that he had seen two men loading a piano and mirrors into a truck, but that he thought that her company was moving out of the building. The thieves were never caught, and there was not even enough evidence with which to confront the theater group about the robbery. Viola did not rent her studio out after that. She preferred to work extra jobs in order to pay the rent rather than go through such an experience again.

Viola always gave the impression of being totally prepared in rehearsals. She was a master at coming up with movement phrases "on the spot," and she had trained her company to pick up the movements quickly. It was rare that she was unprepared. Her self-imposed schedule was to arrive at the studio at 8 a.m. and begin her day by giving herself a forty minute warm up class. Then she taught the advanced class, did company business, or worked on her choreography while a company member taught the intermediate class. After a short lunch break, rehearsal began, usually lasting until at least 5 p.m. More company business or rehearsal on a solo for herself was followed by teaching a beginner class. If she did not teach that class, Viola stayed and worked on something relating to the company, or, if needed, she played the piano for the class. She usually got home around 8:30 or 9:00 p.m. For years, she maintained this schedule five days a week while the company was in New York. Saturdays, she came home by 3 or 4 p.m. Often she went to the studio alone on Sundays to work by herself on a new piece or on her own dancing. Rarely did she take a day off. Even though she complained about her strenuous schedule, she loved her work. Dancing, the company, and hard work were a way of life for Viola. She seemed not to know how to handle free or idle time.

One of the first dances that she choreographed in the new studio was a work called *Survey* (1971). Choreographed and performed in silence, *Survey* was approximately forty minutes in length. It was very difficult for the dancers, requiring extreme stamina and endurance. The dance began with a series of very slow movements which the dancers were asked to perform in any order and in any direction that they chose. The first movement phrase was packed with difficult balances, and it was almost impossible for the dancers to cover any mistakes. As the dance progressed, it gradually picked up speed, and toward the end of this very long work, when the dancers were close to dropping from fatigue, they had to dance their fastest. Several in the company remarked that the hardest part of performing *Survey* was taking the curtain call after the dance was over. All they wanted to do was to go to the dressing rooms and collapse. Taking a second or third bow was difficult, as no one had much energy left to be gracious to the audience. Every time I had performed *Survey,* I ran directly for the men's room to throw up.

Viola once told a friend that she remembered a woman telling her that she had not enjoyed watching *Survey.* She had not been bothered by the length of the work or the lack of music, but by the fact that she could see and hear just how difficult it was for the dancers to get through the piece. At some point, the woman had stopped seeing the work and began worrying about the dancers' health.

When Viola's mother was diagnosed with Alzheimer's and eventually was placed in a nursing home in a suburb of Chicago, Viola decided to choreograph a solo for herself based on her mother's illness. Not wanting to use her mother's real name, she titled the dance *Mildred.* "My mother's name was Dora," Viola said, "which is a name hardly anybody has now, and when I started out making it I wanted it just to be about the woman. I didn't want it to be specific. It turned out to be much more about Mutti than I had realized. Mildred also seemed to me to be a name that people didn't use very much anymore, and it wasn't Dora."

She wanted to perform the dance in silence because she was afraid that any music she chose would lend too much atmosphere or the wrong quality to the solo. Then she hit upon a wonderful idea of having the company members stand in the back stage area and call out the name Mildred with different voice qualities and accents. "This had to do with Mutti imagining that people were calling her, because she thought she had to do things for a lot of people and she didn't really like that.

It wasn't that she didn't love them, but she had to do things that were very difficult for her to do," Viola explained. "So, the sounds were something that I imagined she would think. They're always calling 'Mildred, Mildred, Mildred,' but also, I think it was me calling. Mutti was difficult, but I really loved her very much, and I remember when she died I thought, 'Well, it's wonderful for her to be rid of this pain, this agony that she was in, but I'll just never see her again."

The dance proved to be very effective and interesting when seen from the audience. The first time that she performed it was at the Brooklyn Academy of Music, and the union stage crew liked the idea so much that they chimed in, calling out "Mildred" as well. The name was said sometimes quickly, or sometimes slowly. Sometimes it sounded loving or angry or hurt. Viola claimed that she did not react to the names being called out; she was such a good actress that I think she must at least have been affected by it. She used several facial expressions in the solo, and I am certain that these were related to her hearing the people calling out "Mildred."

The Brooklyn Academy of Music crew seemed really to enjoy Viola's work, and when Viola was going over the books with her manager at Artservices later that month, she discovered that the crew had not charged the company for its services. This was totally unheard of in the theater. The men told Viola's manager that they had thoroughly enjoyed working with Viola and her company, and that they knew that we must be an extremely poor company, judging from the low-budget look of things. Viola was very touched by this gesture and sent them all a gracious thank-you note.

The first big break for the company came in the spring of 1972, when a member of the French Ministry of Culture, Michel Guy, was to come to watch a rehearsal. He was in New York scouting for new dance companies to participate in the Ninth International Paris Dance

Festival, and acting on the advice of Artservices. Viola and the entire company were excited and nervous about his watching rehearsal, because we all knew it was also an audition for the festival.

On the day of Michel Guy's visit, Viola arrived at the studio to find that one of the male dancers, Larry Clark, was injured, Rosalind Newman was ill with the flu, and I was very sick with a cold. In the spirit of "show biz", however, everyone was there ready to perform. Nothing short of a broken leg was going to stop any of us from trying to help Viola get the performing gig in Paris. Many of the dancers had never traveled abroad and were anxious to go.

The guest of honor arrived, along with the company manager, Mimi Johnson, and the dancers proceeded to show Michel Guy the repertory. Everything was going along smoothly until, in one of the dances, Rosalind and I collided, my arm smacking hard into her already dripping nose. There we were, this brand-new modern dance company dancing away, trying to get a date in Paris with everything going wrong that could go wrong. Everyone in the company was certain that we had danced our worst and not presented the company as being of the professional caliber that Michel Guy expected.

The dancers were crushed and, more importantly, terrified that we had ruined Viola's big chance at having the company take part in the festival. To our astonishment, Michel Guy stood up at the end of the rehearsal and applauded with great enthusiasm. His eyes were wide with excitement, and he asked Viola right then and there whether her company would be part of the dance festival in Paris. She, of course, said yes.

The Ninth International Paris Dance Festival was held on the outskirts of Paris at the Theatre de la Cité Internationale. It had a terribly small thrust stage, and the stage floor and backstage area were very dirty. To make matters worse, a huge set which belonged to one of the other companies was stored in the stage left wing area. This made entering onto and exiting from the stage very hazardous. The dancers were not too bothered by this, however, because we were dancing in Paris, France! As far as we were concerned, we had made it to the big time. The other American dance company to perform at the festival was the very young Twyla Tharp Dance Company.

The performances went well in spite of the small stage, and during our brief time off, the company members wandered around Paris, enjoying the sights. There was a huge party at the end of the festival, and awards were to be given for best choreography, performance, and the like. Everyone in the company was excited and hoping, of course, that Viola would win one of the awards. Her dancers considered her to be the best, and we hoped that the French judges would think so, too. We all knew that the French had loved Viola's dancing in 1964, but this was seven years later. Would they remember?

The big gala party arrived, and the awards were announced without Viola's name being included among them. The company's spirits were beginning to sag, when all of a sudden the emcee, a faceless voice over a PA system, said, "This year we are pleased to present a new award for Creativity and Expression, and that award goes to Viola Farber and Bif Clinton."

While everyone was applauding, Viola was looking around, wondering who the heck Bif Clinton was. It was Anne Koren who finally figured out that they were talking about me. Somehow, Jeff Slayton had gotten translated into Bif Clinton. Viola and I went up and accepted the award. Because I couldn't speak French and Viola spoke it fluently, she did all the talking. The award that was presented to Viola and me was a very small wooden star that had been painted gold. It was a cheap item that was probably thrown together hastily on the day of the ceremony. Viola, however, was thrilled to have been singled out and very grateful for the award. She kept that little painted gold star for many years, but somehow it was misplaced in one of her many moves.

At the end of that same first trip to Paris for the Farber company, Michel Guy treated the entire company to dinner at the famous Maxim's Restaurant. Remy Charlip happened to be in Paris and joined us for dinner. Everyone was shocked to find that the meal consisted of what looked like beef stew, and that it tasted more like English cooking than French cuisine. Viola knew that the dancers probably looked very much out of place, as none of us could afford the type of clothes worn by the regular patrons of Maxim's. Nevertheless, we had a wonderful time and Michel Guy made the company feel very much at ease, so we were soon mingling with the "rich folks."

Viola in Legacy, *1968. Photographer: Teresa King*

Left to right: June Finch, Andé Peck, Viola Farber in Viola's Curriculum, *1970.*
Photographer: Teresa King

Viola Farber and Jeff Slayton in Tendency, *1970. Photographer:
Teresa King*

Viola Farber in Mildred, *1971. Photographer: Jack Mitchell*

Viola Farber in Tendency, *1970. Photographer: Teresa King*

Viola Farber and June Finch in rehearsal for
Curriculum, *1970. Photographer: Mark Lancaster*

*Left to right: Andé Peck, June Finch, Anne Koren, Larry Clark, Rosalind
Newman in Farber's* Survey, *1971. Photographer: Teresa King*

Viola Farber and Jeff Slayton, circa 1972. Photographer: Terry Stevenson

Jeff Slayton and Viola Farber in Route 6, *1972. Photographer: Mary Lucier*

Andé Peck, Viola Farber and Jeff Slayton in rehearsal for
Route 6, *1972. Photographer: Mark Lancaster*

Left to right: Jeff Slayton, Viola Farber, Andé Peck, Anne Koren
in Farber's Poor Eddie, *1972. Photographer: Mary Lucier*

Chapter Four

The Viola Farber Company (1973 – 1981)

VIOLA AND I FINALLY GOT to take our much needed honeymoon a full year after we were married. We decided to drive down the coast and spend a week at the Meher Spiritual Center in Myrtle Beach, S.C. The Center is a beautiful retreat with lovely cabins, a lagoon with a resident alligator, many pine trees, and hordes of copperhead moccasins. One had to carry a flashlight around at night in order to assure that one did not step on the snakes that came out to drink from the lagoon. It was a wonderful week away from New York, the company and the worries about where the next rent check was coming from. It was here, too, that through a series of teasing each other that I nicknamed Viola "Dos" and she began calling me "Dimt." There were many variations on these names, but those were the two that endured. Privately, we rarely called each other by our real names. Perhaps this was a way to separate our professional and private selves.

Around this time, 1972, Viola began working with composer Alvin Lucier, who not only composed the scores for several of her dances, but also became the company's Music Director for several years. The first dance of Viola's that he composed the music for was an extraordinarily beautiful work titled *Dune*. To many who saw her work, *Dune* was one of Viola's best creations, and Lucier's music was just as powerful as the dance. It was inspired by a vacation that Viola and I took to Cape Cod in the month of September, and the dunes that we saw there. The movement was lush and full, and the quality of the work was warm and inviting. *Dune* gave one a similar feeling of peace that one gets sitting by the ocean. The duets were tender and loving, unlike some of Viola's other works that some viewers found filled with violence.

Dune was choreographed for seven people. She related the following about what inspired her to choreograph *Dune*. "One of the beaches that we used to go to had fifty foot high dunes, and there were few people on the beach. Occasionally small groups, a couple, or a solitary person would appear. Sometimes people would roll or run down the dunes to the beach, singly, or two people together, which was illegal, but very beautiful. The ocean was cold and calm. The dance starts with a woman moving slowly from stage right to stage left, sometimes stopping, sometimes moving sharply, before continuing on her slow path. The dancer is still upstage right for three minutes, then she moves down stage and leaves. The other six dancers appear briefly and leave. People dance together, alone. They come, go, and stay a while."

Lucier was an electronic music composer, which some audience goers find difficult to listen to or sit through. Up to this point, Viola's work had mainly been seen in silence or very familiar music. Lucier's music was a new stretch for the company, but it also helped to bring Viola's work into the arena of the rest of the "Avant Garde" choreographers in New York. Cunningham had been working with electronic music from the mid 1950s, but his company had not truly become well-known throughout the United States until the late 1960s. Lucier was among that generation of composers that followed after John Cage. Cage is considered by many to be the father of electronic music. Other works of Viola's that Lucier composed for included: *Poor Eddie* (1973), *Soup* (1973), *Spare Change* (1973), *Willi I* (1974), *No Super, No Boiler* (1974), *Houseguest* (1974), and *Motorcycle/Boat* (1975). The score for *Houseguest,* a solo for me, did not include electronic music, but the sounds of doors slamming. These sounds were not recorded, however, but were made by Lucier himself walking around the aisles of the audience and slamming the exit doors. After several performances of *Houseguest* Lucier and Viola agreed that the dance would be performed in silence because members of the audience kept complaining that some weirdo in the audience kept making too much noise slamming the doors. *Houseguest* was a particularly difficult dance to perform; full of extremely hard technical feats, one following right after the other. I would have to spin on the floor without using my arms, spiral up to balancing on one leg in relevé. After a brief pause, while my upper body was tilted to one side, I had to turn without any preparation. I went from one difficult turn into another without the normal dance preparation in between. Without any music to help phrase the movements, I had to find my own phrasing. The slamming of doors had helped me with the atmosphere of the solo at least, but without it, I was totally on my own. Scary! It took me a good year to find the phrasing for that solo that totally pleased Viola, and when I did she asked me how I had come up with it. "I'm out there singing. Can't you hear me?" I answered. Viola simply smiled and walked away. I do not know if she approved of my method or not, but she never bothered me about the phrasing in *Houseguest* after that.

During the summer of 1972, the company was invited to share a three week residence at American University in Washington, D.C., the same university where Viola had gone to school for one academic year. The other company at the residency was the Bella Lewitzky Dance Company. Although the residency was very successful for the company, the conditions under which we had to work were far from ideal. Classes for the students were taught on hard gymnasium floors and for several classes, the Farber company taught on one side of the gym, while on the other side, separated by a folding wall, the Lewitzky company taught another class. Music for the two classes filtered through the folding wall, making it difficult for the students and the teachers to concentrate.

Most of the company classes and rehearsals were held in a converted attic studio which was small, low-ceilinged, strangely proportioned, poorly ventilated, and painted bright orange. If not there, then the company used one of the gymnasiums that was situated directly over a sauna. The closeness, the color of the paint, and the heat and humidity often caused tempers to flare and patience to wear thin. Another factor which made the residency difficult for Viola was that the whole company lived in one two-story house which the company rented in order to save money. For four weeks, we were together almost twenty-four hours a day, working, eating, and sleeping in close proximity of each other. Except when she was in our bedroom, Viola had no privacy from the company members.

It was in that orange studio that Viola began choreographing a new dance, a quartet, for herself, me, Anne Koren and Andé Peck. It was clearly a dance about irritation. Viola had taken the emotions and feelings felt in that small American University studio and turned them into a dance. In her own words: "Our bodies in the dance are often twisted, pulled off center, the legs jab the air and paw the floor, we fall, push, are pushed, we interrupt each other in the middle of movements, get in each others way, etc."

During this residency, Viola and Bella Lewitzky were invited to be interviewed by one of the local Washington, D.C. radio stations. The interviewer had obviously not done the necessary homework before the two women arrived, for at the beginning of the live interview he introduced Ms. Lewitzky as a member of the Viola Farber Dance Company. In her usual cool and elegant manner, Ms. Lewitzky responded with a statement that, although she would be honored to be a dancer in Ms. Farber's company, she in fact had her own company which was also in residence at American University. These two strong women enjoyed each other's company and had high regard and respect for each other as artists, but their work was miles apart in both quality and style. Bella Lewitzky was trained by and performed with Lester Horton, whose technique was nothing like the Cunningham approach to dancing, or to Viola's. There was nothing similar in either's approach to choreography or in their teaching of dance technique. During the three weeks those differences in teaching styles challenged the students who studied with both.

Back in New York, one of the male students who attended classes at Viola's studio at the time was a young man from China. He spoke very little English, and because everyone had trouble pronouncing his name, we called him Eddie. Because of his lack of understanding of the language, Eddie was either late to class or he came to the wrong class level. One day after Eddie had shown up late yet again and then left in frustration, Viola said, "Oh, poor Eddie!" Well, it somehow became a running joke among the dancers in the company, and Viola decided to title the dance that she was choreographing *Poor Eddie* in honor of that young Chinese man.

Many dancers, who are studying choreography, always ask how one comes up with title for dances. Some of Viola's titles came directly from the making of the dance, such as *Duet for Mirjam and Jeff*, which was given that title because it was a duet for those two dancers. In the case of *Poor Eddie* and many others of Viola's works, the title had nothing to do with the dance, but came from some situation that took place in her life during the time that she was choreographing. Her solo *Seconds* (1965) got its title because Viola had been making up movement for classes that she had been teaching, and so felt that the solo was made up of leftovers from those classes. *Route 6* (1972) was a trio that got its inspiration from a trip that Viola and I took on a two lane highway, Rte. 6 in Massachusetts. As previously mentioned, *Dune* (1972) was inspired by a trip to the ocean. So, an audience member who was unfamiliar with Viola's work may have been very confused while watching a dance and trying to connect what she or he was seeing with the title of the dance listed in the concert program.

In the fall of 1972, Viola's company was asked to perform at the Anta Theatre in New York on the Umbrella Dance Series. The theater is located in the Broadway district, so for Viola this felt like the "big time." What was a little odd about the way the series was organized was that each company would share a program with another dance company, not always one that was compatible. Such was the case of the Farber company's first experience on the Umbrella Dance Series, for it was paired off with the Alvin Ailey Dance Theatre.

One could not ask for two more different companies. The audience for the Ailey Company was made up of people whose taste in dance differed from the audience for the Farber Company. Alvin Ailey was an extremely talented black choreographer whose work was just one generation behind. He often choreographed to jazz and Negro spirituals. His costumes were elegant and his work was a little more "traditional" than Viola's generation of choreographers. So, after the Farber company finished performing each of its two works, *Dune* and *Route 6*, only half of the audience applauded enthusiastically, and the same thing happened after the Ailey company danced. Since the Ailey company was much better known at the time, its "half" of the audience was a great deal larger than the Farber company's "half." Viola found the entire experience embarrassing and unpleasant. The dancers did not feel this way; of course, as they were extremely thrilled just to be dancing in a theater on Broadway, even if they were considered a "second string" company. Everyone has to start somewhere, is how they looked at it.

Viola fumed for days after that first Umbrella Dance Series. She put blame on Artservices, and then on the people who organized the series. How could they do this to her? How could they be so stupid? Listening to Viola rant and rave about this, I began to realize that she was somewhat embarrassed by what had happened, and was feeling very insecure about her work. It took weeks to convince her that her work was just a strong as anyone else's, and better than most. I am not truly certain that she was ever convinced of this fact.

One of the fun things that did happen during that series, and talked about for many years afterwards by the company, was how the dancer Judith Jamison was backstage. Jamison was one of the most beautiful modern dancers of her generation. She had a huge presence onstage, and although not the strongest dancer technically, she was an amazing actress and could hold an audience's attention indefinitely. Backstage it was the same. Jamison held court in her dressing room, and everyone who could fight their way backstage after the performance, wanted to see her. I remember her sitting at her dressing room table before the concert began wearing a bright red dress, and with her feet propped up. As we walked by her room on the way to the stage, Jamison smiled and wished us all good luck, or as dancers say it, "Merde!" There was no false airs about her. She was genuinely warm to us all.

Viola and I were in St. Louis, Missouri in the summer of 1973 teaching a summer workshop when we got the news that her mother had died at age 82. I only met Dora Farber once, and she was already pretty ill. At the time she could no longer speak English, and her German was almost gone as well. She would mainly speak in garbled German, only making sense occasionally. She also seemed to cry most of the time. I was standing at the foot of her bed, when she said something that Viola and her sister, Elisabeth seem to understand. They both looked at me and laughed. When I asked them to explain what Mutti had said they told me that she had wanted to know if I was cold because I was standing there with my arms folded. I told them to tell her that I wasn't cold, but that I didn't know what else to do with them since they were so long. This seemed to please Viola's mother and she smiled.

The thing that struck me about Dora Farber was that at her late age her hair was still almost solid black, with very little gray in it. I asked Viola if Mutti dyed her hair, and Viola said that she didn't. She thought that it might have to do with the fact that Mutti had a bit of Mongolian blood in her ancestry. Her hair was thick, almost jet black, and extremely straight; very much like Asian women's hair.

Dora Farber died on July 13, 1973 after a long battle with Alzheimer's. Viola flew to Chicago to help with the funeral arrangements while I stayed in St. Louis to teach. The rest of the company arrived before Viola returned and we rehearsed for the upcoming performances without her. Viola, like the trouper that she was, returned in time for the concert. She was extremely sad, of course, as she had been very close to her mother and loved her very much. I do not remember her crying as much when her father died as she did after her mother's death.

Viola and I were rehearsing later that year when I noticed a lump on Viola throat. It was only noticeable when she arched her upper back and neck. I asked if she knew what it might be, but she had no idea. On examination at her doctor it was discovered that she had a tumor on her thyroid gland, and that it had to be removed. Viola was very nervous about the operation, but knew that it had to be done in case it turned out malignant. We checked her into the hospital and after I had gone home a young intern came into her room and told her that the tumor was very close to her vocal cords and that she may lose her voice. Viola immediately called me at home and was very upset and crying. I made a call to her doctor and he was furious that an intern had said this to her the night before her surgery.

Fortunately the operation went well, the tumor was not malignant and the vocal cords were not affected. When she woke up from the surgery the first thing Viola did was test her voice, and she was thrilled, of course, to find that she could speak. Two months later it was very difficult to see where the surgery had happened, as the scar was thinner than a slim, gold necklace. The doctor said that she was very lucky that her skin healed so quickly and cleanly. Viola would, however, be on thyroid medicine for the rest of her life.

As I have said, one of the things that the company had to do on tour was to give lecture/demonstrations in most university settings. During my research I came across many notes among Viola's personal journals. Many of them appeared to have been written for articles that she was writing, or notes for lecture/demonstrations that the company gave while on tour. The following one was among those notes for such an event.

> "I am interested in the diversity of physical phenomena, in the relationships of beings and things to each other; in love, hate, anger, indifference, affection. I would not like to live in a tropical climate - I welcome the change of seasons. Some animals move very slowly, some with lighting speed, some do both and in between. The textures of simply the outside of our bodies are many and varied."

I think that what Viola was writing about was how she saw

movement, and how she liked to choreograph. She enjoyed variety, and her work sometimes took on the look of a three ring circus. The audience had to make choices about where to look or which dancer or dancers to follow. Her work changed, of course, through the years, but her early work especially had the quality of organized chaos.

Each choreographer begins her or his dance differently. Viola was no exception to this fact. There are really no set rules or formulas that dictate how a choreographer must work. Classes and workshops in composition and choreography are taught in colleges and universities, and even in some professional arenas. Some choreographers begin by choosing a work of music and letting that inspire them. Others begin with a storyline or emotion, choreograph the movement and then either have the music composed for the dance, or they search out music that fit's the movement or idea. Choreographers like Merce Cunningham create their dances solely separate and independently of the music, letting the dance and the music simply share the same time and space, but each an entity of and to itself.

Viola worked differently on each dance. Sometimes it was a piece of music that gave her the inspiration for a dance. Examples of this were *Dinosaur Parts* (1974) to the music of David Tudor with the same title; *Night Shade* (1975) to Ludwig Van Beethoven's *Opus 27, No. 2*; *Turf* (1978) to Poulenc's *Organ Concerto in G Minor*, and *Bequest* (1981) to Mendelssohn's *Trio in D Minor No. 1, Opus 49*, to name a few. Viola also got inspired to choreograph *Turf* from watching sports reports. The dance's patterns were derived from sports movements, particularly those of a soccer game that Viola had seen on television. Poulenc's music still came before the movement, however. Other times she got her ideas from movement phrases that came to her while preparing to teach. A picture in a museum, the way a person in the street was acting, a drive through the country, or a tragedy in her personal life might cause her to choreograph a certain dance. Several dances were choreographed and the music added later. This was especially true during the years that Alvin Lucier was the company's Music Director. During that period, 1971 to 1976, the company often performed to the music composed by Lucier.

Larry Clark felt that Viola choreographed because she was interested in making dances for herself. The result of this meant that whatever movement that she made up for herself, also became movement for her dancers. There was no story line in Viola's choreography, and she only asked that the audience be actively involved while viewing her work. She rarely choreographed specifically for the audience. Viola made dances that reflected what she saw in the world.

I know that Viola was very concerned with the plight of people in the world around her. She also trusted that the audience was intelligent enough to see and think for themselves without having to "spell it out" to them. Having said this, there is a humorous event that took place between Viola and I in an airport somewhere in the U.S. I can not remember the exact date, and it is not really important. We were married at the time so it had to be between 1971 and 1978. We had some extra time at the airport between flights and so we were walking around looking in the gift shops and book stores. At some point Viola turned to me and said, "Jeff, I think that I know now why most people don't like my work."

"Why?" I asked.

"Well, look at the awful crap that is in most of these gift shops that people are buying! If they like this junk, how can they like my work?"

Somewhere around this time Viola and I decided to take a long week end and drive up to Bennington, Vt. We rented a small cabin-like motel room that was tucked away in the woods just outside Bennington.

That first evening we went to see Judith (Judy) Dunn, who had moved there and who was recovering from surgery. Judy had asked us for dinner, but when we arrived all that was served was tea and cookies. We had a wonderful visit with Judy, but both Viola and I got horrible migraine headaches from not having eaten. I drove us back to the cabin at night, with the oncoming headlights glaring in my eyes, and Viola sat next to me clutching her head in agony. We got something to eat at a local diner, but neither of us could finish our meals, and when we reached the cabin we went directly to bed. It was fall and very cold at night there, so we had turned on the wall heating unit before going to sleep. Several hours later, Viola woke me saying that the wall looked as if it was glowing. At first I thought that she was hallucinating, but when I got up and felt the wall, I found that it was red hot. I turned off the heating unit and opened the window in the kitchenette, and we managed to avert a fire in the cabin. The following morning, we decided to return to New York, but half way home, the jeep that we had borrowed from friends overheated. We had to call road service in order to get the jeep started, and to make matters worse, it began to rain harder than I can ever remember. The drive home took several hours longer than it should have, and we were more exhausted than we would have been had we never gone to Bennington at all.

Although we never took vacations, Viola and I did escape regularly to her small house in New City, where we had wonderful dinners with the Rossins. I remember very nice walks in the surrounding woods, and sitting in front of the fire place drinking coffee at night while we chatted, and of course, chain smoked. The Rossins had a beautiful live-in maid named Bridget, who cleaned the little house for us, fed our two cats, TJ and Eric, and built wonderful fires. I have rarely met anyone who made such great fires as dear Bridget.

In 1974, Viola received a grant from the New York State Council to present outdoor performances in all five boroughs of New York City. These performances took place in 1975 at the McGraw Hill Plaza on the Avenue of the Americas, the Bronx Botanical Gardens, the Staten Island Ferry Terminal on the Staten Island side, the Brooklyn Museum Sculpture Garden, and at the old World's Fair site in Queens in and around the world globe sculpture. Viola titled these performances *Five Works For Sneakers*, based on the fact that the dancers performed in sneakers and wore everyday street clothes. The performance times were not announced in advance, and so the company performed in front of whoever was at those sites at the time. Rehearsals for the events happened very informally only minutes before the actual performance took place, so the people who happened to be passing by during the rehearsal times also got to see the company dance.

The dances for *Five Works For Sneakers* consisted of sections from different works in the company's repertory, with excerpts from several different dances sometimes happening simultaneously. Although it was fun to dance at these events, it was also extremely difficult because of the different surfaces on which we had to perform. At the McGraw Hill Plaza the surface was cement. At the Botanical Gardens it was grass. At the Staten Island Ferry Terminal it was somewhat like marble, and extremely hard. The Brooklyn Museum Sculpture Garden was the toughest because the Sculpture Garden had all the different materials that had been used for New York's city roads over the past century. They included brick, cobblestone, tar, cement and asphalt. The dancers had to adjust to each surface as they passed over it.

The strangest of these performances was at the World's Fair Site in Queens. The company danced next to and underneath the very large world globe sculpture, which also is a fountain. There was no water running in the fountain at the time, but the surface was like the bottom of a swimming pool, and it curved up as it neared the edge. Absolutely no one was there to see the company perform, and so we danced for each other and the company's manager, Margaret Wood.

Viola's favorite performance during the *Five Works For Sneakers* events was the one in the Staten Island Ferry Terminal building. The surface of the floor was easy to work with, and, for the most part, the people who were there to catch the ferry were very attentive. A few people totally ignored the dancers, however, even though the performers were dancing inches away from where they were seated. What Viola found special about it was that near the end of the performance the bell announcing the departure of the ferry sounded. The company continued to dance while the audience got up from their seats and walked to the area where they boarded the boat. This area looked like a large elevator, and the commuters continued to applaud as a solid gate came down, closing them off from the dancers. The gate acted as the curtain inside a theater, except that we kept on dancing until we finished the piece, even though the audience had left. Viola found this very amusing indeed. I remember her saying, "Merce would have loved it!"

Viola choreographed a wonderful dance for a 5 p.m. performance series at Town Hall in New York in 1974. The series was designed for people who worked in New York, but lived outside the city. It was for those who were staying in town to attend a Broadway play or musical at 8 p.m., or for people who simply wanted to see a performance early in the evening before going home. Only an hour in length, the performance gave the people time to eat dinner before the 8:00 curtain time. The stage at Town Hall is long and not very deep. It was not designed for dance, but for chamber music and the like. Viola realized that nothing in her repertory would fit or look good on that stage, so she decided to choreograph a new work especially designed for that specific space and time of day. She felt that these people, who would be coming directly from work, would most likely appreciate something humorous and light.

She went about making an extremely funny dance which included one dancer, Larry Clark, on stilts, herself dressed up like an elderly woman, and many other characters appearing throughout the hour. There was, of course, her usual work as well, but with a different twist to it. The music for this dance was by Alvin Lucier and Pat Richter. Ms. Richter was one of the musicians who played for classes at Viola's studio, and the music she played for this performance consisted of show tunes that the audience would recognize and relate to.

When Viola came out dressed as an elderly woman, with a gray wig, a skirt, "good woman's shoes," and horn-rimmed glasses while using a cane for support, no one in the audience who knew the company recognized her until she began dancing. When she did, the audience broke out in laughter and cheers. One person said later that she looked like a character straight out of the Carol Burnett Show.

The title of this Town Hall work was as funny as the dance itself, and, as was often the case, it had very little to do with what was going on onstage. The dance was choreographed in the White Street Studio. It was winter, and the heat had gone off. One afternoon while we were rehearsing, there was a knock on the studio door. Viola went to see who it was, and it turned out to be a plumber who was there to try and get heat back into the building. He asked Viola if she knew where the super of the building was. She told him that there was no super for the building, as it was a loft building for artists. He then asked her if she could show him where the boiler was so that he could fix it. She said that there was no boiler in the building, that the heat for the studio was a gas heater in the middle of the studio space. She took him to the elevator and told him that the building did have a basement and maybe he could find something down there to repair. As he descended in the elevator, we heard this poor man exclaiming quite loudly in a thick Bronx accent, "No super, no boiler, no nothin." The title of the dance for Town Hall promptly became known as *No Super, No Boiler.*

The performance was a great success, and the dancers were sad to see this piece disappear. This dance had only one performance, but Viola did use several sections from it in another dance a year or so later. With the making of *No Super, No Boiler*, Viola had proved to the critics that she could make funny dances as well as dances that were considered serious art.

Many people, including some dance critics, spoke of violence in Viola's work. As a performer, one did not feel this, but the dancers did experience an amazing sense of energy and vitality. Performing her work not only required a high level of technique, but it also constantly tested the dancers' stamina. When a dancer in the Farber company finished an entire evening of Viola's work, she/he left the theater with very little energy left to do much more that to grab a bite to eat and then go home, or to the hotel room, to rest.

One dance critic said the following.

"Farber's world always strikes me as a dangerous one, no matter how cool and businesslike the performing demeanor. It's full of violence and unsettling encounters: tenderness seems to come only with exhaustion."
Deborah Jowitt, <u>Village Voice</u>, December 1, 1975

Carolyn Brown, the former Cunningham company member, stated, "I remember talking to Miss Craske about it, and she said to me, 'There's a lot of anger in her, and it's got to come out.'" But later on in the interview, Carolyn mentioned how she had then seen a work of

Viola's in Minneapolis that the New Dance Ensemble had performed (*Preludes*, 1988) and said, "It was beautiful. It was not hostile. It was the most lyric, beautiful piece I've ever seen of hers."

On the violence in Viola's work, Willi Feuer saw it this way:

"I never, never ever felt violence as a member of the company. It was energy. She talked about energy. She would come up with movements from pedestrians. When she would walk, she said well here's this man that's crippled or he was on dope and she'd show you some weird kind of unorthodox phrase that was related to that, and the energy that movement portrayed to her, and she would convey that energy to us in forms of movement."

Willi admitted that there was a lot of throwing one's body around, but he never felt that the work was violent. It was more that of super high energy. "I may be way off base here, but you know why I think people thought that her work was violent? I think that Viola had a real dark side to her. She had a definite profound dark side, and I think that in her expressing the dark side of herself or whatever, combined with the energy that she wanted in her movement, the combination of expression can definitely be conceived or portrayed as being violent to an outsider." He added. "Her motivational force for the dances was never in terms of violent display or violent description or anything of that nature. As a matter of fact a lot of it was kind of comical. To me, Viola had a lot of comedy and maybe a dark sense of that fourth dimension thing. She had a lot of comedy and sometimes it was twisted. She put a twist into it that was ironic or maybe it was just twisted enough to make it seem comedic to me."

One of the few company programs in Viola's archives that included program notes, was for the dance called *Willi I* (1974) at Barat College (Lake Forest, IL.) in the Drake Theatre on October 8, 1975. Because Viola did not like to include program notes, one can only imagine that the Barat College Dance Department or the Drake Theatre Public Relations person asked her to do so. Here, in only two sentences total, is what Viola said of *Willi I*.

Willi I is the first new dance I made after Willi Feuer joined the company. It deals with people, their relationships, and the situations they meet and make.

A choreographer cannot be more brief and to the point than that. Also included in this same program, however, is a statement by the composer for *Willi I*, Alvin Lucier.

One day after rehearsal, I asked each dancer what his or her favorite sound was. The answers were wonderful: Viola, church bells; Larry, thunder; Willi, motorcycles; June, ocean waves; Anne, a foghorn; Susan, horses' hooves; Andé, cicadas; Jeff, rocks falling on other rocks. A few months later, Maggi Payne, a recording engineer at the Mills College Center for Contemporary Music, and I tape-recorded examples of these sounds to use as source material for the dance, Willi I.

The material is used in the following way: during a performance, as each dancer comes on stage, I cue his or her sound in and by means of a specially-designed mixer, I move that sound around the audience's space in relation to the movement of the dancer on stage. For example, at the beginning of the dance, as Larry enters upstage left and runs on a diagonal downstage right, I move the sound of thunder from a loudspeaker at the right-front of the audience diagonally back across to the left-rear speaker. As I follow the dancers with their favorite sounds, the audience hears a sonic picture of the choreography. The dancers' movements are a moving score for me to play from. <u>The Fires in the Minds of the Dancers</u> because I believe that people's favorite sounds might be secret hints of how they hear the electronic activity of their brains.

In their October 11, 1974 article in the *Reader*, Chicago's Free Weekly, Sally Banes and Ellen Marzer wrote:

> "*Willi I* is a magnificent piece. It encompasses the best of Farber's two worlds - the epic scope of the group works, with their congested homogeneity, and the close tender focus of the solos. The movements are characteristically Farberesque: limb-oriented, lots of outstretched arms, running, and more running, incredible lifts, split-second interactions that require precise timing and blind faith. And they never stop."

In the same article, Banes and Marzer review one of Viola's solos, *Defendant* (1974).

> ".....Farber is accessible, natural and venerable, in her presence on stage as well as in the kinds of movements she makes. It's as if she takes deactivated components of emotions and gently puts them in your hands. Having made you partner to her introspection

for a time, she leaves you with the residual wisdom from her experience."

Viola observed the world and the people in it, and turned her experiences into art. Because everyone moves in some way or other, people can relate to dancing on a very basic level even if they do not always understand the meaning of a dance. People can look at dancing and have a kinetic reaction to it. A physical response. Viola had the ability to express emotion without telling a story. She choreographed in an era that the phrase *pure movement* was popular, but her work was full of emotion and many varying degrees of energy. Viola often told me that she did not believe that a dance could only contain pure movement, because the dancers in the piece are human and they bring those human qualities with them into the work.

The company danced on two other Umbrella Dance Series. The first was in 1975 at the Roundabout Theatre, and the second one was in 1978 at the Second Avenue Playhouse. The dances performed at the Roundabout Theatre, a total of five evenings, were *Motorcycle/Boat*, *Houseguest*, *Poor Eddie*, *Night Shade*, *Some Things I Can Remember*, *Will I*, *Spare Change*, and *Duet For Susan And Willi*. Generally, Viola included three works on each program. This would change only if she included a short solo for herself, such as *Some Things I Can Remember*, and a short duet. In these cases, the performance would include a fourth dance. Since companies shared an evening during the Umbrella Series, she may have had only two works on one particular night if a dance, such as *Willi I*, was a longer work. The Second Avenue Theatre program included *Sunday Afternoon*, *Solo*, *Lead Us Not Into Penn Station*, and *Turf*.

Although it wasn't funny to the dancers at the time, there is a rather amusing story regarding one performance of the dance titled

Poor Eddie during the Roundabout Theatre's opening performance. Alvin Lucier had set up the tapes for the program that night with the sound technician. He had chosen not to sit in the sound booth this particular night, but was downstairs in the dressing room area. There were four dancers in *Poor Eddie*: Viola, myself, Anne Koren and Andé Peck. The stage manager gave us the "places" call, and the curtain rose as the music began. On a certain sound cue, Anne Koren was to enter first. Right away we knew that something was terribly wrong, as none of us recognized the music. We knew, however, that it was too late to do anything but go one with the performance. Anne's eyes were as big as saucers, but she took a deep breath and began dancing onstage to the unfamiliar music. The rest of us followed when we saw our movement cues, and we somehow managed to finish the dance. The rest of the works performed that night went on without a hitch.

Later backstage, Viola asked Lucier what had gone wrong with the music for *Poor Eddie*. He told her that he was in the dressing room when he heard the music come on over the sound monitor and knew immediately that something was wrong, but that he was too far away from the booth to fix it. What had happened, he explained, was that the sound person had rewound the tape thinking that it had been stored "tales out," which is usually the case as it helped preserve the tapes longer. (This was during a time, remember, when the music for dance performances was recorded on reel-to-reel tape, not digital tapes, CD's or DVD's.) On this night, however, Lucier had already rewound the tape before the performance began, and the sound technician had then reversed it. We danced that night to the music for *Poor Eddie* being played backwards. What was amazing is that we ended exactly on time with the ending of the tape. As far as the audience knew, or the technician in the sound booth for that matter, what they had heard was indeed the music for the dance. It was an electronic score and we did not adhere to any musical meter, melody, or tempo, but we did depend on certain internal sound cues to help us know whether we were on time or not. All the hours of rehearsals had paid off, and the dancers found out that they knew each other's timings better than they thought.

One critic, Robert J. Pierce, brought up the subject of the way Viola structured her dances in his November 20, 1975 article in *The Soho Weekly News*.

"I don't remember now what preceded the section in which the whole company came piling out of the wings in two sloppily converging lines, their feet and bodies chattering crazily, but I remember I wasn't prepared for them to suddenly reverse direction and chatter back offstage. And even later, I remember how surprised I was to see the company suddenly stop the disorder of eight simultaneous solos and segue into the structural discipline of unison jumps and turns, and loose cannons."

Another dance of Viola's that had interesting aspects to it as far as the music is concerned was a dance titled *Night Shade*, danced to Beethoven's *Opus 27. No. 2.*, the first movement of which is more familiarly known as the *Moonlight Sonata*. The dance was choreographed in 1975, and like the music, it was structured in three movements.

Regarding the inspiration for *Night Shade*, the following appeared in an article in 1978 by Jack Anderson, dance critic for the *New York Times*.

Night Shade was inspired by a curious piano recital Miss Farber once attended. The pianist, a grandly gowned woman, made an imposing entrance. But after she had played a few measures, she suddenly got up and marched offstage, to the audience's astonishment. No one knew why she had done this, where she had gone or whether she would ever come back. Moments later, she did return, and without a word of explanation finished the program.

The recital made Miss Farber want to choreograph a dance in which surprising things happened to familiar music.

As mentioned earlier, Viola was a very good pianist. As the curtain rose on *Night Shade*, Viola entered walking from the downstage left wing dressed in a long, black velvet gown. As she slowly made her way across the stage, she stopped only once to stand and wring her hands, while looking somewhat perplexed and anxious. She then crossed the stage and exited. A grand piano was visible behind a scrim in the upstage right area, with me standing upstage of the piano bench dressed in a black velvet suit. Viola then reentered, and stood next to the piano bench looking out toward the audience. After wringing her hands again, she finally sat down at the piano. There was a long pause where Viola seemed to be thinking about whether or not she would be able to play, but she finally did begin playing the first movement of the Beethoven. I was there to turn one page of the music score. After doing so, I exited.

The rest of the company performed the first movement, while I took off the velvet suit and put on a thin brown shift-like shirt over my beige unitard. At the end of the first movement, the dancers exited and Viola walked off stage right and quickly changed costumes.

The rest of the dance was performed to taped music. The second movement was different from most of Viola's work. I entered the performance space in silence, and took my place just right of center, standing in fifth position. On the first note of the music I executed my first relevé in fifth position, revealing to the audience that I was wearing pointe shoes. I stand six feet three inches tall in bare feet, on pointe, I reached an amazing height of seven feet. This brought loud gasps and some laughs from the audience, as no one expected to see anyone in Viola's company on pointe, much less me. The first movement that Viola had choreographed for me was to relevé into fifth position, plié and jump straight up into the air while drawing my feet up close to my torso, and then land in fifth position plié while in relevé. This movement is easy enough to accomplish while bear foot, but almost impossible, and somewhat painful, while on pointe.

After my brief movement solo, Viola entered also wearing pointe shoes, and we proceeded to dance a somewhat classically orientated duet. The difference being, of course, that both Viola and I were wearing pointe shoes. I remember trying to stand up in pointe shoes while executing the difficult partnering movements of the duet. If one does not work in pointe shoes on a regular basis, the easiest of movements suddenly become very difficult.

The third movement was performed by the entire company and was danced barefoot. Viola often said that it was a great relief to take off those pointe shoes, and that her legs felt extremely light during the third movement. Leg lifts and jumps suddenly felt effortless, and our feet were once again squarely on the ground during balances and turns.

On the opening night of *Night Shade*, Viola was informed shortly before curtain time that who should be coming to see the company dance but the famous ballet teacher, Viola's mentor, Margaret Craske. Accompanying her was none other than Sally Wilson, a principal dancer with the American Ballet Theatre. Viola was very nervous knowing that these two renowned ballet figures were going to see her perform on pointe. All she could think about was the time that Miss Craske had singled her out in pointe class for having large feet that would prove to be a difficulty doing the allegro movement she had given the class.

The only pointe training that Viola had taken in several years was the pointe class she gave herself and me in rehearsals. She hadn't had time to take ballet class with Miss Craske in a very long time. Miss Craske and Sally Wilson, however, were very kind after the concert. Craske stated, in her typically English way, that we had done an "admirable job." Wilson was a little more gracious, telling Viola that she loved *Night Shade*, especially the duet.

Night Shade remained in the company's repertory for only one year. It proved too difficult to get a piano in every theater, or to have a stage deep enough to put it there without taking up all the dance area. I do not think that she enjoyed performing in those painful pointe shoes very much. More importantly, I think, was that Viola rarely had time to practice the piano. Her schedule at the studio, and running the company left her very little time for herself. She played the Beethoven beautifully, but she never felt secure about her playing. In rehearsals I would sit next to her at the piano as she played that first movement over and over again, and after each time she would ask me if it sounded ok.

I remember thinking, "She's asking me? I'm not the musician here." But, since I couldn't read music and I was responsible for turning the page, I did not mind going over and over it again. I had to count the bars of music, and did not want to confuse Viola by making a mistake.

Except for the one tour to Paris, the company mostly performed in universities and theaters throughout the United States. Many times the company was asked to teach master classes and to give a lecture demonstration as well as the regular formal concert performances. The schedule was especially grueling for Viola. She taught most of the master classes, taught the company class every day, did interviews on radio and television spots, rehearsed the company and performed. She was adamant that we take company class every morning when on tour.

Performances were generally over at 10 or 10:30 pm, and then the company had to search out a place to eat. Sometimes the presenter would have food set aside for the dancers at the reception following a concert, but more often than not if restaurants were closed, the company found food at convenience stores, all night grocery stores or, when things were really bad, candy and crackers from out of the machines in hotel or motel lobbies.

When the company was on tour, Viola would arrive at the theater or studio early to give herself a warm up class. She then taught us an hour-long class, followed by a very short break. Often during this break Viola had to talk with the lighting designer or the presenter, so it was never really a break for her. The company would then space out each dance onstage. Here again, Viola would often sit in the audience to make certain that we were doing well, so she rarely got a chance to go through the spacing of a dance herself. If she had a solo or was in a duet, she would hop up onstage and begin dancing. It always took a toll on her body; however, as her muscles would get cold while she had been in the house watching, and then not have time to warm up again.

Viola rarely let the company mark movement during a spacing rehearsal. It made sense, as we then knew exactly how the spacing was going to work, but it was hard because it drained that much more energy from us for the performances. She never marked the movement, and we all knew how much work she was doing outside the theater, so we went along with her. It usually paid off in the end.

The Viola Farber Company (1973 – 1981)

In 1976, Viola found that the company was outgrowing the White Street Studio, and the man who lived above the studio was giving the company a very hard time about the music coming from the studio during classes and rehearsals. The lease was running out anyway, so she and her dancers went studio-hunting again. We found a wonderful loft on the top floor of a building on the corner of Broadway and Bleeker, in the area that was later called NoHo, on the lower east side of Manhattan. It was an incredible space. The dance area was a little over thirty-five feet deep and just over one hundred feet long, with no pillars. Viola could, at long last, have a big studio for rehearsals and classes, and a small studio for her private use. She would also have, for the first time, her own private dressing room where she could go to get away from everyone. There was ample space for the company office, storage space and two large dressing rooms. Again, the dancers in the company had to do a major renovation of the floor, but not as much of the walls and ceilings.

As far as I know, this was the first studio in Manhattan where the dancers in the company actually built the studio floor. Michael Immerman, who studied at the Farber studio and who was also a carpenter, build several small sample sprung floors for the dancers to try out and see which worked best for dancing. After we chose the one we liked, we spent weeks laying down the cross beams, then the floor beams, and finally sanding and oiling the floor. We put down all one hundred feet by thirty-five feet of that floor ourselves. Every dancer in the company, plus some of the dancers who studied with Viola, worked many hours each day to produce one of the finest dance floors in New York City. Soon one of the leading ballet schools, the American Ballet School, was calling the company's manager to get the instructions on how to build a floor just like it for their studios. I do not know if they ended up using the plans or not.

During the period that the new studio was being renovated, Viola rented a studio by the hour that was also on Broadway near 8th Street, on the lower eastside of Manhattan. It was a long narrow studio, very dingy, and not a very good floor. The worse problems, however, was that in the middle of the studio there was a loading ramp made of cement, and there was no piano in the studio. For six months Viola taught one class a day standing on that cement ramp snapping her fingers to keep the meter for the students. I did some of the teaching for her, as did Anne Koren. We all snapped our fingers so long that we developed calluses on the ends of them, and the skin would get so dry that it split open. When the company rehearsed there, we had to wear shoes to keep our feet from getting ripped apart. The kind women who owned the studio did not have enough money to fix up the place like it so badly needed.

During this period in the company's history, Viola decided to drop Artservices as her management. She felt that Artservices was spending most of their booking energies on larger companies and their well-known composers. She hired Sheryl Batzer as her manager. Sheryl was a very attractive woman, with a nice personality, and the two women got along very well. All of this occurred around the same time that the new studio opened. Sheryl was thrilled at the size of her office, and Viola was very happy that the size of the new studio allowed her to have her manager right next to where she was working.

Just a month or so after the company moved into this new space, thieves struck again, this time stealing some very expensive sound equipment. Viola was furious, of course. She also knew that because of the expense required to replace the equipment, that the company would no longer have the funds to purchase a new piano for the studio. The old upright that she had bought to replace the stolen on was literally on its last legs. One of Viola's students had inherited some money, and when he heard of the thief, he donated an eight foot grand piano for the new studio.

Shortly after moving into the new studio Viola and I discovered that the little house in New City was haunted by a friend and employee of the Rossins who had died the year before. The woman, who for legal purposes I will call Mary, had been a tutor for the Rossins' eldest child, Mark, who had suffered some brain damage at birth. Mark was handicapped in many ways, but was extremely bright in others, and one of his talents was reading minds. One had to be very careful around Mark because he could literally read a person's thoughts. Mary had become possessive of Mark and also jealous of Viola because she thought that the house should have been given to her, and often tried to spread rumors that Viola was constantly bringing different men up to the house for sexual reasons.

One night Susan Rossin found Mark fully dressed and headed out the front door of their house. When she asked Mark where he was going, he said that Mary was calling him and telling him to leave the house and come to her. When she asked the boy how Mary was calling him, he said, "In my head." Susan was horrified that Mary was using Mark's gift of mind reading to call him out of the house in the middle of the night, and fired her the next day.

When Mary died a couple of years later, her spirit took up residency in Viola's country house. It developed a cold spot, our cats refused to come into the house and Bridget, the maid, said that she often smelled Mary's perfume in the house. The Rossins also had a dog named Belle who accompanied Bridget into the house while she was cleaning it. Belle now refused to come near the place. Several times we saw things flying across the room, and at night locked doors would open and slam shut. The last straw came, however, when Mary's spirit pushed Viola and then Mark's new tutor down the stairs. Both Viola and the other woman spoke of feeling two hands on their back and hearing soft laughter. We moved out of the house right after that and Susan Rossin turned the house into a pottery studio.

Even after Viola and I had abandoned the wonderful little house, and it had been renovated, Susan told us several times that Mary was still playing tricks on her. Susan had kept our refrigerator in the house, and often while she was there Mary would unplug it. Susan did find, however, that when Mary started to act "naughty," that if she read from one of Meher Baba's books, Mary settled down.

Right after we gave up the country house Viola discovered that she had a very large tumor in her uterus that had to come out. Viola went into surgery and due to the size of the tumor, the doctor decided to perform a complete hysterectomy. She was in the hospital for about a week, and was, of course, in a great deal of pain, but the operation went well and she recovered quickly. The apartment that we had recently moved into was on West 16th Street in an old brownstone building. It was a one bedroom apartment on the second floor, and the steps were very difficult for Viola to use. We decided to take a two week vacation from the company so that Viola could mend. I had also torn a groin muscle in rehearsal and needed the time off myself.

Since we not longer had the country house, Viola called her dear friend Jasper Johns and asked if his country house was available. He said yes, so we packed up and drove up to Stony Point, New York. Neither of us had ever seen the house, and when we arrived we found that it was a lovely three story house built on the side of a mountain. There were stairs to get to the entrance and stairs to get to each level of the house. Viola and I burst out laughing, as here we had left our apartment to avoid climbing stairs and were now faced with twice as many. We decided to stay and make the best of it. We planned our day so that we only had to go up or down a minimum of stairs. There was a very large kitchen down on the lower level, and a huge sitting room with an enormous fireplace. We actually had a wonderful time, and it was the longest vacation we ever had together in our nine years of marriage.

While at Jasper's house, we invited Susan and Buddy Rossin over for dinner as they lived not far from there. Viola and I managed to fix a lovely dinner and the four of us had a great time sitting around the fire talking. We did say to each other later, however, that Buddy did not look well. He had had a heart condition for some time, but seemed to have it under control. Just a short time after we got back to New York Susan called us to say that Buddy had died. It was a great shock to both of us, as Buddy had been so kind and generous to us through the years, and he was especially dear to Viola who had known him much longer than I. Not long after his death Susan sold the big house and moved into a much smaller house on the Steiner Community property.

Viola, in her usual way, went back to work much sooner than her doctor advised. Two months after her surgery, she performed on stage with the company.

Touring with the company was often great fun for all of us. It was a small enough company, five women and four men, so that it sometimes felt like family traveling together. That first nucleus of dancers, June Finch, Andé Peck, Larry Clark, Anne Koren and myself, stayed with Viola for about five years, with Willi Feuer, Susan Matheke and Jumay Chu joining the company shortly thereafter.

No matter how long Viola performed or how many dances she choreographed, the fact that she had danced with the Merce Cunningham Dance Company haunted her constantly. She danced with the Cunningham Company for a little over twelve years, from 1952 to 1965, and her choreography was influenced by his movement style. This problem confronts many new choreographers who first danced with famous companies such as Cunningham, Taylor, Graham, Nicholais or Tharp. One review that Viola proudly quoted came in the February issue of Dancemagazine. The author of that article was Robb Baker. He wrote the following: "Viola Farber has accomplished the well-nigh impossible in today's dance world by establishing a movement style completely her own."

Many interviewers asked Viola what influence Cunningham's work had on her own choreography. When I interviewed Viola, I asked her whether it was the movement Cunningham had given her in his dances, or the movement that he had not given her that most influenced her choreography. "The latter, I think." She said. "It was what I didn't get from working with him. Very much so. I think in a way (that) he had a much greater effect than I often admit, because sometimes I did things when I was on my own in defiance. And that is certainly a great influence."

In 1976, Viola was asked to be part of collaboration with Robert Rauschenberg, David Tudor, and Alvin Lucier on a video for dance. The project was to be funded by the Museum of Contemporary Art in Fort Worth and by the National Endowment for the Arts. Taping took place at the museum and the editing in Dallas. The director for the video was Dan Parr, who was affiliated with the museum.

Viola spent months working on the choreography for this work, and the dancers were fitted for the costumes, which were designed by Robert Rauschenberg in New York. Everyone enjoyed working on this dance. It was the first piece to be choreographed in the new Studio, and finally we had the room to dance full out. We then traveled to Fort Worth and for only one week went through hours and hours of tedious rehearsals and video taping. Most of the time was spent waiting while the crew got the correct lighting and camera angles. By the time that Dan Parr was happy with these, we felt like we were dancing our worst. Standing around caused our muscles to get cold and stiff.

Rauschenberg had designed costumes that were simply leotards and tights, but they were dyed the most beautiful bright solid colors. Each dancer had three different colors. Each section of the dance was shot three different times with the dancers wearing a different color each shoot. If one is familiar with Rauschenberg's work, one can imagine the collage effect that he was after. In the final version of the video, the dancers changed colors in the middle of a single dance movement. The idea and the reality were amazing.

After one week, the majority of the dancers flew back to New York. Viola and I stayed in Dallas while she, Dan Parr and the other artists edited the video. Viola returned late each night totally frustrated because for the first time in her life she felt thrust into the male chauvinist's world.

"They are destroying my dance," Viola said on the third day of editing. "You can't see an entire dance phrase or an entire dancer's body during the whole video."

Viola was frantic and wanted to leave, but was convinced that she had to stay and protect what she could of her work. To Viola, Dan Parr was so impressed with Robert Rauschenberg that he was only listening to him. He was also not very familiar with dance, much less Viola's work. He relied on his instincts as a film maker, noting only what looked interesting to him on camera. Viola could see that the dance she made was being rearranged and torn apart. It did not resemble anything of what she felt she had choreographed. The video was given the title *Brazos River* by Rauschenberg because he had seen a river near Dallas with that name and liked the sound of it. So, Viola felt that she didn't even get to title her own dance. By the time she left Dallas, Viola wasn't speaking to anyone involved with the project. She was angry, frustrated, and rapidly making herself ill.

Months later, *Brazos River* had its premiere showing in a studio in Soho to a very small and exclusive art crowd. After the showing Viola was given a copy of the video. When we got back to our apartment, she threw her copy of the video in the trash and never discussed it again. *Brazos River* was shown once in Fort Worth at the Museum of Contemporary Art, and this was the end of that dance.

Years later, I happened to come across a copy of *Brazos River* and I actually felt that it was a wonderful video. Viola was correct that it didn't do justice to the dance she made, but it was a beautiful work of art. It looked like a moving painting by Rauschenberg, and the music score was wonderful. It is truly sad that so few people got to view it. Fortunately, Viola's anger was short-lived and everyone involved remained friends.

A solo that Viola choreographed for herself in 1977 was titled simply *Solo*. It was only three minutes long, but for those who saw it, it was one of her strongest solos. Viola did not particularly want to choreograph a solo at the time, but felt that it was important for her to have one on the program. She had also been asked to perform on a dance series at Brooklyn Academy of Music (BAM), so she needed this solo in order to appear. She asked me to watch the rehearsal of *Solo* once it was finished. When it was over, she asked, "Is it too boring? Are you sure that it isn't too short?" She felt that the dance was not long enough and that it was too austere. She was also concerned because there was no music for the dance. I assured her that the dance was wonderful, but I knew that she never believed me. Her insecurity barred any ability to listen to any praise.

The dance series at BAM was called *Modern Dance From Isadora to Pilobolus*. The director of this series, Anabelle Gamson, came to Viola's studio to see a rehearsal of *Solo*, and said that it was perfect for the series. In dress rehearsal, however, when Viola saw what other choreographers were performing, she felt that the solo was totally out of place.

"The context is important as to how something is viewed," Viola explained. "And I felt that it was in the wrong context. Not that there was anything wrong with the program. Not that there was anything wrong with my solo. But the two should never have met." The other dances were produced with beautiful costumes, lighting, and music. *Solo* was performed in silence, lit very starkly, and Viola wore a simple black leotard and black tights. "I did it in spite of my awareness of how out of place I was. I think it dropped like a lead balloon. There was not much applause," she added.

Solo did not drop like a lead balloon, however. Harvey Liechtenstein, the director of BAM, liked it very much, it was reported. Paul Taylor loved it, as did many; many others who saw Viola perform on that series. It was not an easy dance to digest, and it was over almost before it began. Audiences never applauded very enthusiastically for *Solo*, but it could be said that it was one of those dances where one had to be familiar with Viola's work to really appreciate it. People may have misunderstood the dance's meaning or didn't like it, but whatever the reason, *Solo* was a dance that caused a great deal of discussion among people in the audience.

"Paul Taylor called me and said that he had seen the performance of *Solo* and that he thought it was wonderful." Viola added. "I said, 'Oh, but Pete (his nickname)! I was so out of place in that!' He responded in a typically Pete fashion, 'But Viola, you're always out of place. That's what's so wonderful!' He meant it as a compliment, but for me it was too close to the truth." Upon reflection she said sadly, "I'd rather he hadn't said it."

In 1977, a little less than two years after the new studio on Broadway and Bleeker opened, tragedy struck the company again. The owner of the building couldn't afford the property taxes, and therefore he was forced to sell the building. Because of some obscure New York law relating to property selling because of back taxes, the tenants' leases were no longer valid. Suddenly everyone was being told by the new owner that they had to get out, because he was turning the building into co-op living lofts.

At first, it looked like the company was the only business that was going to be allowed to stay in the building. Things began to go from bad to worse, however, when the landlord took a liking to the company's manager, Sheryl, and kept trying to get her to go out with him. When it finally became clear to him that Sheryl was not going to do so, he told Viola that the company had to vacate the loft at once.

Viola hired lawyers and fought the landlord for months. He, however, had more money to fight with, and he was also harassing the company and the students by changing the locks on the door that led into the building's lobby, and turning off the power to the elevator so that the dancers had to walk up nine flights of stairs to get to the studio. Once he went so far as to change the lock on the studio door that led to the stairs.

Viola tried everything to get the landlord to let the company remain in the building. She even went to her friends at The Village Voice, and they printed an article about the company's situation. The Village Voice article almost backfired on the company, however, when the landlord's lawyers threatened to sue Viola for slander. She did get the fire department to make the landlord quit changing the locks on the lobby door and the elevator. The only reason he agreed was because the fire department said that he was in violation of New York City and state fire codes.

After months of legal hassles, the company had to pack up and move out. Choreographer Lucinda Childs was gracious enough to let the company rehearse in her studio until Viola found another space. Not only was everyone involved angry at the new landlord for throwing them out, but they were broken hearted at losing their lovely new studio. The loss of this studio also hit the company financially; a loss that the company could ill afford. Not only had all the legal hassles been costly, but the move of the studio brought about a drop in the number of classes that Viola could offer, and a drop in the number of students paying for classes.

After about six months, the company took up residence in the Madison Avenue Baptist Church on the corner of 31st Street and Madison Avenue. Diane Byers, a former student of Margaret Craske, owned the studio and rented out the space to the company. Byers was an excellent teacher of ballet and in the process of building a large following of students. It wasn't a perfect match, mainly because ballet students use rosin on the floor to keep them from slipping. Modern dancers dance barefoot, and the rosin cuts into their feet. The situation was handled by putting down a dance floor that suited both dance forms. The studio was a lot smaller than the Broadway/Bleeker studio, and there was no office space for Sheryl, so she was forced to manage the company out of her apartment. The dancers stored some of their costumes at home, and stored the electronic equipment in a small space behind the studio.

Even with this new space, Viola could not offer the number of classes that she had in her own studio, nor could she rehearse the company as many hours as before. The loss of income eventually forced her to let Sheryl go as well. After all her hard work, Viola again found herself at square one.

During the legal battles over the studio, Viola was diagnosed with Hepatitis A. It was no small wonder that she became ill because of what she was going through, but it only increased the pressure on her and she was unable to work, which meant less income. I decided to look for temporary work elsewhere, in an attempt to supplement our income, and found a guest teaching residency in the dance department at California State University in Long Beach. Viola was not happy that I would be gone for almost four months, leaving her to fight the landlord alone and then move the company into the new space, but I could not find enough work in New York to pay our rent. My leaving was the beginning of the end of our marriage, and losing the Broadway/ Bleeker studio was the beginning of the end of the Viola Farber Dance Company's life in New York.

While I taught in Long Beach, Viola met a man named of Curtis Roosevelt. He was interested in learning about Meher Baba, and initially connected with Margaret Craske. Knowing that Viola needed distraction from her company problems, Miss Craske sent Curtis to speak with Viola about Baba. Miss Craske did not expect Viola and Curtis to fall in love. The age difference between Viola and I had begun to bother Viola. People who met us for the very first time would ask if we were brother and sister, or mother and son. They rarely connected us as husband and wife. Curtis was only a year or two older than Viola; he was straight, not gay like me, and not an artist. Viola found these qualities extremely likable.

When Viola would write or call me in California, her letters and phone conversations included Curtis's name more and more often. I began to suspect that something was going on, but hoped that my suspicions were incorrect.

I returned to New York on Christmas Eve of 1977. As I entered the apartment building on West 11th Street where Viola and I lived, I saw a man standing in the lobby. He was tall and wearing a very expensive looking overcoat and hat. Even though I had never met him, I knew right away that it was Curtis Roosevelt. I took the elevator up to our apartment and found Viola putting on her coat and gloves, obviously getting ready to go out.

"Curtis is waiting downstairs for you isn't he?" I asked.

"Yes." Viola answered.

"I've been gone four months. It is Christmas Eve, and you are going out with him anyway?" I said as I set my suitcase down and began taking off my own winter coat.

"Yes, Jeff. I am."

As I watched Viola go out the door that night, I knew that our marriage was over. I was sad, but not surprised. What hurt was the way Viola handled it. To go out on a date the night that I returned from California was very painful to say the least. It was, however, not unlike Viola to do. As generous as she was with her talent, Viola always did what she wanted in her personal life, no matter who got hurt.

We did not tell the company of our separation. The company was scheduled to perform on another Umbrella Dance Series in January of 1978 at the Second Avenue Playhouse, and then go to Chicago for a residency at Columbia College. Viola did not want to upset the dancers in the company, so we would meet each morning and walk together to the studio or to the theater. While in Chicago we shared the same motel room for the entire time that we were there. When I left the company in August of 1978 and moved to Los Angeles, it was as big a surprise to the company and our friends, as our marriage had been. Viola and I had once again been extremely private about our personal life. News always spreads rapidly within the dance community, and it was not long before everyone knew of our break up. Our marriage had shocked the community and our separation caused an even bigger reaction.

As in the past, Viola did not give up, but continued to teach, choreograph new works, and tour with her company. She hired a new male dancer, Robert Foltz, to replace me. Jumay Chu and Andé Peck left the company to join the Lucinda Childs Dance Company, and they were replaced by Karen Levey and Joël Leucht. The company continued to tour the United States, but struggled financially. Viola asked me if I would guest with the company when it toured the west coast, and I agreed. I was not in any of the group works, but only danced in duets with Viola, or performed the solo *Houseguest*.

Between 1969 and 1980, Viola choreographed more than fifty works for the company. During this time, when the company was not on the road, she taught daily technique classes at her studio to help support the company. These classes did not bring in a lot of extra income, however, after the rent was paid, and so she had to go on the road by herself and teach in residencies or choreograph dances for other companies, solo artists, or dance students in university or college dance departments or programs throughout the world. Companies that commissioned works by Viola included the Repertory Dance Theatre in Salt Lake City, Utah; the Ruth Currier Dance Company which was at that time based in Ohio; the Nancy Hauser Dance Company in Minneapolis, MN.; Ballet Theatre Contemporaine in Angers, France; Ballet Theatre Français in Lyon, France; Janet Gillespie and Present Company; and soloists such as Ze'eva Cohen, and Susannah Payton-Newman, among others. She did teaching residencies in the dance departments of the University of Utah, Salt Lake City; University of Michigan, Ann Arbor; University of Minnesota, MN., and Ohio State University, Columbus, to name only a few. Her schedule was grueling, and the bigger the company grew, the harder Viola worked.

The subject of the violence in Viola's work continued to plague her. During an interview in 1979, Angela LaMaster of the <u>Cityside</u> newspaper in Milwaukee asked about the violence in her work. Viola was sick of discussing this subject and tired of defending her work. She skirted the issue in the following manner:

Q. One review says that you used some very violent movement.

A. There is also very tender, very gentle movement. I choreograph about human situations. I don't use the elements of chance in my work, but I give my dancers some freedom in using the material - for example, in some pieces they can choose which partner they want to dance with.

In the <u>Cityside</u> interview with Angela LaMaster in 1979, Viola worded her answer to how much influence Cunningham had on her work this way: "Well, I've been out of his company for 14 years. Oh……..the answer would be very boring….or else it would take four hours."

Viola challenged her dancers to take risks with movement. Taking the movement "to the edge," was the life of her dances.

She also wanted the dancers to be part of the making of her dances. "I think that was very important to me. I found it very strange initially to tell people what to do. I thought that it was an odd position to be in. So that was one way of trying not to do that [telling people what to do all the time]. I also was very aware of the limitations of one person…. me….perceiving what somebody could do and what they couldn't do, and what they should do and what they shouldn't do. Although, God knows, I have strong leaning in that direction," Viola laughed.

She did not want to assume that a dancer could not jump in a particular way. She choreographed the movement, gave the rules, and let the dancer discover her/his limitations. It was Viola's way of not letting the dancers be stopped by her perception of them.

When I told Viola that the dancers in her company felt that they had a part in what the audience saw of her work, she smiled and said, "They did. And that was only possible because of the kind of dancers you were."

It wasn't totally because of who we were, however, or what type of dancers we were. Yes we were strong dancers and very willing to do anything Viola asked of us, but it was because Viola had an enormous part in training us how to do her work and allowing us to feel secure in taking on that responsibility.

Like much "avant-garde" choreography, Viola's work did not have a story line, and if you asked each audience member after a performance what a particular dance was about, you would probably get as many different answers as there were numbers of people in the theater. An example of this was Cunningham's dance titled *Winterbranch*. Some viewers thought it was about a train wreck and others thought it was about the concentration camps during World War II. Viola, however, was always inspired by something in particular while choreographing each work. It could be the illness of a family member such as in *Legacy* (1968), or a situation that might happen on a trip, such as in *Route 6* (1972) and *Motorcycle/Boat* (1975). It could be influenced by an event or relationship in her personal life, such as in *Solo* (1977) or *Private Relations* (1978).

Like many artists, Viola's sensibilities were more honed than the average person's. She seemed to see and understand the world's problems more clearly, and to be deeply affected by what she saw. She was able to translate these feelings into abstract movement, and into dances that expressed how she viewed the world without being overly narrative. Miss Craske described Viola as too intelligent to be an intellectual. However, many feel that she was a genius. Her intellect constantly clashed with her emotions, but Viola knew how and when to put what she saw and felt into her work. She knew how to express to the audience the essence of what she saw and felt, without demonstrating a specific situation, or making the audience feel that her art was her psychiatrist's couch.

Dandelion, which was choreographed in 1978, got its inspiration from a request that I made of Viola. It was after we had separated and I was living in Los Angeles, but still dancing part time with the company. I asked her why she never made a dance that wasn't totally packed with her usual technically difficult movement phrases. I asked would she ever consider choreographing a dance where the dancers could simply have fun. She thought about it and agreed, and the result was *Dandelion*, which used simple pedestrian movements such as walking, running, falling down and jumping. The dance was very successful, both with the dancers and with the audiences. I haven't a clue, however, where the title came from, and as was often the case with her when titling her dances, Viola may have simply enjoyed the sound of the word.

When asked if she cared what the audiences or the critics thought about her work, Viola said that when she choreographed, she never thought about the audience. She was well aware that each audience consisted of hundreds of different individuals, and that she could never please all of them. Viola made dances that interested her; dances that made a statement on what was important to her at the time. As for the critics, she did not pretend not to care about what they wrote, as she knew that when the dance was over, the only thing that remained was what was written down on paper by the critics. For Viola, her dances did not exist unless the dancers were performing them, and she liked that idea a great deal. She tried not to get hung up on the written word, and felt that what the critics said about her work was often not relevant to what she was doing. She never had a set formula for her choreography as the things that interested or engaged her were constantly shifting.

She loved speed and quickness, both in how the dancers moved and in how they thought or handled her ever changing movement phrases.

There was a quote that was taken from a French newspaper or magazine that I found in Viola's belongings after her death. Unfortunately, the article did not list the name of the newspaper or magazine, the author or the date, so I was unable to seek its source out. Judging from its contents, it seems to have been written around 1980. The quote is one that I think Viola would have enjoyed. She must have, because she saved it.

"The particular charm of Viola Farber may perhaps be for many; a very strong emotion that cannot be solely the product of a feminine or masculine entity."

In the same article, Viola describes how the idea for *Private Relations* came while taking a walk in Nancy, France. Viola says that she was very lonely at the time and decided to go into a museum and look at paintings. She found the artworks not very good, but very moving, and composed the dance in her head as she walked back to where she was staying. *Private Relations* was choreographed in New York in 1978, right after she and I had separated. To many, *Private Relations* was one of her best works.

In the fall of 1978 I formed my own company, Jeff Slayton & Dancers, in Los Angeles. I called and asked Viola if she would fly out and appear as a guest artist on the first performance which was taking place at California State University, Long Beach where I was teaching part time. She said yes, and we performed the duet titled *Doublewalk* (1978) which had been choreographed while I was on the last tour with her company in Chicago. The concert was a big success and the reviews for the duet were wonderful. Viola and I had a great time working together again, and the dancers in my company fell in love with her immediately. None of them had met or studied with her before, but all of them had, of course, heard about her or read about her in books about Merce Cunningham.

In 1980 Viola traveled to Denmark to teach. The struggles of maintaining an income can be see in this excerpt from a letter that she wrote to me on July 9, 1980.

> Today Ulla (from Finland) and Nana (From Sweden & New York) showed up in my afternoon class. It was lovely to have them because it is slow slogging with the dancers who've been here. I sometimes want to say, part of the way through class, let's all give up and go home. One problem, I think, is that there are no mirrors, so that the students can't see how unlike what they do is from what I've showed them to do. Haven't seen Toni Lander at all. The ballet classes happen in some other, doubtless much more elegant, location. The accompanist can not play anything but 4's, and those in only one tempo.

****

Here is a second letter that Viola wrote two days later, also from Copenhagen.

> Saturday - July 11, 1980
> People here are extremely pleasant, but no one told me that all stores close at 1 on Saturdays, and I teach until 3:15. Can you imagine my despair at going to 2 closed book shops, seeing lots of English paperbacks in the windows and having no way of getting at them? I have had a sore throat and headache

thing for more than a week and had hoped to spend the weekend reading, dozing, drinking orange juice. The orange juice store was closed too. But I did come home and sleep. Strangely and mysteriously the students have learned a little something during the week. They are Danish and Swedish and Finnish and Norwegian and English and Swiss, and two seem to be American.

Tomorrow I am going to meet 2 French cultural attachés from the embassy (French) at 1. I hope they give me some food. On July 14, Bastille Day, I've been invited to a reception at the French Embassy.

I have gone to two chamber concerts that were sort of pleasantly dull, and if my legs are up to it I'm going on a guided tour of the old city, which I read about in my "This Week in Copenhagen." There are really quite a few things here that I'd like to see, but I work by myself before teaching my 1 one hour and 45 minute classes and usually want to put my legs up after that.
Enough rambling.
Take most excellent care of the best and dearest Wit.

Love -

Old Dos

Viola and I were still calling each other by our nicknames. This was two years after we had separated, and we officially divorced in June of 1980. Throughout all this time we had remained close and dear friends; soul mates that found it impossible to live together. The divorce closed a chapter in our marriage, but opened another door into a deeper and meaningful friendship.

Left to right: Viola Farber, John Conlon (actor), June Finch, and Alvin Lucier (musician/composer) in Farber's No Super, No Boiler, *1974.*

Photographer: Mary Lucier

Alvin Lucier, 1974. Photographer: Mary Lucier

Viola Farber, Sneakers, Dances In Public Places, *1974, IDS Building lobby in Minneapolis, MN. Photographer: B. Hagen*

Viola Farber Dance Company in Sneakers, Dances In Public Places, 1974, IDS Building lobby in Minneapolis, MN. , 1974,. Left to Right: Viola Farber, Anne Koren, Andé Peck. Photographer: B. Hagen

Viola Farber Dance Company in Sneakers, Dances In Public Places, 1974, at the Staten Island Ferry Terminal Building, Staten Island, NJ. Left to Right: Viola Farber, Susan Matheke, Jeff Slayton, Willi Feuer, Anne Koren, Andé Peck.

Left to right: Viola Farber, Jeff Slayton (front), June Finch, Willi Feuer in Farber's Willi I, *1974. Photographer: Johan Elbers*

Left to right: Jeff Slayton, Andé Peck, Anne Koren, Viola Farber, Willi Feuer in Farber's Willi I, *1974. Photographer: Johan Elbers*

Left to right: Viola Farber (at the piano), Willi Feuer, June Finch, Susan Matheke, Andé Peck in Farber's Night Shade, *1975. Photographer:*

Jeff Slayton, Viola Farber in Night Shade, *1975.*
Photographer: Susan Cook

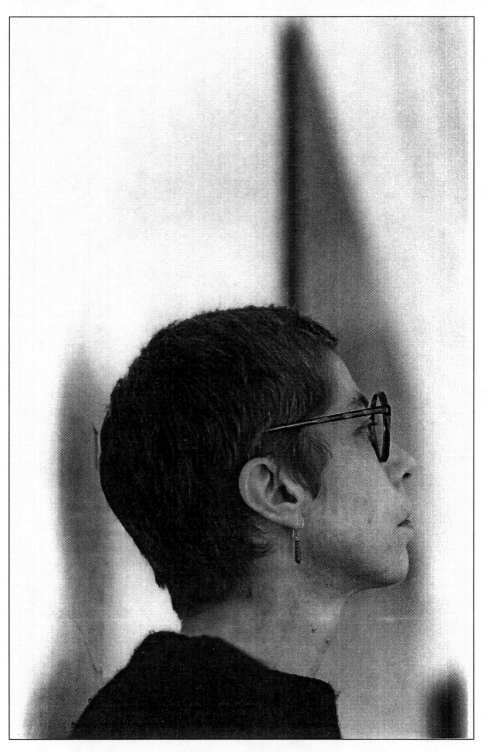

Viola Farber watching company rehearsal, circa 1976.
Photographer: Susan Cook.

Farber company in rehearsal, Broadway/Bleeker studio, circa 1976.
Left to right: Viola Farber (seated), Larry Clark, Anne Koren, June Finch,
Willi Feuer, Jeff Slayton, Susan Matheke, and Andé Peck.
Photographer: Chuck Osgood

Composer/musician David Tudor preparing his sound equipment
for Brazos River, *Fort Worth Museum of Contemporary Art,*
Fort Worth, TX., 1976.Photographer: David Wharton

Robert Rauschenberg with Director Dan Parr on the set of
Brazos River, *Fort Worth Museum of Contemporary Art, Fort
Worth, TX. 1976. Photographer: David Wharton*

Larry Clark, Andé Peck, Jeff Slayton on the set of Brazos River, *Fort Worth Museum
of Contemporary Art, Fort Worth, TX., 1976. Photographer: David Wharton*

Farber company in Lead Us Not Into Penn Station, *1977. Left to Right: Anne Koren, Willi Feuer, Susan Matheke, Larry Clark, Andé Peck, Jumay Chu, Jeff Slayton. Photographer: Johan Elbers*

Farber company in Turf, *1978. Left to right: Viola Farber, Andé Peck (on floor), Larry Clark, Jeff Slayton. Photographer: Johan Elbers*

Left to right: Jeff Slayton, Viola Farber, Irene and Bob Aikin (Viola's sister and husband), Elisabeth and Lawrence Lanzl (Viola's eldest sister and husband), 1978, at the Aiken's home in Woodside, CA. Family photograph.

Viola Farber, Jeff Slayton, 1978, Woodside, CA. Family photograph.

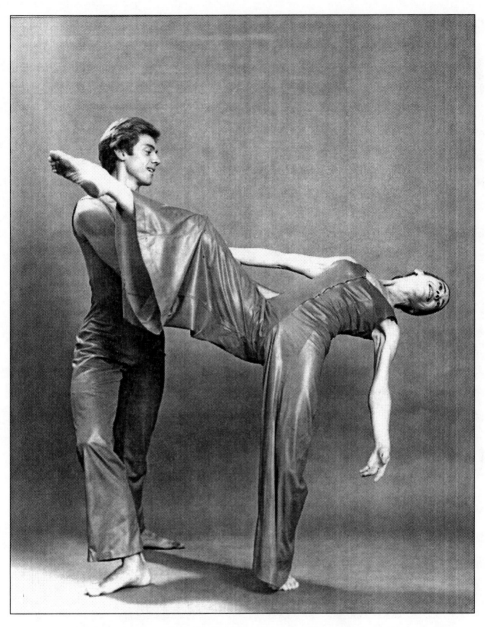

Michael Cichetti and Viola Farber in Farber's Bright Stream, *1980.*
Photographer: Susan Cook

Farber's Untitled, *1980. Left to right: Joël Leucht, Larry Clark, Jumay Chu, Andé Peck, Anne Koren, Michael Cichetti, Karen Levey. Photographer: Unknown*

Jeff Slayton and Viola Farber in rehearsal at the Abbaye de Pont a Mousson, France. Circa 1980. Photographer: Unknown.

Susan Matheke, Larry Clark in Spare Change *(1973), choreography: Viola Farber. Photographer: Mary Lucier*

Chapter Five

The European Company

IN 1980, VIOLA WAS OFFERED a three-year contract as the director of *Le Centre National de Danse Contemporaine d'Angers* (The French National Center for Contemporary Dance, the city of Angers), better known as the CNDC. The first offer did not state what part her company would have in all this if she accepted the offer. She did not relish the idea of leaving the United States; however, the work of keeping her company afloat financially in America was taking its toll on her physically and emotionally. She was forty-nine years old and felt too old to start over in a new county.

She flew to California to work with me on a new duet titled *Just Correspondence,* and we spent many hours talking about the pros and cons of her moving the company to France. The duet was titled *Just Correspondence* because our relationship had, over the past few years, been carried on by just that, correspondence. We were seeing less and less of each other because of the distance between our living places. In her letters, Viola was constantly writing to me how difficult it had become to keep her company, pay the dancers, and to keep classes going. I reminded her of a long letter that she had written me, stating how tired she was of trying to make a go of things in New York, and I urged her to take the job in France.

After discussing the offer with her partner, Curtis, and the dancers in the company for almost a year, Viola decided to accept the French government's offer and, in August of 1981, packed her belongings and moved to Angers, France. The French government agreed to allow Viola to continue her company in France as long as half the company members were French. So, five of the American dancers in her company, who agreed to re-locate to Angers, went with her. Here is a copy of one of the first letters that I received from Viola after she had moved to Angers.

Another reason for Viola accepting the job in Angers was that Curtis Roosevelt had been hired to be the President of Dartmouth College in Devon, England. They would still be in different countries, but at least on the same side of the Atlantic Ocean.

Angers, September 8, 1981
Dear Sweet Jeffet -

What a day! A letter and a telephone call from you - what a treat. And, perhaps because of it, I even got something set on the (new) company. I'm using the Villa Lobos "Bachianas Brasilieras", so far only No. 1, will also do No. 5, which Joan Baez sings but I have a cassette tape of Rostropovitch's wife singing it very dramatically. I would like us to do a duet to No. 5 - it suits us.

Dear Dimt, don't you know that we'll both always feel lonely? I find myself, frighteningly, acting with Curtis quite similarly to the way I was with you after a few years. Perhaps worse, because I think of you so much and when we were married (before you left for

California) and together I assure you I never thought of anyone else. And there's always the damned work. I'm in a way happy to be here alone and not bothering some poor person with my stupid preoccupation with the work I don't do so grandly anyhow. Thank God for Baba - otherwise it wouldn't make much sense to me. Anyhow, sweet Ditling, I know that it's lousy to be lonely, but I also know that people admire, love, and respect you tremendously. And I love you more than there is, and I wish you could be here to show them what DANCING is.

I've had some wine - quite a lot.

Take excellent care.

Much love -

Dos

P.S. Please continue to write.

The letter below was written a month later. Viola had been working non-stop on making dances, getting ready for a December performance. Her mood was a little upbeat still, but it shows how hard she was working, and she shared with me an idea for a new dance. She rarely called me Jeff in her letters except when she was not feeling well. Here again are excerpts.

Angers, October 10 (I think)

It's Saturday

Dear Jeff -

It's windy, rainy, gray, and I'm tired, lonely, etc. Had no pianist for class this morning, nor will I have one

Monday. I had my haircut (very well) by a dear young man who laughed and said, "particularly in Angers" when I told him that the only thing that I didn't like about my haircut was people starring incredulously at me. Also bought a pink and green Indian bedspread and a pink cyclamen plant - you know how well I do with them - to put some un-grayness into the apartment.

I teach, try to make dances, although there's not really much time for that, and go to meetings and have meetings here, etc. and feel old. I'm on the track though, of a nice dance, that I hope I can make - creepy and maybe a little funny. Have gotten 19th century fashion books from a museum to see how people held themselves then. So far have just had people improvise on given movements and situations - next week have to put it all together. The women and the French men do beautifully in it. Bob doesn't, so I'm going to give him a contemporary duet with one of the women using the same movements - and it will be a future dream that the others have.

I'm sleepy and cold. Will climb into the bath tub and go to bed. One of the dancers in the company gave me her salts from Brittany to put in my bath, which I thought was lovely of her. She had heard my complaints about my feet. Another told me today how happy she was to be working with me - that every day she learned something even when she couldn't learn it. You will, I hope and think, enjoy them in June.

Much love from a Fibity Dos

Fibit was one of the many nicknames that I gave Viola, Dos being the main one. Fibit was the name I used when she wasn't feeling well. The next letter came a month later; I had not heard from her for a while by either letter or telephone. This was very unusual, as most of the time we spoke over the telephone at least once a week.

Angers, November 5 (1981)

My dearest Jeffet -

I so much love getting your letters that I feel doubly and triply askew for not having written to you recently. But of course there are reasons.

1. I have not had time to write.
2. I have not had time to go to the post office.

It has been complicated and not entirely pleasant here since the stagiaires (students) arrived. There is not enough room and not enough time for them. They are also not all terrifically nice - more like the cliché about French dancers than the dancers in the company, who continue to be wonderful. The details are boring, but ugh!

Lots of Paris critics are descending on Angers to see our performances here and I can't get the damned mystery [she was choreographing a new dance that involved a murder.] off the ground. The way it's going, it would take about 2 hours to do it. I need some help and advice and there's no one to give it. Oh, what shall I do?

I have had several glasses of wine to ease my way out of rehearsal and into the night. Being here makes me understand how easy it could be to take to the bottle. Fortunately, I'm not constitutionally fit for that.

Dear Dittling, take care and write, and I will and do think of you and your most beautiful dancing.

Love, Love, Love -

Dos

The problem of dealing with the students that Viola mentions briefly in the above letter came to a climax a month or so later. In France, at that time, the students were paid to study at the CNDC. They were selected by audition and came from all over Europe, not solely from France. Being a student there was considered a job, and they had a union that protected them from any employment abuse. In their minds, Viola had been unnecessarily strict with them and was demanding too many hours of dancing from them. She told me by phone that one of their complaints was that she made them take a technique class every day, and, since they were getting paid, she did not think that this was asking too much of them. She also demanded that they show up for class on time, and if they were late, or if they missed a class, she had part of their salary cut.

The students filed a complaint and called in a union representative. When this person first arrived, Viola said, his sympathy was with the students, and he told Viola as much. After he had been there a few hours and listened to the students' complaints, he told Viola, "These students are spoiled and awful. Do what you will with them," and he left. Viola took him at his word, and when students missed more than three classes, she fired them. Soon she had no more discipline problems, and the students who were left ended up loving Viola and she them.

The dancers from the two countries were quickly looking like they had been dancing together for years. The opening performance was fast approaching, but Viola had put together a season's worth of repertoire in record time. Here is the list of dancers, musicians, and directors for the CNDC:

Centre National de Danse Contemporaine
Angers, France

Artistic Director:	Viola Farber
Administrator:	Anne-Marie Chaulet
Artistic Director Ad joint:	Leone Mail
Assistant Artistic Director:	Patrick Le Levé
Administrator:	Henri-Pierre Garnier
Public Relations:	Genevieve Vincent
Artistic Secretary:	Pascale Bouvier
Secretary of Direction:	Michèle Bouveur
Lighting Design:	Alain Manceau, Didier Ponchon
Company pianist:	Dominique Lofficial
Costumes:	Therese Labeyrie

The Company

Assistants to Viola Farber: Michael Cichetti, Joël Leucht
Rehearsal Directors: Anne Koren, Robert Foltz, Karen Levey
Dancers: Michael Cichetti, Didier Deschamps, Jean-François Duroure, Anne Koren, Chantal de Launay, Karen Levey, David Liebart, Joël Leucht, Nadège Macleay, Mathilde Monnier, Sylvain Richard, Claire Verlet.

Administration: Marie-Paule Amann

(Other dancers who worked with Viola during her time in Angers as guest artists and/or guest teachers included; Andé Peck, Jumay Chu, Mary Good, and myself.)

When asked, the French dancer, Sylvain Richard, said the following about her first meeting with Viola at the CNDC. "My first impression was of a woman of strong and rigorous personality. (Viola was) Someone who loved to dance and wanted to share this passion with others; very generous with her art, but very demanding of people. She was interested as much in the potential of a dancer as in his or her technical achievements; skills were important, but personality was just as, if not more, valuable."

Sylvain had seen Viola's company when they performed at Beaubourg in the early 1980s, when the company was on tour in France. This was before Sylvain auditioned for the CNDC. She related her thoughts after seeing that performance.

"I remember thinking that I would really like to be able to join them and dance like that. It was not so much the choreography that attracted me, but the way the dancers performed; the physicality of the movement, the sense of fullness, the way that they pushed themselves to the limit. They made the movement come alive."

The CNDC was housed in a beautiful, rambling three-story building with three very small studios. Viola lived in two large rooms on the top floor, right next to her office and the offices of her staff. It was far from an ideal living situation, because she was never away from her work or from the people with whom she worked. During the first few months, the dancers managed to go to Paris on weekends, but Viola was always in that building. Some of this was self-inflicted, but most of the time she had to stay in Angers to ensure that the CNDC and the company were run the way she wanted. Viola had worked hard all her life and by this time knew no other way to live. She often complained how hard everything was, and that she never had any free time to herself, but even when she did, she rarely took advantage of it. The company, and now the CNDC as well, always came first for Viola. Anyone with a role in her personal life had to accept this.

In Angers, Viola did not have to worry about paying the rent or the salaries for the dancers; all that was taken care of by the French government. She was, however, extremely busy all the time, especially at first. Her contract began in September 1981, and the first performance of the company was scheduled for early December. That meant that she had to audition dancers, train them, and choreograph new works for them. She decided to revive one of her older works, *Dandelion* (1978), for this concert, but would have to choreograph two entirely new dances in just three months. Sylvain thought, and I agree, that working in France and with French dancers caused Viola's work to evolve into a more intimate and psychological choreography.

In addition, Viola was in charge of the school and taught not only the company classes each day, but at least one of the classes for the students. After the classes and rehearsals were over, Viola then had to meet with her staff and go over all of the business that was involved with running a school and a company. Even though she made a fuss over this, she enjoyed the challenge. One difficult problem was trying to keep the American dancers happy. The French dancers who were taken into the company had to learn her technique and choreography in record time, while the American dancers also had to adjust to living and working in a foreign country. The American dancers wanted to go to Paris on the weekends, but Viola had a deadline and needed them in Angers.

Most of the French dancers had only seen Viola perform with

the Cunningham Dance Company on film, never live. A few had seen her own company perform in France, but the majority of them had never studied with Viola. Sylvain saw a film of Viola dancing with the Cunningham company and remembered thinking what "an extraordinary and very personal dancer" she was. Like most that saw Viola perform, she thought that she was unique as a dancer. Sylvain described Viola's performance in that film as "intense and lyrical."

The two new works that Viola choreographed for the new company were *Cinq Pour Dix* (1981) and *Attente* (1981). Needless to say, everyone was exhausted by December, and nerves were on edge. The new company, however, premiered to rave reviews and Viola was to learn that the French audiences and critics remembered her from her days with the Cunningham company, and that they still adored her. She soon found out that they loved her choreography, and that her work in France would help establish her reputation as a choreographer in the rest of Europe.

While the company was enjoying its new success, however, Viola's personal life was slowly falling apart. The distance between she and Curtis, plus all the attention that Viola was giving to the company and the school, were putting a huge strain on their relationship. The two rarely had time to see each other, and both had very stressful jobs.

After all her teaching, rehearsing, and dealing with the company and school business was done each day, Viola was left alone with herself for the remainder of the evenings. She hated eating out alone, and she disliked the way the people of Angers looked disapprovingly at her short hair and her clothing. She let her hair grow long again, and she purchased a few new dresses, trying to "fit in," but she never felt at home. What is odd is that most of the people who worked in shops or restaurants knew Viola by name and that she was the director of the CNDC. They also attended the performances of the company when it performed in Angers. The town welcomed Viola with open arms, but, as was her way, Viola never learned to accept the fact that she was loved. She only noticed the people who looked at her with odd expressions, not those who looked at her with great admiration and respect.

In 1982, Viola asked me to join her company as a guest artist for a tour of France. She had begun to perform less and less with the company because the age difference between herself and the dancers was growing wider and wider; and yet she still wanted to dance. I was brought in only to dance in duets with her on the programs. We performed the last duet that we had choreographed together, titled *Doublewalk* (1978), and an older one titled *Default* (1972).

When I arrived in Angers, I found a very tired, extremely nervous and very thin Viola. Something was wrong on with her, but I could not quite figure out what it was. She seemed almost paranoid. She was also suffering with a toe on her left foot that was so painful while she wore shoes that she had begun using a cane. When we walked together in the street, we held hands and I literally had to hold her up. I remember thinking that she was going to break my hand and arm from the force that she used. As the days went by, I realized that it was not just the toe that was causing this, but that her entire self was in need of mending. Her relationship with Curtis was growing more and more strained, and the burden of maintaining the company and school was wearing her down. For the first time since I had known her, I felt that Viola was about to crack emotionally.

During the tour, however, her spirits seemed to lift and we had a great time on stage, as well as long talks into the night in the hotel rooms. By the end of my three weeks, I felt that she was going to be all right, but looking back now, I know that I was wrong. Her emotional health was to deteriorate drastically during the new year. The toe problem was taken care of later in the year in New York. Viola had a rare and strange bone disease, which was cured by her doctor removing the entire middle joint of the affected toe, the toe next to the big one on her left foot. Fortunately, it did not cause any problems with balance, and her dancing returned to its full strength. Her emotional wellness, however, did not.

Later in the summer of 1982, Viola flew to California and taught for six weeks at the Long Beach Summer School of Dance which was run by Joan Schlaich and Betty Dupont and sponsored by the California State University, Long Beach Dance Department. We collaborated on a new duet which we titled *Meanwhile Back In The City* to an original score by Ruby Abeling who was the Music Director of that department. We had a wonderful time, and almost every day after work Viola had me drive her down to the beach for a swim in the ocean. She looked radiant and happy when she left, but that look was short lived.

In spite of her unhappiness in Angers, or maybe because of it, Viola continued to work there and produced four new works for the company between September 1981 and the end of her time there in 1983. These new works were quite theatrical in nature, and she learned to direct the audiences' eyes to what she felt necessary for them to look at. The works still had her signature of organized chaos, but the chaos was less prominent and less distracting. The theatricality was very attractive to the French audiences, and Viola knew this.

In 1983, the London dance critic for the newspaper <u>Passion</u>, Allen Robertson, wrote the following in his review.

> Not only is Farber having a distinct effect on the
> school (the Centre National de Danse Contemporaine
> in Angers), France seems to be having an equally strong
> effect on her work. The dances she has created since
> arriving in Angers have a new-found sense of ease that

fills out her speedy, fiendishly strenuous choreography with a ripe, almost voluptuous tone. There was a time when Farber's work looked as if someone had accidentally pressed a "self-destruct" panic button. Now, her choreography luxuriates in a new expansiveness. Without losing its multiplicity of focus or its throbbing sense of urgency, her work now has a quality of breadth and depth that, at times, approaches the monumental.

The French members of the company were beautiful dancers and performers, and when I returned to France in 1983, I was amazed at how quickly these incredible dancers were able to grasp the essence of Viola's work. This is a great testament to them and to Viola's teaching and coaching. The American dancers had also blossomed as they had not in New York. Perhaps it was because in France they did not have to work at other jobs in order to pay their bills. Also, their free time was limited in Angers because the hours in the studio were longer than those in New York. Dancing was a full-time job in France, and when they did have time off, they were in a foreign country where the language, for most, was a huge barrier. Their energies were concentrated on the dancing in a way that they had never been before with Viola's company.

As stated earlier, there was a cruel side to Viola that often caused friction within the company. Unfortunately, the dancers never had a way of expressing their frustration with this darker side. They adored the woman, and were in total awe of her as a choreographer. None of the dancers in the company wanted to be anywhere else, but none of them knew how to cope with Viola's temper. Viola felt that she was always right, no matter what, and she rarely, if ever, apologized to anyone after one of her rantings. The closer anyone got to her, the harder she was on them. However, Viola criticized, abused, and scheduled herself far more than anyone else in the company or in the school. She never asked anything of anyone that she did not ask doubly of herself, and when she had mistreated someone, she always suffered privately.

Upset with how hard she was working, her strained relationship with Curtis, and feeling so alone in Angers, Viola began to transfer her anger to the dancers by rarely allowing them to enjoy their weekends. She took to scheduling rehearsals on Saturdays, which no longer allowed them enough time to travel to Paris. Viola was jealous of their freedom and the fact that they had friends with whom to share their free time. It was a four hour drive to Paris, or a two hour train ride. Without thinking in those terms, Viola seemed to make certain that the dancers were as lonely and as unhappy living in Angers as she was. If one of the dancers got up the nerve to ask Viola for the entire weekend off, he or she had to deal with her wrath. She was a master at cutting a person into little shreds with a single glance and a minimum of words.

Viola was under a great deal of pressure constantly to produce new works at the CNDC. This meant extra rehearsals whenever the company was not touring. She had to keep the dancers working longer than perhaps even she wanted to be with them. She was extremely lonely. Those around her were her students or her employees, and not always her friends.

Sylvain Richard related that she felt that working with Viola was "essential" for her, and that she had become the kind of performer that she was because of the time she spent working with Viola in Angers. Viola gave her self-confidence, a strong technique and "a strong love for movement."

"But," Sylvain added. "She was a difficult woman to get along with on a day-to-day basis; she was very demanding and pushed us hard, sometimes to the point of breaking."

What made this cruel side of Viola so difficult to endure was that she was usually very gentle and loving, and she had a wonderful sense of humor that could totally delight and endear her to everyone. She spoke three languages, German, French, and English, and could move in and out of all three without a hitch. She played the piano and had roomfuls of books, all of which she had read. Viola could converse with anyone about anything, and she could use her charm to win over almost anyone whom she thought she needed to win over to her side. When she was angry, however, everyone felt it. Like a prickly rose, Viola scratched and impaled with her thorns anyone who came too close to her.

During a Christmas trip to New York in 1982, Viola decided not to renew her contract with the CNDC. She contemplated moving to London to be near Curtis once her contract was up. She also would have liked to move back to New York, but did not have a job or apartment to go back to.

New York, January 3, 1983

Dear Jeffet -

I, as usual, have to continue to fuss right around with CNDC affairs. At least I don't have to go back right away.

Have not yet started to pack up my things. The worst thing, of course, will be to go through papers - ugh! I will consult by telephone about our things and send you the Rauschenberg poster unframed and insured. Don't yet know what I'll do about London, New York, Kansas City?

Went to a fancy Rauschenberg opening the late afternoon of New Year's Eve. Some of the work was extraordinarily beautiful. He seemed very much like a movie star. Saw few people I know, but I hear some came after I'd left. Did see Jill Johnston who has aged beautifully.

Lots of love, dear Wit -

Dos

In the summer of 1983, Viola and I shared a residency at the International Arts Festival in Arles, France. It was a particularly hot summer, and we taught in a gymnasium that had skylights which allowed the sun to bake down on us all day long. The technique level of the majority of the students was that of beginners, and the condition of the floor was anything but desirable. After teaching, we rehearsed a new duet that was to be performed at the end of the three-week festival. Exhausted, we then went back to our hotel rooms and tried to bathe or shower in rooms that had little or no water pressure. Viola and I set up a routine of starting the water in her bathroom, and then going into my room to have a cup of coffee. After her tub was full enough for her to take a bath, I went to my room and showered in what little water was trickling out of the showerhead. We then went to a nearby restaurant that we liked and had dinner, and then went back to the hotel. From 8 p.m. until 1 a.m., movies were shown outdoors in the plaza right outside our hotel rooms, so that we rarely got a full night's sleep.

Near the end of the first two weeks, the rest of Viola's company arrived in Arles for the last performance together as a company. Viola's energies were spread even thinner now that she had to add rehearsal time for the company to her already exhausting schedule.

When the time came for the dress rehearsal for the performance, we discovered that we were going to have to perform outdoors on a makeshift stage made up of scaffolding covered with plywood and a vinyl dance floor over that. We also found that the stage was not only small, but very shaky and overly resilient. The composer, Alan Evans, was playing live, and the piano that he was given by the festival was a very old upright placed on the ground next to the stage. Alan was very good-natured and tried very hard to make the best of the situation.

In the middle of the rehearsal for the first group piece, the poorly constructed stage gave way on one side and collapsed under the weight of the dancers. Luckily, no one was injured, but Viola was so angered by this and many other events during the festival that she told the director that the company would not be performing. The director was frantic, as many critics from all over Europe had arrived to see and review the last performance of this extraordinary company, and to see Viola and me perform together again. We discussed the situation and agreed not to perform the duet, but not to punish the other dancers by not letting them perform. They would dance, but she and I would not.

During that performance, I sat in the audience and cried because the dancers and Viola's work looked so beautiful. Viola had reached a peak in her creativity, and the dancers were doing their best. It almost broke my heart to see this extraordinary company coming to an end. Worse still, they had to dance their final performance on such a horrible stage and in front of a very small audience.

If that were not enough, in the middle of the dance for which Alan Evans was playing, the back of the old upright fell off. Then the front panel went, and one of the pedals broke. Alan continued to play throughout all this, even though his leg had been hit by the front panel as it fell. Throughout this mayhem, he somehow managed to create beautiful music. It was both a nightmare and an amazing experience.

Although Viola and I did not perform that day, one critic wrote a rave review of our duet. Viola believed that this was done on purpose, not from any oversight on the critic's part, but because he or she knew of the awful conditions under which the company had to work, and wanted to show his or her support. Viola and I agreed that it was very strange to hear how beautiful and amazing we were in a duet that we did not perform.

Sylvain thought that one of the things that made Viola's choreography strong, and that set her apart from other choreographers, was "the quality of her dance, and the way the performers threw themselves into the movement, and not her arguments." By "arguments," I presume that she meant Viola's views or her personal emotions.

Viola's job in Angers was now over. She was exhausted, and tired of constantly teaching and choreographing new works, and she wanted to be with Curtis in England. She had never enjoyed all the politics that were involved in running the CNDC, and she was happy to leave Angers. She would miss France, but not the CNDC. She felt sad, and a little guilty, about the dancers who were now out of a job; especially the American dancers who had sacrificed so much to be with her in France. She felt positive, however, about her decision to disband the Viola Farber Dance Company, and to resign her position as the Artistic Director of the CNDC. She was ready to move to England and to try to make a life with Curtis. She knew that this decision would impact greatly on the lives of the dancers, but she felt that, for her own sanity, it was the right thing to do.

Thus ended the Viola Farber Dance Company, and what a harsh ending it was. But, considering how difficult the rest of Viola's life had been, it is not surprising that the company ended in this way. From its beginnings in 1968 to its final performance in 1983, the company had been held together solely by the determination of Viola and her dancers. Even without having to pay studio rent those last three years, Viola still had to fight to produce the kinds of works she wanted, and she had to struggle with the management at the CNDC. She never, in all her years as artistic director, had a period when she could just be the choreographer or a dancer in her company. She always wore several hats, doing several jobs within the company, and she was always exhausted and unwell. Viola never had the luxury of time to think about what she would like to work on, or the luxury of having unlimited time alone in the studio to create.

It was very sad news to all when Viola announced that she was leaving France and even more so that she was permanently giving up her company. She was not just disbanding the French company, but giving up the idea of having a company anywhere. Many felt that her work had reached a point where there was a chance that she might gain the international attention she deserved. The money was there. The time was there. But it was not meant to be, because Viola was simply too tired to fight any more, and more importantly, she wanted to have a chance at living a normal life with Curtis Roosevelt in England. For the first time in her life, Viola was ready to put love before her work. She was fifty-two years old, and, for better or worse, ready to settle down.

Viola had a huge impact on French dance and on the French dancers. She left behind a new way of approaching modern dance, and she had trained a new generation of French dancers to go forward and teach, or at least incorporate, her style of movement. Below is a brief insight into how she felt about dancing, which Viola expressed during my interview with her:

"Movement was and is still at the core of all my pieces and I demand great physicality of my dancers. But it is also essential for me to reveal the person behind the dancer."

In Sylvain's words, "I think everyone who studied or danced with her was never the same afterwards. Viola was a strong, tenacious, hard-working, passionate and generous woman, but, I fear, very lonely."

Viola sent me this letter just after she moved to London, where she began teaching at The Place and at the London Conservatory of Contemporary Dance in the fall of 1983. It shows how tired and depressed she was.

London, August 30, 1983

Dear Jeffet -

I didn't write and mail earlier in the day because I still didn't know the whole address - now I know:

c/o of Wilson

32 South Eaton Place

London, SW

England

It was lovely to talk to you the other day. I'm happy the last performance went well and was seen. Wish you all success and happiness for the next year.

I went to a concert at the Royal Albert Hall this evening. Tomorrow I want to go to a play with Ralph Richardson - he's the actor who played the drunken, drinking host in that wonderful Pinter play we saw years ago. I feel so rotten, ugly, nowhere, that I'm not really interested in seeing or hearing anything, but am trying with tooth and claw and thinking of Baba to climb out.

Started teaching today. The "students" range from age 11 to I'd say 35, and can't even count to 2. I kept making things simpler and simpler, trying not to come to a dead halt - a real challenge - 4 more days. I'd so much like for them to learn something.

Next week I'll be in Paris. I start with the stagiaires

there on your birthday. Then I'll either come back to London (if they get enough "professional" students) or to Dartington or maybe even to New York for a week, how's that for clarity and precision?

Take good care, dearest Dimt. I'll think of you on your birthday (even more than usual).

Much love - Dos

Viola first traveled back to New York to take care of some personal business and to see friends and family. She then moved to London where she got part-time jobs teaching at The Place and the London Conservatory of Contemporary Dance. She did not choreograph in England that first year, but she did return for a six-week stay at the 1984 Long Beach Summer School of Dance, during which we collaborated on another new duet titled *Last Waltz*. The duet was given this title because, at the time, we both thought that it might be our last opportunity to perform together. Luckily, it was not. She also choreographed a very large group dance with six men, all over six feet tall, and about fourteen women. It was a long and exciting dance titled *Day's Return*. Viola was not happy with the composer of the dance, but she became very fond of some of the dancers in the workshop. She related to me how different they were from the dancers in London, who, according to her, seemed rigid, tentative about moving, and somewhat lazy. She loved the American dancers because they were willing to try anything and seemed totally fearless in the way they approached new material. Viola could excuse anything except laziness. She said that she hated to see anyone waste their talent, and she often told students that, if they were going to waste their talent, they should do it where she did not have to watch.

Viola was far from idle during her first year in London, however,

and she did find an outlet for her creativity. She choreographed two
dances for the London Conservatory of Contemporary Dance, titled
Venom and Antidotes and *Autumn Edge*. Her work was well received
by the few critics who saw it, and, by all accounts, the dancers at the
London Conservatory of Contemporary Dance enjoyed working with
her. She did complain that rehearsals were difficult because whenever
another artist's dance was being rehearsed, the director either pulled
dancers out of Viola's rehearsal or canceled the rehearsal altogether. The
same thing happened with Viola's technique classes. Her work always
took second place both at The Place and at the London Conservatory
of Contemporary Dance.

Viola's journals from 1983 illustrate her depression while she lived
in London. What this letter does not directly say, is that Viola and
Curtis were having problems. Viola suddenly found herself without a
company, a home, a permanent job, and possibly without Curtis. She
even thought of suicide.

London, August 31, 1983
I am writing this journal, not because I find myself so
interesting - quite the opposite. I am bored and almost
sickened by how I feel, how I look, how I think, how
I sometimes act. If it weren't totally "wrong" in every
way - Baba particularly of course - I would see no reason
to go on living, but even that is part of what makes me
tired - that sentence. I mean everything about it.
Stuffing watercress into my mouth - vitamins. My
civilization is not very deep. Desperate efforts to uncork
wine with corkscrew, resulting in crumbled cork that
still can't be pushed down and broken glass from lip of
bottle - no consumption of wine. Rings on sitting room

table. After living with Curtis the possibility of having them myself in spite of careful saucer usage is enough to make me consider genteelly slitting my throat. Here's a good sentence, thought, and (sick) I feel it strongly: I WANT TO GO HOME, BUT THERE ISN'T ONE FOR ME. Make Baba my home. I try to think that Baba's arms are always around me, but I don't feel them. They are anyhow. As I wrote to Susan, Baba is not a painkiller.

London, September 1, 1983

Went to see "The Real Thing" tonight. Forced voices, Max in a perpetual demi-plié parallel position at beginning, banal dialogue - awful - left at "interval." Having bought corkscrew, came home, opened wine, and DRANK. Tried to phone CR, but nothing but steady buzz. Baba embraced me. Baba held my cheek to His. What sort of animal monster am I to want more?

Devon, October 1983
In coffee shop during my long between classes break. Weekend at Dartington Meeting at TSW - guitarist and "Pandora" artist - both ghastly in different ways. More discussion with no conclusion, at end of long session, about Kevin Crooks' and my project. To CR's house

- scotch and dinner - friendly, efficient, calm. CR's feet - then he to bed in studio, I in bedroom. Beautiful room - (We picked roses in danger of cold night by flashlight before dinner.) No sleep, cold in all ways. Finally took pillow and blanket to "music room" and stove. Tears all day. Abject pleading with CR - agreement no doors closed - to station. Greeted by Sheila who most apologetically said that I had to leave in order for sale of house contract to be signed - solicitors, referees, etc. I "quite all right, I do understand." Fortunately she then left so when the crying went on I could make noise. Call to Susan, she phoned back later. Eyes swollen almost shut this morning. Going on and on.

I found this very interesting outline in Viola's journals that was also written in London in 1983. It appears to be an outline of her career and accomplishments. It does, however, turn somewhat strange at the end.

London, 1983
Black Mountain College - Katherine Litz, Merce, John Cage, David Tudor, Charles Olson, Franz Kline.

New York - Merce, Katie
Beginnings of MC company -
Never knowing which of 2 works were what
Seeing first C (Cunningham) performance - Audio
- Impression that class was more beautiful than "dances."
Summer with M. at Black Mtn.

Paul Taylor - Jack and the Beanstalk, beginnings of

No pay - many jobs

First C tour - no place to stay before arriving in Los Angeles

Chance

Story - Paired

World Tour

Rauschenberg - difficulties

Starting own company

Teaching for Merce - advanced class - making of dance in class - etc.

What is important about dancing -

The total uses of oneself very obviously - the impermanence of action - the crisis of the moment - the possibility of and inevitability of constant change. The use by dancers of new strengths, even weakness not discovered by choreographer. The expressive possibilities through combination of strength, risk, vulnerability. The readiness, alertness necessary to respond to new situations at the moment, while totally exposed.

Audience - faith that by letting them participate in all of above one is presenting something that has to do with everyone's life. (Sometimes too much, since often audiences prefer to be distracted from their lives rather than continue to deal with life during an evening out.)

Music - musicality

Music for dance

Alvin Lucier - working together - growing apart

Dances in public places

Raising money - NEA - private wealthy people.

CNDC

Company - students in Angers - addition of pedagogy

students

Decentralization

State and city

Albeit

In 1984 Bennington College offered Viola a teaching position. Here is a brief passage from her journals mentioning the possibility of moving to Bennington, VT. Viola did not take the job. This was the last entry in her journals. If she wrote any others, she did not keep them.

London, 1984

Bennington has called to ask if I'm interested in a teaching job there. I will go there to look when I'm in New York beginning of April. I don't think it matters very much where I am at this point. The mixture of boredom and pain is not, I think, caused by geography.

Miss Craske said at Myrtle Beach during her talk in the library one day that Baba takes things away so there's more room for Him. I think that's a lovely idea, but after trying, trying, trying to make the emptiness inhabitable for Him, I can only come to the conclusion that for whatever reason, this is not so in my case. I can, and have, put on an act for a while, and then it falls flat.

I was very concerned about Viola's emotional state, and wrote a letter to Margaret Craske sometime in early 1984, asking whether she had any advice as to what I could do to help Viola. Here is what she wrote back.

New York, February 1984

Dear Jeff,

It was good to have a letter from you, telling me of your life and the way that Baba communicates with His love and has helped you through the very difficult Viola situation. She has contacted me once or twice by telephone weeping copiously for part of the call. In a strange way Baba is wiping something away. Of course, the Curtis situation is not good and does not appear to be improving.

About the dancing? Who knows? She seems to get plenty of work, but not quite what she had envisioned. Well my dear, we have to leave our Vi in Baba's hands.

Good-bye and many thanks for writing.

Much love,

Margaret Craske

Sometime in 1982, Curtis had convinced Viola to apply for a Guggenheim Foundation grant to bring several members of her former company together for a film project in England. Viola had applied several times before for such a grant, but had always been turned down. Rosalind Newman, a former member of her company, received one before Viola did. I think that this suggestion of Curtis's was an attempt to make Viola happy. He could see that she was growing bored and restless by simply teaching in London. He had also heard Viola's stories about working with the dancers in California, and knew that she was itching to choreograph for dancers who understood what she was about.

The grant proposal listed the dancers Viola wanted to work with, and that the dance, produced under the grant, would be filmed, converted to videotape, and distributed throughout America and Europe. The organization that Viola and Curtis contacted to do the filming was Television South West Limited in London. They agreed to the project and listed Kevin Crooks as the man who would direct the filming.

Viola was certain that she would be turned down again by the Guggenheim Foundation, but to her surprise and delight, she was awarded a rather large grant, which, along with financial help from Dartington College in Devon, made it possible for her to pay for the round trip airfare for six dancers in the U.S., and for three in France. It also paid the dancers a small, but sufficient salary for two weeks. She called me and asked whether I would be one of the dancers. She was honest with me and explained that she again needed someone closer to her age to perform with, and that she needed desperately to talk to me about what was going on in her private life. She had called me several times during the months before this, upset and crying. I experienced the same feeling that I had had back in 1982 that she was rapidly falling apart. I agreed to the project, and just after Christmas in 1984 I flew to England, arriving a few days ahead of the other dancers.

Curtis and Viola met me at the airport and drove me to the dormitory in Dartington where I would be staying. Although the entire building was empty for Dartington's winter break, they told me that there was a maid who would clean my room each day. We then walked through a path that led from the dormitory building through a beautiful 12th century cemetery and directly to Curtis's house. It was no more than a five-minute walk. They then walked back with me and told me to come to dinner around seven o'clock.

During dinner, Viola hardly ate and rarely took her eyes off her plate. She appeared extremely thin and nervous. When she did look at me I was struck by the combination of panic and resignation in her eyes. They seemed to scream for help, but at the same time they looked empty and defeated. I was very worried about her, but did not say anything that night. Curtis seemed his usual self; polite, charming, but extremely detached. He did not appear to be worried about Viola's health.

The next day, Viola invited me over for breakfast. Curtis was at his office, and so we had a chance to talk. She told me that Curtis had found someone else, and that he was probably going to marry this woman in the coming year. She was frantic. She had given up everything for this man, and now he was dumping her. I told Viola that she could come and live with me in California, but she refused. We finished breakfast and went to the studio. When all else failed Viola, she chose the studio.

The other dancers arrived a few days later, housed in a different dormitory building than I, and we began rehearsing on Viola's new dance on January 2, 1985. Viola immediately came to life when the studio, a very large 12th century dinning hall, was filled with dancers whom she knew and loved. There were moments on that first day when it appeared that she was going to be all right, but at other moments her eyes got the far-away glaze that I had noticed a few nights earlier.

It was like old home week, however, and we all enjoyed catching up on all our news, taking class with Viola, complaining about getting older and laughing a great deal. The dancers who were there for this project included Viola, Jumay Chu, Didier Deschamps, Anne Koren, Karen Levey, Joël Leucht, Andé Peck, me, and an English actor named Michael Dower.

The first week end after the start of the project, Viola and I decided to go to dinner at one of the local restaurants. Curtis was in London, and we used his car to get there. We did not invite any of the other dancers because Viola needed to talk. Later, as we were driving back to Curtis's house, it began to rain and turned very cold. When we got out of the car, Viola could not find the key to the house. We searched her purse, her wallet, her coat and the inside of the car, but the key was nowhere to be found. Viola began to get hysterical in a manner that I had never seen before. She was trembling and terrified, and said that Curtis was going to be furious with her. I told her not to worry, that we would find the key and all would be fine, but the more we looked, the more I knew that the key was lost. We tried all the doors and windows, but the house was locked up tight. I suggested that we go to my dormitory room and look through her coat and purse again.

Once inside my room, we emptied the entire contents of Viola's purse and wallet onto my bed. The key was not there. Viola was so upset that she made me do it a second time, as she was certain that she had put the key in her purse or wallet. I told her that it was getting late and that she should sleep with me that night and we would get someone from the college to open the house in the morning.

Neither of us got much sleep that night. Viola cried softly all night long, trembling and repeating over and over that Curtis was going to be furious. I assured her that he would not be angry and that we would all laugh about it in the morning.

When morning did come, Viola reached into her purse to get her lipstick, the only make-up that she wore, and out of the purse fell the key to Curtis's house. To this day, I have no idea where that key had been; I know that we had searched through that purse many times. I can only think that it was some crazy trick of Meher Baba's and that it had a purpose in Viola's and my life. If so, I still do not know what that purpose was except to bring Viola and I closer together, and to help us take care of each other.

We rehearsed in a dance studio on campus, but filming took place in the very large and very cold dining hall. The floor was beautiful and resilient, but it was extremely slippery. As with the filming of *Brazos River* in Texas, we all had to stand around waiting for what seemed like hours while the lights and camera crew got everything just right. When they were finally ready, we were freezing and our muscles felt as if they would never move again. Viola had choreographed herself in only two very short duets, one with me and one with Andé Peck, and was acting mainly as director of the dancing. It appears, too, that she had not learned anything from the Texas experience, as she very soon lost control of what was going to be recorded with regard to camera angles. She had managed to keep the dance in its original sequence, but the camera was not always getting the entire dancers' bodies in the frame.

Gordon Jones had composed a beautiful score titled *January* because the filming was taking place in January, and so the dance took on the same title. We only had one week of filming, and, as suddenly as it had begun, the project was over.

Now fifty-three years old, Viola was rapidly going to pieces emotionally, in spite of everyone's help and in spite of the wonderful experience of working with her favorite dancers once again. During the filming, the dancers had been amazed at the way her entire physical being changed whenever she stepped in front of the camera. The performer emerged as soon as the camera rolled, but immediately afterwards her age and posture returned to those of someone in great emotional despair. Viola needed professional help, but there was no time then to get it for her. It was incredible to all how she managed to get through that week of rehearsals and the week of filming without ending up ranting and raving. She was wonderful to everyone and never once lost her temper.

She and I discussed what was going on with her emotional health, but we never burdened the other dancers with any of it. Viola managed to give all of us a wonderful working experience, even giving the dancers a class every morning. Her work and her love of dancing came before her own health.

I remember looking at Viola as I drove off in a taxi toward the airport. She looked small and almost transparent. I was truly concerned about her emotional health and wondered how on earth I could help her.

As before mentioned with *Brazos River*, Viola hated the finished editing of *January*, but everyone else who has been lucky enough to view it, loved it. It is a beautiful film, and Viola looks gorgeous in it. The dancers are amazing to watch, and the work is brilliant. The dancers who worked with her knew that Viola was a genius. *January* illustrates the essence of her work. It shows the way in which Viola saw the world, how she viewed people and their relationships to each other. How she accomplished this when she was in such personal turmoil is a mystery to me. Perhaps pain and turmoil were part of what made Viola tick. She seemed to thrive when situations surrounding her were at their worst.

The finishing of *January* marked the end of an era for Viola. She would never again choreograph a dance for the dancers who had given her so much of their lives, and over whom she had had such an influence. They were not only strong technically, but were intelligent and could handle the type of strong, energetic choreography that Viola created. They had to be able to think "on their feet," to make choices onstage about where to take a phrase, who to do it with, or how to change the phrase when another dancer challenged them with a different dynamic. They had to do all this while keeping an eye on the rest of the cast and keeping track of time. They had to be part of the entire dance, not just soloists sharing the same space. Viola depended on them to realize her vision of each and every dance in her repertory. They had to be able to shift from what looked like improvisation to unison dancing, and to make it look seamless.

Dance critics labeled these dancers as having remarkable strength and rapport; marked individuals; to have equal measures of security, drive, and charisma; stark, unadorned bodies in motion; high-powered; to posses energy, speed, tension; dizzying; elegant. The descriptions go on and on. Even critics like Arlene Croce, who did not like Viola's choreography, praised the dancers in the company.

The Viola Farber Dance Company usually received excellent reviews wherever it performed, but because of poor management the company never became as visible and well-known as did the Cunningham, Taylor, or Tharp companies. Viola never created the type of management that could promote her company the way it needed in order to achieve national or international acclaim. Her focus remained on the artistic work, and she did not possess the ability or the funds to hire high-powered management, nor was she lucky enough to find an excellent manager who was willing to work for little money and the love of the work. Viola did not possess the ability to play the business games that would further her career as a choreographer. She refused to go to parties or receptions that other artistic directors attended and she lacked the foresight to see their necessity. She understood the importance of the business side of the company, but simply could not do her part in making it be successful.

The company was, however, one of the first "Post-Cunningham" companies in the United States. It was a powerful company, and very prominent during its twelve year life span in New York City. Many aspiring young dancers flocked to Viola's studio in hopes of getting into her company. A large number of dancers who were performing with other prominent companies began studying with Viola after seeing her dancers perform. The Farber studio was one of the "hot" places to study during the 1970s, and Viola's company was a favorite amongst many dancers in New York.

It is sad that more people throughout the United States and the rest of the world never had an opportunity to see this amazing company perform. One critic credited Viola with helping to revitalize modern dance. Another said that she had accomplished the near-impossible by establishing a movement style completely her own.

Most unfortunate, too, is the fact that few records of the company exist. A few videotapes dating back to 1979 are preserved at the New York Library of Performing Arts. These tapes, however, were done before video had become as sophisticated as it did later on, and these tapes are slowly fading. The library does not have enough funding to restore the tapes, or to transfer them onto digital tapes or CDs. Viola did not keep notes on her dances and they were never notated; therefore, the majority of her work will be lost forever if these visual records are not preserved.

After finishing *January*, Viola concentrated her energies on her teaching in London. She and Curtis went their separate ways, and Viola began to see a psychiatrist and was put on antidepressants. Her mood changed slightly, but our telephone conversations were still filled with her crying and saying how much she hated living in London.

One amazing event did take place in London, however. Every day as Viola was leaving her apartment, she saw a woman next door working in her flower garden. After a while, they began to say hello to each other, but that was all. A couple of months went by, and finally the woman told Viola that it was silly that they only spoke each morning, lived next door to each other, but had not had the opportunity to get to know each other. She invited Viola for tea the next day.

Viola arrived at the woman's apartment and was shown into very cozy rooms filled with beautiful, old furniture. The woman asked Viola to be seated while she went into the kitchen to prepare the tea. Viola was restless and wandered over to the fireplace mantle and began to look at photographs that were lined up there. One of the photos caught her eye. It was of a man standing alone in what looked to Viola to be her birthplace of Heidelberg, and she somehow thought that she recognized the man's face. She did not understand how she could, as she was only seven years old when her family immigrated to America.

When the woman came back, Viola pointed to the photo and said that she thought that she knew this man and asked who it was. It was the woman's father whom she had not seen since World War II because he and her mother had divorced, and they had moved to England after that. When Viola asked where she had been raised, the woman said Heidelberg, Germany. Viola told her that she, too, was from Heidelberg and asked the man's name. He turned out to be Viola's father's employer, the very one who had paid her family's way to America. The woman was very happy to have this news of her father as her mother had never told her anything but horrible stories about him, and she thought that perhaps he had been a member of the Nazi party during the war. She was very grateful to Viola for finally providing a good memory of him, and to find out that he had not been a Nazi.

Viola continued to teach at The Place and at the London Contemporary Dance School. The Place was, at that time, considered by Viola to be a shrine for the Martha Graham dance technique. She felt that it was even more "old Graham" than Graham's own teaching. Viola was teaching there at the time she mentioned this, so this would have been some time in 1985 or 1986.

A letter written to Robin Howard, the founder and director of The Place, which was found in Viola's personal journals, shows what obstacles she felt she was up against while teaching in London. The letter was not dated, and it is not known whether she actually mailed it. I also have no idea who the Richard is Viola mentions in the first paragraph.

For Robin -

I have just read Richard's summary of his private conversation with teachers at The Place.

It seems to me that there is a controversy going on at the LCDS (London Conservatory of Contemporary Dance) that no longer exists anywhere else in the Western world: is Graham technique the only valid contemporary dance technique? In France there are numerous dance companies and independent dancers who have never done a "contraction" in their lives. They dance, some of them, extremely well. (And many of them have had their initial continuous training with me or members of my company.) In the United States, where dance has flourished, and specifically in New York, it has not been considered necessary since the early 50s, when I arrived on the scene to sit on the floor for a long time in order to learn to dance, unless one wanted to dance in the Graham Company. If, as Robert Cohan seems to believe, Graham technique is the only worthwhile contemporary dance training, one must ask what, then, is the meaning of the word contemporary and for what expression of dancing is the student being trained? My resentment of Bob, which is very mild, is not that he isn't around the school very much, but that, not being around, he makes judgments, suggestions, and decisions in a situation with which he has at present less than a nodding acquaintance.

I knew when I accepted to teach at The Place that it was a Graham school. I was tired from the multiplicity of duties and responsibilities of my work in France and quite happy simply to have a teaching job. I am no longer tired. But I am disturbed by what seems an extreme lethargy, lack of curiosity, adventure, and sheer pleasure in moving that pervades the school. I am also more and more aware of the difficulty of teaching students to use their body in a way different from what they are used to. Put in a simplified manner; lengthening and lifting the muscles rather than squeezing and clenching, using minimum force rather than maximum - opening rather than holding tight. Moving with a basic simplicity, like a finely toned human being, and not heroically "like a dance" - this latter being again a very limited and stereotyped idea of what that must be.

Contemporary dance started as individual expression. Surely we cannot say that only one of these individual expressions hold the ultimate range of possibilities in moving, the only truth. The world of dance now is many faceted, how can one specific technique particularly one in which the emotional and dramatic expression is intrinsic, be the only contemporary technique to prepare a potential dancer, potential teacher or amateur?

I am frustrated and amused at being considered "the alternative technique" of which the students are meant to get a little taste when they have achieved "the basics." The frustration lies in my never being able to get with the students to the fullness of dancing that is possible in what I do, because there is such a confusion for them in the process of shifting from mental and physical habits which have been presented to them as basic necessities for dancers.

Can we open the situation? Can we recognize that not everyone is suited mentally, spiritually, emotionally, or physically to just one kind of anything? Can we give students choices? I am told that I don't believe in discipline. I believe very much in discipline, it's the only way to get to anything. But I think we lack discipline, a true, inner discipline, in the school and therefore have to be authoritarian to keep things from falling apart too badly. I feel our students are both spoiled and oppressed - an odious combination.

If the decision is to be that LCDS is a "Graham School" (I still certainly understand this was its purpose at the outset) my alternatives are 1. To leave, since I really believe that what I can teach is more valuable than the place it can have in such a situation. 2. To stay, teaching as well as possible in the circumstances and try to do lots of things outside the school, with dancers who choose to work with me.

Other thoughts: Rather than have regular weekly courses in subjects related to dance, let's get some exchanges going. We are in London, which must be full with resident and visiting artists, thinkers. Music classes might, for example, be a series of sessions with a professional, working musician who would work with students for a limited time on a project of choice.

Sessions with theatre (drama) people, nutritionists,

kinesiologists, lighting and costume designers, painters, video artists and technologists, biologists, etc. would be of interest.

Technology plays an important part in contemporary life and art. I am stupid about it, and not terribly interested, but it seems to me that students, whose skills and interests are not necessarily mine and who are generally going to be around in the world longer, might be very interested and stimulated by some work in that area.

Choreographers might come in and talk about some aspect of their work - working with composers, the business and administrative aspects of their work, etc.

Community work - I know that Richard Mansfield is involved in this. Could students not also perform, teach in community areas? Can people from the neighborhood and people specifically interested be invited to come and see what happens in the school? I realize that this poses security problems, but mention it anyhow!

The letter ends there. It is clear that Viola was upset but that she had regained some of her strength to fight back. I do think that not much changed at the LCDS, but Viola choreographed two more dances for them in 1987. These titles were *Bank Holiday* and *Passing*. I know why she named the first dance: she was always complaining to me over the telephone that every time she turned around there was another bank holiday in London. She hated holidays because she was living alone and had nothing to do on those days off, or anyone do anything with.

Viola also made two works for a company in London called the

Extemporary Dance Theatre. The titles were *Winter Rumors* and *Take-Away*. She also choreographed a dance titled *Preludes* for the National Youth Dance Company in London. Thus, she managed to stay busy outside The Place or the LCDS. In between, she was also making trips back to the United States looking for work, but without success. She did make the short list for a tenure track position at Texas Christian University, but they chose a younger teacher for the job. Viola was then fifty-six, and I am sure that the search committee at TCU did not want to hire a teacher who would retire a few years later - - not that Viola would ever have retired.

Finally, in the fall of 1986, a job became available that Viola could consider taking. A former company member, Karen Levey, had left her part-time position at Adelphi University and was now teaching part-time at Sarah Lawrence College in Bronxville, New York, a short train ride from Manhattan. The chairperson who had begun the dance department there, Bessie Schoenberg, had retired a year or so earlier, and the faculty was not happy with her replacement. They were looking for a new chairperson, and Karen suggested Viola. Viola called me and I told her to go for it because Sarah Lawrence College was close enough to New York City that she could live in Manhattan and commute by train. She liked that idea and sent in her application. In early 1987, she flew to New York and interviewed for the job. She had agreed to teach that summer for six weeks at the American Dance Festival in Durham, North Carolina, and thought that, if she got the position at Sarah Lawrence, that she could use the time before to look for a place to live.

I flew to Durham to spend a week with Viola, and to take class with her again. She still had not heard from Sarah Lawrence College and was becoming discouraged about having to go back to London. The next to the last day that I was in Durham, word came that the job was hers if she wanted it, and she told them yes. When she hung up the telephone, Viola began to dance like a school girl around the apartment she had rented in Durham. I was very glad to see Viola happy and excited about working again. My mother was visiting us from Richmond, Virginia, and the three of us went out to dinner to celebrate Viola's good news.

Viola flew back to London in late July of 1987 and gave her notice to The Place and the LCDS, packed her suitcases, and flew to New York. She was unable to find an apartment in New York that she could afford, as rents had almost doubled during the time that she was in Europe. She did, however, find a one bedroom apartment in Bronxville. She soon had her furniture taken out of storage and moved into her new place. Her furniture and paintings (some of them by Jasper Johns and Robert Rauschenberg) had been in storage since the summer of 1981. Viola was finally back in the country she loved and near the city she called home.

Viola Farber in Bequest, 1981. Photographer: Lois Greenfield

Chapter Six

Sarah Lawrence College

THE NEW JOB AT SARAH Lawrence frightened Viola a little, but I reminded her of all that she had done in her life that prepared her for her new position. She had run a dance company and school for fifteen years and choreographed hundreds of dances. She certainly was capable of running a college dance department. She knew how to do budgets, write grants, and organize people. At age fifty-six, she knew that this might be her last full-time job. She feared that, because she had not finished college, the other faculty members on campus would look down their noses at her. Instead, everyone welcomed Viola with open arms, and the other faculty members were very impressed with her credentials. Even though she had not finished college, she had had years of learning from life experiences.

Disaster struck immediately, however. There was a freak snow storm early in the fall semester. Viola's apartment was located at the top of a very steep hill, and on the morning of the storm Viola began her trek down the hill and slipped. She knew that something serious had happened to her left wrist because, when she tried to get up, she couldn't. Viola sat in the snow for more than twenty minutes before someone came to her aid. X-rays showed that the wrist was shattered in several places, and that it needed to be operated on to repair the bone and place metal pins that held the bones in place. The operation affected her so severely that Viola was unable to return to work for the remainder of the semester. She would have to wait until January 1988 to begin her job again.

Like all new chairpersons who are brought in from the outside, Viola set out to revamp the dance curriculum and some of the part-time faculty. Her ideas were not popular with some of the faculty, but the majority liked the changes. Her full-time faculty consisted of herself and dance historian Rose Anne Thom. Karen Levey was a part-time faculty member, and Viola hired a former member of the company Dan Wagoner & Dancers, Emmy Devine. One of the part-time faculty instructors who Viola kept on was her old friend, and Baba follower, Marie Adair, who taught ballet.

The next two years at Sarah Lawrence College went very well for Viola. She began to implement many of the things that she had written about in the letter to Robin Howard (see Chapter Five) several years before, bringing in guest artists and having the dance students exposed to subjects other than dance. Sarah Lawrence is a liberal arts college, and all students are required to divide their curriculum into three different areas of study. Consequently, there were no dance majors. This did not sit well with Viola, but she had no choice but to accept it. She did, however, set about requiring the dance thirds, as they are called, to take more dance technique and choreography courses than were required with the previous chairperson. Soon it was difficult for many of the students to be called just "dance thirds," as they were taking so many units in dance, but somehow they made it work. Viola fought hard for these changes and won. She also began an outreach program in which the dance students taught classes at a high school in Yonkers,

New York, and performed some dances of their own choreography for the high school students. Viola kept her students abreast of what was going on in the rest of the arts, and she kept all of them very busy.

On one of my visits to Bronxville, Viola and I were discussing the teaching of dance in a university or college setting as compared to teaching it in a professional studio. We agreed that it was very different, and very difficult. Dancers in school tended to put their grades ahead of dancing, whereas dancers in the professional world danced because they loved it. Viola seemed to feel that the dancers at Sarah Lawrence College were not growing as fast as she would have liked, and she was frustrated by this fact.

The next day, I went to watch Viola teach. It had been almost twenty years since I had first seen Viola teach, and the students at Sarah Lawrence College were dancing with the same kind of energy and abandonment I remember witnessing back in the late 1960s. Viola still had her magic, and the dancers were just as eager to learn from her as were those in the past. I later told Viola that she had nothing to worry about, that the students in her department were doing just fine.

Viola's position first came up for review after she had been at Sarah Lawrence College for two and a half years. Here are excerpts from a letter she addressed to the committee for her re-appointment, dated September 5, 1990. It demonstrates some of the ways she changed the department and how she was implementing the ideas that she had mentioned in her letter to Robin Howard.

> Since coming to Sarah Lawrence College in January, 1988, I have made what I thought were necessary and/or desirable changes in the curriculum and part-time faculty of the Dance Department. The number of part-time faculty has been reduced and,

of the number now existing, each one teaches more classes, thus providing greater stability for students and perhaps more involvement for faculty. It seems to me that there is now greater respect for each other among the faculty despite a healthy diversity of particular interests, approaches, and dance backgrounds. We no longer have a Friday Guest Teacher, a long tradition in which I participated in the 60s. To provide a broader acquaintance with dance possibilities, styles, and ideas, we have invited guests to teach and lecture; among them Sara Rudner, dancer and choreographer; Beverly Emmons, Sarah Lawrence alumna and well-know lighting designer; Charles Honi Coles, tap dancer; Glory Van Scott, actor, dancer, playwright; Youssouf Koumbassa, African dancer; and Sun Ock Lee, Korean Zen dancer. I plan to continue to invite guest teachers and lecturers.

One change that Viola made in the curriculum was to require each dance student to take at least one dance technique class each day. This was intended to bring the student's work level up to meeting the same demands as those of the rest of the dance students "in the world," as she put it in her letter. She goes on to explain how she and Shirley Kaplan, a faculty member in the Theater Department, shared guest teachers; what a "very rich and exciting experience" it was for the dance and theater students, and how they wanted to continue to collaborate and involve faculty and students from the music department as well.

In regard to the community outreach program and the student concerts, Viola wrote:

I have talked with Bob Cameron about working in the wider community this year, perhaps at PS 30. Many students, I think, would like to be generous, and dance is, in any case, an activity to be shared. I think that it should be possible to do this within the present curriculum. We intend also to continue the lively work that students in Rose Anne Thom's very lively teaching conference have been doing in Bronxville schools.

We consider it important, among some of the Dance faculty, to present another informal dance faculty performance. Some of us think that our first and last, in spring of '89, was enjoyed by our students and helped them subsequently to work with increased awareness and attention. We enjoyed doing it.

It is important, I think, for students and faculty, to continue to change what we do and how we do it, within the constraints inherent in our situation, as we see interests and needs, and our perceptions of them, change.

Viola went on to describe how she and the dance faculty were going to try to resuscitate the Dance Group, a student dance organization which "has subtly suffered a lingering and unheralded demise." She mentioned that Emmy Devine was the faculty advisor to the Dance Group, and that this student organization could "then organize extra curricular activities which students find interesting and lacking in the Department's daily round. In this way they can be responsible for seeing a project from inception to completion through their own organizational energy, desire, skill."

Knowing the importance of academic politics and saying all the right things in her re-appointment letter, Viola added at the end how fortunate she felt to "work in a department with such an excellent tenured faculty as well as guest and part-time faculty. They all do their work with attention, gravity, grace, and humor."

On February 18, 1990, Viola's mentor and long time teacher, Margaret Craske, died. She had taught Viola to dance correctly and had helped guide her along a spiritual path. Miss Craske had been like a mother to Viola, as well as a teacher. Viola had always turned to Miss Craske for advice and comfort. The death of her dear friend shook Viola to the core, and she wept for days. Baba had said not to weep for the dead, as they were on to the next life and were very happy to be with God. But Viola could not help it, and she called me almost daily to talk. Miss Craske's ashes were taken to India and placed not too far from Meher Baba's tomb. Viola vowed to go to India to see that spot, and she did.

Viola was ill off and on for the rest of the 1990. She was fifty-nine, working far too hard at Sarah Lawrence College, smoking too much, and generally being very unhappy. She felt alone and unwanted. This woman, who was loved by hundreds of dancers throughout the world, lived alone and could not find happiness anywhere. She now longed to be back in France, the country that she had run from to be with Curtis. Suddenly, the CNDC did not look as awful as she had thought back in the days when she was working so hard to keep her company alive. She realized, however, that she could not go back; that the French no longer wanted Americans running the CNDC. Viola knew in her heart that that was as it should be. American choreographers had run the company and taught in the CNDC students for decades, and now the French had found a modern dance style of their own. It no longer imported American modern dance, it was French.

Viola did not choreograph any dances that year. She seemed

depressed and unable to pull herself together enough to move forward. I went to visit her for Christmas and helped her file away papers and clean up her apartment, and we sat and talked for hours.

The night before I was to leave, we decided to call up Peter Saul and wish him a happy New Year. He was living in Ithaca, New York, and teaching ballet in the dance department at Cornell University. As we were talking to him, I sensed that something was wrong, and I asked him if he was all right. He said that he was bedridden and everyone he knew was away for the holidays. He was so ill that he could not get out of bed. I told him that I would fly to Ithaca the next day to be with him.

The events of the next three months did not help to raise Viola's spirits. Peter was diagnosed with acute leukemia in January of 1991 and died in March. Viola had known Peter since the late 1950s. Both had studied ballet with Margaret Craske at the Old Metropolitan Opera House, each were followers of Meher Baba, both had danced with the Cunningham company, and they had collaborated on at least two modern dance concerts. Viola took Peter's death very hard, partly because it happened so quickly. It was a great shock for all of Peter's friends, but with the help of her spiritual beliefs, Viola managed to hold herself together.

Peter's remains were cremated, and in early June of 1991 Viola, Tex Hightower, Donald Mahler, and I and my aunt Julia met in Myrtle Beach, South Carolina, to bury his ashes. We waited almost a year after Peter's death because we had difficulty finding a date when all of us were free at the same time. Viola was busy at the college, Donald was teaching all over the world, and I was in California. We buried Peter's ashes on property very near the Meher Spiritual Center. We felt that it was an appropriate place to bury the ashes because it was against the rules to spread human ashes on the Center's land. We dug a hole, said a prayer, and then went out to lunch and told stories about Peter.

During this trip, we all noticed that Viola looked pale and thin. She had a terrible cough and was complaining of a migraine headache that did not go away. At one point, Donald said to me that he thought we would soon be back in Myrtle Beach burying Viola's ashes.

I asked her whether she had been to see a doctor recently, and she said no. She did say that she had stopped smoking a few months earlier, but that her chest and side hurt all the time. When my aunt and I drove Viola to the airport, I made her promise that she would see a doctor when she got back to Bronxville.

I stayed in constant touch with Viola and kept reminding her of her promise, and so she did go to a doctor. The x-rays showed that she had two malignant tumors in her left lung. All the years of smoking had finally caught up with her. The doctor said that the only treatment for her was to undergo surgery and then chemotherapy. He advised Viola that the operation was extremely dangerous and that she might not survive. He added that she would not survive without the surgery. Viola agreed to have the operation at New York Hospital in early July. Viola knew that her father had died of lung cancer, and she was, rightfully, terrified.

I was teaching at the American Dance Festival at the time and was unable to be with her during the operation, but several friends in Bronxville were there with her. When Viola checked in, she took along a picture of Meher Baba and put it on her bedside table. Her doctor asked who the man in the picture was. She answered, "His name was Meher Baba, and he is God." Viola said that the doctor did not flinch, but that he did smile.

The operation turned out to be very successful, and Viola pulled through with "flying colors." When she was awake enough to speak with her doctor, he pointed to the picture of Meher Baba and said, "I don't know exactly who that guy is, but he sure worked miracles with you!" It was Viola's turn to smile.

I found out that most patients who go through lung removal surgery have to be put on a heart pump or a respirator, or both. Neither of these had to be done with Viola. The doctor said that he could almost see her body healing itself as he was sewing her up. He was totally amazed and had never seen anything like it during his entire practice. Viola was not surprised at the power of Meher Baba. Although she had been terrified, as would anyone, she had put her life in Baba's hands.

I arrived in Bronxville about a week or so after Viola returned home from the hospital, and I was with her during two sessions of chemotherapy. She was nauseated and lost almost all of her hair. Her skin turned yellow, and she could not stand the smell of coffee. Viola had been drinking many cups of coffee a day for all of her adult life, and during that time even the odor of it made her ill. I was still smoking, but pretended that I had quit. I stayed with her all day, and then just before bedtime I told her that I was going for a walk. I smoked a cigarette and then chewed two sticks of gum before returning. If she knew that I was smoking, she never said anything. I am certain that she did know. Other odors made Viola nauseous as well; odors that Viola had once loved, like those of roses or honey. Her entire sense of taste had been turned up-side-down.

After Viola's second chemotherapy session, she insisted on going home the minute that the nurse took the IV out of her arm. The doctor had wanted her to stay a day or so longer to monitor her, but she was adamant. She lived on the third floor of an apartment building with no elevator, and I had to carry her up the stairs because she was too weak. She immediately went to sleep, and I went out for a smoke. When I returned, I found Viola wide awake and complaining of severe chest pains. A few minutes later, she was screaming from the pain and begging me to get help. I did not wait to call an ambulance, but picked her up, ran down the three flights of stairs, and drove her to the Bronxville Hospital Emergency Room.

About an hour later, a doctor came into the waiting room and told me that Viola's chest pains were nothing serious, that she was simply dehydrated. He said that she should have remained in the hospital after the chemotherapy and that they could have hydrated her before releasing her. I was just happy that she was not dying. I had feared that either she was having a heart attack or that her incision had torn open. A few hours later, we were back in Viola's apartment and she slept the rest of that night.

When the bill for her hospital stay came, Viola found that she owed a great deal of money, her insurance had not covered everything. I called Jean Rigg, who had been the manager for the Cunningham company while I was a member, and asked whether she knew anything about handling health insurance issues. She offered to come and look through Viola's papers and hope to sort things out. She did, and Viola ended up not having to pay as much as she had feared.

A lovely story involved Jasper Johns, the famous painter who had been a dear friend of Viola's since the late 1950s. He came to visit Viola, and I made tea for them while they sat and talked. When it was time for him to leave, he handed Viola a package, which he had been holding, and told her to open it after he had left. When he was gone, Viola opened it to find that Jasper had given her a book with a title that she did not like.

"Why on earth would Jasper give me this book?" Viola asked, as she began to open it. "Oh! My God!"

The book turned out to be hollow on the inside. It was a fake book for storing things that one might want to hide from plain view, and it came with a note which read:

"Here's a little something in case you need it. Love, Jasper."

Inside the book was a legal size envelope containing a large sum of cash? Viola used the money from Jasper to pay her friends for groceries, and for taxi cab rides to and from the doctor. His very generous gift had taken the edge off Viola's money worries.

Viola's friends among the Sarah Lawrence College faculty, together with her Baba friends, rallied around Viola during this time. Among those friends were Karen Levey, Annie-Claude Dobbs, Pauline Watts, Emmy Devine, Mary LaChapelle, John Yannelli, Jennifer Michaels, and Jasper Johns. Merce Cunningham was very good about calling Viola as well. One Baba friend, Virginia (Ginny) Sadowsky, had a lovely home in Armonk, New York, not too far from Bronxville. When Viola was strong enough, she often went to Ginny's for a long weekend, and sat outside in the sun. Here she could rest completely, read, or simply sit by herself without worrying about telephone calls from the college, or about people having to climb the three flights of stairs to her apartment to bring her food.

Jasper Johns also had his staff bring Viola whatever she needed. They delivered food, a radio, books, and other items that Viola needed and was unable to get on her own. His generosity was overwhelming.

The Sarah Lawrence faculty took over Viola's classes and ran the department while she was ill, and they still found the time to stop by and visit her. Karen Levey, especially, did a great deal for Viola, bringing her food, teaching extra classes, going to student rehearsals, or simply being there for Viola to share her fears. Viola often mentioned of how much Karen had helped her get through her illness.

With her usual style, Viola recovered rapidly from the surgery and the chemotherapy, and her incision was almost invisible within months.

Her doctors had wanted her to have a third session of chemotherapy, but she refused. Instead she chose to seek alternative medicine from a homeopathic doctor in Spring Valley, New York, who gave her a mistletoe extract to be injected. Viola gave herself these injections on a regular basis for several years, and her cancer never returned. Her love of coffee and her hair, however, did return. When her hair grew back, it was a darker blond than before, with three round patches of gray in the front. She kept the short haircut, and I teased her that the color reminded me of a calico cat.

To everyone's amazement, Viola traveled to France in 1992 to collaborate on a new dance with the now famous French choreographer Mathilde Monnier, a former member of Viola's company, and with Anne Koren, who continued to live in Paris after the company closed down.

Another person who performed in the dance was former company member Joël Leucht, who was living in France and dancing with Mathilde's company. The dance that resulted from this collaboration was titled *Ainsi de Suite*. The dance was full of humor as well as seriousness. There was a very strong solo by Viola that was inspired by her struggle with cancer. One section of the dance involved the three women wearing black dresses and sporting blond wigs, while Joël danced madly around them. *Ainsi de Suite* was a delightful dance which premiered in Lyon, France, in 1992.

Viola did not choreograph anything else for at least two years. Instead, she focused her energies on the students at Sarah Lawrence. When I asked her once why she had never choreographed a work for her students there, she took her usual long pause and then said, "Because I want them to make dances that come from inside themselves, and not from me." Then, after another long pause and a deep, deep sigh. "Besides, I am simply too busy all the time here." It was obvious that she missed choreographing, but that she was too busy running the department.

The next time I saw Viola, which was some time in the winter of 1993, she was again walking with the aid of a cane. She had been suffering with arthritis in her left hip for several years, and the pain had become unbearable. She told me then that she was seriously considering hip replacement surgery, but the thought of going "under the knife" again frightened her.

Viola was now up for tenure at Sarah Lawrence College, and, as in most colleges and universities, she needed letters of support from colleagues. She had to write a letter to her review committee stating why she thought that she deserved to be awarded tenure. The process tenure review is time-consuming and arduous, exactly the kind of thing that Viola found boring and unnecessary. She thought that a person's actions and accomplishments should be proof enough, if indeed anyone in the administration was paying attention. Her letters and telephone conversations were full of resentments at having to go through this process, but she did it anyway.

Viola asked Karen Levey to write a letter of support for her. Karen's letter is long, but so beautifully written that I asked her permission to include the entire document. It demonstrates what Viola brought to the dance department and how she reached out to the community as well.

February 22, 1994

To the Advisory Committee:

Viola Farber has earned my admiration and deepest respect over the many years that I have known her. There are a variety of reasons for this, among them: her ability as a great teacher, her creativity and willingness to take risks, her intelligence and vision, her sense of loyalty to the work, to dance and to art. In the history of dance, Viola Farber has made an extraordinary mark. Her place is eternal.

In London, Viola was described as "one of the great teachers of modern dance" and as "one of America's most intriguing choreographers." Her record speaks for itself - honors and awards, directing accomplishments, teaching experiences, choreographic projects including repertory and special events, television and film. Viola's expertise as a judge, panelist, teacher, director, choreographer and critic has been sought after worldwide.

For any artist who has had the experience Viola has had of being a soloist with the Merce Cunningham Dance Company, a recipient of the Gold Medal for Creativity and Expression in Paris, France, the founder and director of her own dance company and a master teacher for professional dancers throughout the world - to choose to accept the responsibility at Sarah Lawrence College of directing its Dance Department - creates a rare opportunity for remarkable events to occur. It is truly a meeting of the minds and a challenge for those willing to pursue the goals.

Viola's artistic leadership is profound and the results of the changes she has made in the Dance Department since she became director are significant. More and more of the students excel to an advanced level of achievement. The high standards set by Viola prove necessary in order that the students are prepared for the possibility of work as dancers when they graduate. The demands set forth and the lessons learned result in commitment to hard work, self confidence, maturity, willingness to accept greater responsibility, productivity and stronger, more beautiful dancing -- attributes truly within the Sarah Lawrence tradition. There now existed a clear direction and a strong momentum towards excellence due to Viola's vision and deep understanding of the process necessary for training dancers. Viola insists on a code of behavior that demonstrates respect and common courtesy towards the teachers, the musicians and other students - as practiced generally in the dance world. This helps create order and form so that everyone can get on with the work of dancing.

Her concern has also focused on including as many guests as possible to complement our faculty in order that our students benefit from a variety of techniques, disciplines and points of view. These experiences not only provide diversity but are wonderful and exciting opportunities for our dancers to feel connected to current events in the dance world. Many of our recent graduates are now performing in companies or shows, choreographing and producing their own work and/or teaching dance. The interest shown and effort made - especially recently - by Viola to explore possibilities for the enrichment of the dance program through the hiring of guest teachers, involvement in outreach programs, variety in curriculum and choice of faculty - have helped to build a strong sense of community that extends into the professional arena.

Despite a life threatening illness, Viola has met the challenge set before her - to structure a program that will result in training people how to dance as well as they can and prepare them, as best can be, to seek employment as dancers. I am aware that some students are intimidated by the rigorous demands, the strict approach and the quality of work required. I think Viola has struggled with finding a way to honor her set of standards and at the same time teach students who have not made a full commitment to the dancing at this time. The rapport improves as the students appreciate the value of Viola's teachings. Viola has been more and more accessible to the students. Besides spending countless hours at rehearsals, her office is most often full of students waiting for advice, support or a friendly chat. As a director and as a colleague, Viola is hard working, supportive and clear about teaching methodology. Viola's commitment to the department is enormous. She has set the stage for growth and creativity for both the faculty and the student body. I never stop learning from Viola Farber.

Sarah Lawrence College can only gain by having as a faculty member, such a world renowned artist, a master in her field, a brilliant teacher, a woman with a vision and strong points of view. A contemporary artist in the truest sense, Viola Farber has shown courage by using her wisdom to reshape a program to successfully teach students skills and give them the tools necessary to learn how to dance and how to make dances - thus preparing them - if they so choose - for a career in the arts.

The Dance Department is continuously moving towards excellence under Viola's guidance - a process that is never ending and always challenging. I firmly support that Viola Farber be granted tenure.

Sincerely and most respectfully,
Karen Levey
Guest Faculty, Dance

The list of guest faculty and artists that Viola hired during her tenure as director of the dance department included David Capps, Jay Hoggard, Deborah Jowitt, Harry Pickens, Marcia Siegel, June Ekman, Dianne McIntyre, Susan Marshall, David Thomson, Jelon Vieira, David Zambrano, Elliot Capland, Yoshiko Chuma (School of Hard Knocks), Steffan Clemente, Ernesta Corvino, Charlie Moulton, Eiko Otake, Steven Petronio, Elizabeth Streb, Charles Honi Coles, Lucinda Childs, Beverly Emmons, Sun Ock Lee, David Dorfman, Barbara Grubel, Eiko & Koma, Joanne Robinson Hill and Andrew Hill, Ellen Cornfield, Thomas Baird, Lance Westergard, Douglas Nielsen, and Doug Elkins. The full-time dance faculty included Emmy Devine and Rose Anne Thom, and some of the regular part-time faculty included June Ekman, Willi Feuer, Karen Levey, Marie Adair, and Max Luna. The lighting designer who worked with the dance students was Penelope Dannenberg, and the musician/composer was John Yannelli of the Sarah Lawrence Music Department.

Viola wrote to the Advisory Committee why she thought that they should award her tenure. Even though she felt that the entire process was unnecessary, Viola wrote quite eloquently.

February 14, 1994

To the Advisory Committee:

It is possible for anyone who likes to see what the components of the dance curriculum are, and what is required for a 1/3 dance program by looking in the college catalogue. The structure has remained much the same throughout my time as director of the dance program. The details, however, always change. These changes occur through variations in conditions within the college, through shifts in dance faculty, and because of the continuing work of the faculty within and outside the college, which inevitably brings with it changes in emphasis, focus, and methodology. The courses change according to the perceived abilities, needs, and potential of our students. The courses I teach are: Advanced Modern Technique, Advanced and Intermediate (Modern) Technique, Advanced Composition, and Choreography.

The world, as we all know, is changing rapidly, and although I don't always feel obligated to change with it, even if I could, I feel an obligation to be aware of what is happening in my field. I make an effort to see a variety of dance concerts in the city, and to attend professional rehearsals in order to be aware of current technical demands on dancers, and contemporary concerns in choreography and sound for/with dance, not to copy anything, but to be realistic about preparing students for possible work in dance.

I worked in New York during a time of wonderfully fresh beginnings, of hard work and a strong dedication to that work, for a sense of community among artists, even of wonderful parties. But I do not welcome nostalgia in large doses.

Our students have, I think, come to accept the necessity for consistent and focused work, and may even be getting some pleasure for it, and I was delighted with our December concerts - the lack of heavy, earnest expressions of "the modern dance," the abundance of fantasy, mystery, humor, light, good dancing, as well as, in one case, an intelligent roughness combined with unusual form, breadth, and invention. The strong participation of John Yannelli (musician and composer) and students from the Music Department contributed to a lively situation. This could only have happened in the atmosphere created by the entire dance faculty, the members of which function both independently and in support of each other.

I'm interested in continuing to open the Dance Department to the outside world and the college community. Dance students from Rose Anne Thom's Teaching Conference are presently working at P.S. 30 in Yonkers, in the kindergarten class, and are enthusiastically received by teachers and students. The Composition class plans also to work in Yonkers public schools, our students presenting some of their own work and adapting their own class assignments to the needs of children.

The Theater Department, Multicultural Affairs, and Physical Education Department have joined with the Dance Department in sponsoring 12 sessions of tap dance classes taught by Jim Tate, an alumnus of Sarah Lawrence. We have invited guest artists from a variety of cultures and movement disciplines to work with the dancers. These master classes have often been open to the entire college community. Most recently, our guest was the Brazilian artist, Jelon Vieira, who spoke about the genesis and development of capoeira as a martial art and dance form in Brazil, and taught, with an assistant, a class in this discipline.

I look forward to increasing interaction among the Dance, Theater, and Music Departments. I hope to do some work in connection with Shirley Kaplan's "Floating Cathedral." I welcome the imminent possibility of working with Harambe and other student groups to make available to the college a greater exposure to diverse movement forms.

I hope this is useful to you in assessing the work I do.

Sincerely,

Viola Farber

While going through the tenure review process, Viola was also dealing with a far more serious issue. Her long time and very close friend for over forty years, Susan Rossin, was diagnosed with cancer. The cancer had spread throughout most of Susan's body before it was discovered, and had reached her brain. This was a devastating blow to Viola, as the same doctor that had helped her with the alternative medicines for cancer had been Susan's doctor for many, many years. Viola was angry that he had not spotted Susan's cancer much sooner, and that now her dearest friend was going to die.

Viola made numerous trips to Spring Valley, NY, to see Susan, and until the disease took away Susan's ability to speak, they had many long and wonderful talks. Susan asked Viola to watch after her son, Mark, who now lived and worked at the Steiner community. Mark was then in his forties, but still had the IQ of a twelve-year-old. Viola promised Susan that she would call and visit Mark; a promise that she kept. Susan died on April 30, 1994.

Unfortunately, the pain in Viola's left hip was getting worse, and she was finding it difficult not only to teach, but simply to walk. She and I talked a lot during that time, and I encouraged her to go ahead with the hip replacement surgery. She agreed, and in the spring of 1994 she again entered the hospital. When Viola was shown to her room, she noticed that it was a private room. She told the nurse that there must be some mistake, that she was certain that her health insurance would not cover a private room. The nurse went and checked. When she returned, the nurse told Viola that the room had already been paid for in full.

"How can that be?" Viola asked. "Who paid it?"

"A Mr. Johns," the nurse replied, and left.

Jasper had come to Viola's rescue again. He simply could not stand the thought of Viola in a semi-private room, sharing it with someone whom she might not like, or worse, someone who was extremely ill. Viola remembered telling Jasper that she was going into the hospital, but she knew nothing of what he had planned. Viola was, of course, overwhelmed and grateful for Jasper's repeated show of generosity.

The next time I saw her, Viola was walking normally and teaching dance classes as if nothing had happened. Her doctor had said to her that the hip replacement was to relieve the pain, <u>not</u> to make it possible for her to dance again. Viola simply smiled at him and replied, "What's the use of having a new hip put in if I can't dance?" She could no longer jump or run, but did everything else. Once again, she went full steam ahead, worked twelve hours days, and taught more classes than anyone else in the department.

In 1995, Viola received a request that she simply could not refuse. Ralph Lemon, a dancer whom she had known since he had studied with her at a residency in Minneapolis years before, asked her to work with him. At first, Viola thought that the offer was for her to choreograph a new dance for his company. She adored Ralph and said that she would be honored to work with him. His company was receiving excellent reviews, and Viola had asked him to teach part-time at Sarah Lawrence. When she found out that Lemon wanted her to collaborate with him on a new duet and for her to perform with him during his company's New York season at the Joyce Theatre, Viola was both thrilled and concerned. Her concern was that she was now sixty-four years old, and aside from the physical limitations that now confronted her, she worried that it might appear that Lemon was dancing with his grandmother. Viola had long been an admirer of Lemon's work, and never gave much thought to age differences in general, but she knew that this would definitely present a new challenge for her.

The two friends, mentor and student, began work in August of 1995. At first they sat talking to one another, and exchanging ideas. In a New York Times article by Jennifer Dunning, dated October 3, 1995, Viola is quoted as saying, "To work in preparation for something is frightening, but also just wonderful. It's like waking up to something again, but in a different way. In the same article Dunning describes watching a rehearsal of Viola and Lemon. "Mr. Lemon began flinging himself into a whirlwind solo of leaps and turns. When he finished, Viola called out teasingly, 'Enjoy it while you can!'" Then she began to roar with laughter."

By the end of their rehearsal period, they had choreographed a duet that drew standing ovations for Viola and rave reviews in the New York

Times and the Village Voice. The Lemon company performances ran for one week at the Joyce Theater, but Viola performed the duet on only three nights. The dance was titled *Threestep (Shipwreck)*. Ralph Lemon wore a bright red unitard and Viola was costumed in a beautiful, long gray shift dress over gray tights and leotard. The duet also included the cellist Michael Mermagen as a third performer. The dance had no message or storyline, but, as Anna Kisselgoff wrote in her review (New York Times, October 5, 1995) of *Threestep (Shipwreck)*, the two "offer a dialogue of contrasting personalities and styles." She said of Viola, "She looks ascetic, with her close-cropped hair and a long gray robe, but she cannot suppress the wit that erupts from the clarity and suddenness of her movement." Ms. Kisselgoff went on to say that "Ms. Farber's star presence, which recalls that of Mr. Cunningham, is obvious from the start, even when her back is to the audience." And my favorite line, ".......Ms. Farber becomes more of a benevolent white witch; elbows up, she lopes around the stage and casts her spell on both Mr. Lemon and the audience."

Dance critic Tobi Tobias wrote the following in her review.

> *Threestep (Shipwreck)*, originated in a specific biographical relationship - that of its two performers and co-chorographers, Lemon (black, male, in his physical prime of 43) and his onetime teacher Viola Farber (white, female, at 64 the gallant if physically compromised survivor of lung cancer and hip-replacement surgery). Despite some images suggesting a tender and mysterious emotional rapport, *Threestep* functions as an occasion for Farber to wipe the stage with Lemon, she's so distinctive and compelling. As a star with Merce Cunningham, she was a cool, technically remarkable presence; here,

making the most of her limitations, discarding self-consciousness as if it were beneath her contempt, she's like one of those astute, ancient witch-women invented by Isaak Dinesen. Her movement -wild in the extremities, erratic in its rhythms, its shaky center concealed under a swirling gray abbess's gown - - looked like a force of nature let loose to astound anyone still clinging to conventional decorum.

Douglas Nielsen said to me after seeing the duet in New York, "Jeff, Ralph was wearing bright red and Viola gray, but I could only see Viola!" This had nothing to do with Ralph Lemon's abilities as a dancer or as a performer, but demonstrates the power of Viola's performing presence. There were few dancers who could compete with her. Even Merce Cunningham knew not to put himself next to Viola for very long.

In 1996, at age sixty-five, Viola flew to Setubal, Portugal, and choreographed a large group work for a company called CE DE CE. She sent me many letters while she was there, telling me how much fun she was having, and how beautiful the dancers were. She gave the company daily classes and choreographed a large work called *Dreams of Wind and Dust*, a beautiful title. Viola was still "weaving her magic" throughout the world.

The last time that Viola and I performed together was in June of 1996 at the American Dance Festive in Durham, NC. Viola had just finished a semester sabbatical leave from Sarah Lawrence, and she appeared more rested than I had seen her in years, even though she had traveled and taught a great deal during her semester away from her position as chairperson. Her teaching jobs had taken her back to the CNDC in Angers, France, and to the London Contemporary Dance

Company in England, as well as to teaching independently in New York.

We had been hired by Charles and Stephanie Reinhart to teach. Viola agreed to teach only the first three weeks and I the full six weeks. We shared a rented condo and soon were back to holding hands while strolling across the campus of Duke University between classes. We began working immediately on a new duet, which we titled *It's Been A While*, since it had been more than ten years since we had last danced together in England during the making of the dance for television, *January*. We each had to teach three classes a day, Monday through Friday. At five o'clock each evening, we met in The Ark, a beautiful old church that had been turned into a very lovely dance studio, and rehearsed for one and a half to two hours.

If you have ever been to Durham during the summer, you know how hot and humid it gets there. Viola had survived the removal of one lung and had an artificial hip, and yet it was still difficult to keep up with her. There were times when the heat got to her; her face flushed with heat, but she simply sat for a few minutes and then said, "O.K, let's go." It was a wonderful and awe-inspiring three weeks, working with Viola. I had known her for thirty years, and I never became tired of being around her, dancing with her, or simply sitting and listening to her tell stories of her latest adventures.

Natalie Gilbert and Beverly Botsford were two composers and musicians who played for some of our dance classes at the festival. Natalie played the piano and Beverly percussion. We asked them whether they would write a score for our duet and perform it live. They watched the duet and agreed to work with us. They later decided that they did not have the time to write a score, but wanted to improvise the music as we performed. Viola and I loved the idea and agreed.

We had hoped to perform the duet on one of the smaller stages that of the Reynolds Auditorium, which the festival used at Duke University, but Charles Reinhart refused. Instead, we had to settle for The Ark. Usually more than three hundred students attend the American Dance Festival each summer, with more than twenty faculty members. There also is a large staff who work in the festival offices. The Ark is big, but not big enough to accommodate all of these people. On the afternoon of the performance, Viola and I watched as the audience grew larger and larger, as suddenly, the space that we had been using during rehearsal was growing smaller. We looked at each other, smiled, and nodded to the musicians to begin.

In rehearsals, Viola had been able to do everything she wanted to do, but her usual full strength had been absent. During the performance of *It's Been A While*, however, I felt that we had slipped back to a time to when we were much younger. Whatever that thing is that happens to performers took over, and we were sailing. There were runs, jumps, small leaps, lifts, and funny moments in the duet, and Viola was doing it all as if she were in her forties, not her sixties. When the duet finished, the audience went wild and gave Viola a standing ovation. They cheered, clapped, and stomped their feet and did not let her leave the performance space for a very long time. They all knew about the trials that she had endured with her illnesses, and they were acknowledging her fortitude and personal triumphs as well as her amazing talent.

When the applause finally stopped, Charles and Stephanie Reinhart came up to congratulate Viola and me. Stephanie commented that the duet should have been performed on the Reynolds Auditorium stage because there were so many students who could not fit into the Ark and who had missed the performance. I had no idea what Viola was going to say to Stephanie, because we had originally asked to use the big stage and Charles Reinhart had refused. I expected Viola to explode into one of her rages, but instead she stared hard into Charles' eyes and said, "Thank you, Stephanie. I quite agree!" She then turned around, took my arm, and we strolled out of the Ark.

Douglas Rosenberg, the videographer for ADF, had arranged for a scholarship student to videotape the performance of *It's Been A While*. When Viola and I went to get a copy of the tape, we learned that the camera had broken, and that Mr. Rosenberg was not at the performance to help. Viola was furious that not only had we not been allowed to perform the duet onstage, but now there would be no record of it. Fortunately for us, however, an ADF student who was in Viola's choreography class had brought her own camcorder and videotaped the performance, so that there is a record of the duet in Viola's archives.

Viola left Durham feeling very much elated and loved, but it turned out to be the last time that Viola choreographed a new dance. She did act as one of the adjudicators for the Northeast Region of the American College Dance Festival in 1997. A colleague of mine, Jim Sutton, called me and told me that he was going to be the ballet person on the adjudication panel at this festival. I told him to call Viola and see whether they could travel together, as I thought that the two of them would enjoy each other's humor. They did travel together, and when the festival was over, both of them called me and thanked me for suggesting this. Both expressed how much they had enjoyed meeting each other, and that they had laughed all the way there and back during the trip.

In 1997, Viola also traveled to Roanoke, Virginia, where she was honored as one of the women on Hollins College's Landscape of Modern Dance Series. The series honored women in the field of modern dance who showed outstanding achievement in their field, both as teachers and as choreographers. Donnafaye Burchfield, the chairperson of the Hollins College Dance Department, produced a wonderful video in which Viola was interviewed and which included excerpts of Viola's performing career and her choreography.

I traveled to Bronxville to see Viola once during 1997, and we drove to visit her godson, Mark, at the Steiner community. Viola looked radiant and seemed to be very happy. She was working too many hours at Sarah Lawrence, but she had always worked too hard. She loved to complain about the hard work, but I knew by this time that it was what she enjoyed most in her life. She simply did not know what else to do but to work, and as she loved dancing so much, she worked hard at that.

Viola taught all day at the college and then spent several hours in the early evening watching students rehearse their dances. No one made her do this, and she even complained to me about having to be there because no one else would do it. I have my doubts whether Viola ever asked anyone else on the faculty to stay, but perhaps she did. I do know from the way that she talked about the rehearsals that she enjoyed them. If that had not been the case, she would not have talked about it so much. Viola never discussed, at great length, things that bored her, but would simply dismiss such subjects.

In Donnafaye Burchfield's video on Viola, there is a wonderful moment when Viola is sitting by the mirrors in one of the Sarah Lawrence dance studios observing a student rehearsal. The student had just shown her dance to Viola and John Yannelli, and was seated on the floor in front of them waiting to get Viola's critique. Here Viola demonstrates again her ability to "cut to the chase" with her remarks, giving both a supporting statement and stating what was wrong with the dance in the fewest words possible.

"You have made a beautiful dance. And, that is very nice!" (There is a long, pregnant pause here before Viola speaks again.) "But, if they don't dance it well, (another lengthy pause) it isn't a pleasant experience."

As in her technique classes, Viola did not consider it right to spoon-feed her students in order to teach them choreography. She wanted them to think for themselves, and to come up with their own ideas. She wanted them to make dances not in order to please her, but to choreograph dances that came from within themselves, and perhaps to choreograph dances that were original and fresh, not simply dances that were carbon copies of hers or of any other artist.

Viola believed that there were really no rules to making a dance. It either worked or it did not. She believed, of course, that there was a craft to making dances. She believed in teaching young dancers some of the ways in which they could come up with movements, and how to put those movements into a framework that would later aid them in their choreography. She hoped, however, that by not insisting that they follow a set of rules laid down by her, they might one day come up with some truly wonderful new ideas of their own and choreograph an entirely different and creative dance.

One only has to look to Merce Cunningham as one who broke all the rules in the late 1940s and early 1950s that were considered the "right" way to make dances. Cunningham, of course, went on to become one of the leading choreographers of his time, and he continues on into the twenty-first century to test the limits of his own choreography. Viola was part of that ground-breaking era, and she hoped to pass her experience of that time on to her students at Sarah Lawrence College.

Company rehearsing Attente *at the
Centre National de Danse Contemporaine d'Angers, 1981.*

Photographer: Pierre Petitjean

Viola Scheffler, Viola's Godmother, 1988.

*Viola (center) with her two sisters Irene Aiken and Elisabeth
Lanzl, Cannon Beach, OR. 1988.   Family photograph.*

*Viola (center) with her two sisters Irene Aiken and Elisabeth Lanzl
clowning around at Cannon Beach, OR., 1988; family photograph.*

Viola Farber, shortly after her battle with cancer, with Mathilde Monnier in Montpellier, France, 1992. Photographer: Brian Ashley

Viola Farber at Sarah Lawrence College,
Bronxville, NY, 1995, Photographer: Brian Ashley

Viola Farber, Ralph Lemon in Threestep (Shipwreck) at the Joyce Theatre in New York, 1995, Photographer: Sara Krulwich

Chapter Seven

Our Lady of the Leaves

"I have seen January winter afternoon for more than 60 years now. A kind of beckoning twilight, the delicate skeletons of trees. It's an invitation to something that you only think is happening sometimes when you're younger. Well, it's all there, and I'm here in it and I'm not a bare tree with no questions. When I feel the way I'm feeling now, it seems that my body would not make a dent on the softest surface, that I am no obstacle to anything wanting to go squarely through me and out the other side."

Viola Farber Slayton
From her journals (circa 1996)

EARLY IN 1998, AT AGE sixty-seven, Viola began to experience temporary dizziness and numbness on the left side of her body. These "events," as she called them, only lasted for a few minutes, but they greatly concerned her nonetheless. She visited her doctor in Bronxville,

Dr. Anne Galloway, who performed a series of tests, but found nothing wrong. By all appearances, Viola was healthy. Trying to put this out of her mind, she agreed to perform in the very first *From The Horse's Mouth* performance at the Dance Theatre Workshop (DTW) in April, 1998 in New York. *From The Horse's Mouth* was conceived and directed by choreographers James Cunningham and Tina Croll.

From The Horse's Mouth was designed to showcase well known veteran dancers who had a lot of years of experience behind them. All the performers were asked to wear black costumes, and Viola wore a long, black, shift-like robe over a black shirt and trousers.

The performers also included such dance notables as Pat Catterson, Yoshiko Chuma, Terry Creach, Tina Croll, James Cunningham, Carmen De Lavallade, Stuart Hodes, Elizabeth Keen, Sharon Kinney, Stephan Koplowitz, James Martin, Wendy Perron, Kathryn Posin, and Cathryn Williams. *From The Horse's Mouth* would be repeated several years in New York, San Francisco, and Los Angeles, featuring famous and primarily mature dancers from each of these cities. Linda Tarney, who performed in later versions of the dance, said, "Dancing in *From The Horse's Mouth* was like dying and going to dancer's heaven."

Sharon Kinney videotaped the series and included interviews with each of the performers. It is a wonderful documentary for which Sharon Kinney later won an award. On it is wonderful footage of Viola performing a solo comprised primarily of torso and arm movements. A little further in the tape, she is seen cavorting with Carmen De Lavallade and James Cunningham.

Viola managed to get through the performances without being dizzy or experiencing any numbness. She told me, however, that once on the train ride from Bronxville to New York, that she almost fell trying to walk to her seat, and that the "event" lasted for more than fifteen minutes. Because it passed, and because all the tests had come back negative, she brushed this off as pre-performance nerves.

During the early summer, the "events" began to happen more and more frequently. Viola went back to Dr. Galloway, who sent her to a specialist in New York. An MRI of her head showed nothing, but a CAT scan showed that Viola had a very small hole in her heart. The doctors prescribed Warfarin, which is a blood thinner, and the "events" stopped for a while.

Viola's nephew, Eric Lanzl, was scheduled to get married to Edith, a Norwegian woman, in October of 1998, and because she was feeling better, she decided to fly to Norway to attend the wedding. Eric is the son of Viola's eldest sister, Elisabeth, who lives in Chicago. When I talked to them all later, I was told that the wedding had been beautiful, and that Viola had had a wonderful time. She even stayed up to enjoy the wedding reception, which went on into the early hours of the morning. Viola herself told me that, although she had not looked forward to the long plane ride, she had really enjoyed the wedding, meeting all of the bride's family and seeing part of Norway. She returned to Bronxville seemingly recharged for the beginning of school.

Viola also attended the wedding of a former company member, Larry Clark, and his wife Piper on Block Island, Rhode Island. Everyone commented later how beautiful and healthy Viola looked. On the day following that wedding, Pam Tanowitz, a former graduate of and one of Viola's favorite students at Sarah Lawrence College, was getting married in Brooklyn, NY., and so Viola chartered a small airplane and flew to attend that wedding as well.

Karen Levey said later, "I will always remember Viola climbing up into that tiny two-person, one-engine plane that had a woman pilot, and flying off in order to make Pam's wedding. Andé Peck and I stood at the little airport and waved her off in disbelief and absolute amazement at her energy, her loyalty, and her courage. Knowing for sure what a true jet setter she was!"

In the fall, Viola had gone back to her regular working schedule, which began around 7:30 am and ended late in the evening. At age sixty-seven, she was not only handling all the administrative work that comes with being the chairperson of a dance department, but she continued to teach modern dance classes and choreography classes, and to attend many rehearsals of student works. When I talked to her about retiring, Viola laughed and told me that she could not afford to retire, and that she would most likely be teaching well into her eighties.

Then in early November, the dizziness and numbness returned. Viola had always had a quick temper, but now she was getting angry more easily and more often. Her colleagues said that she could fly into a rage at the slightest provocation, only to return moments later to apologize. In the past, Viola had rarely apologized for anything she did, but now she was doing so all the time. She told me that she was always angry and screaming at people, but that she did not know why. People who had known and worked with Viola over the years said that they were concerned about her; but that they thought her behavior was due to overwork.

Many of Viola's friends tried to convince her to retire from the college and go back to taking on short teaching residencies or choreography jobs. Viola refused. She said that she was sick of traveling and would rather stay in one place. Over the years, she had survived benign tumors, cancer, pneumonia, a hip replacement, and endless flues and colds. It seemed that her bad habits of not eating right, rarely getting enough sleep, and always being at her office long before anyone else in the dance department arrived were finally catching up with her.

Viola could have afforded to retire, but the truth was that she did not want to retire. Viola loved to work, and she got enjoyment out of complaining about it. She loved the students, and she took great pleasure from seeing them grow as dancers and choreographers. She felt young around them, and she had a wealth of knowledge to share with them. The dance department, and its students, took the place of her former company, and she put as much passion and hard work into that department as she had in everything else that she had ever done. With that passion she rebuilt the Sarah Lawrence College Dance Department.

In the meantime, two wonderful things happened to Viola. First, officials in France informed her that she had been awarded one of France's greatest honors by naming her an *Officier de l'Ordre des Arts et Lettres* (Officer of the Order of Arts and Letters). This was a great honor for Viola. This is one of the highest awards given to French artists, and only a handful of Americans have ever received it. The French ambassador told her that the award ceremony was scheduled to be held in Paris in February 1999, and that he would mail an airplane ticket to her. Viola was extremely excited and honored by this award. She called me and sounded alive and thrilled about the trip.

She was also contacted by Martha Myers, the Dean of the American Dance Festival, and told that she was the recipient of the 1999 Balasaraswati/Joy Ann Dewey Beinecke Endowed Chair for Distinguished Teaching Award. Ms. Myers asked Viola whether she would agree to teach for three weeks at the festival in Durham, NC and that the award ceremony would be held on June 13, 1999. Viola did not relish returning to teach at the ADF, but she agreed.

When Viola called me, she joked that neither of these awards came with any money, but I could tell that she was very excited, touched, and honored by both. She was beginning to think, too, that perhaps her career was not over simply because she was sixty-seven years old, and that perhaps she could afford to retire from Sarah Lawrence College after all. Her good friend, Jasper Johns, had offered to subsidize her retirement, and she called me to discuss the matter. I told her that Jasper considered her family, and I encouraged her to give his offer serious thought. Viola said that she would, but that she did not want to be obligated to anyone. I assured her that Jasper would not attach any strings to his offer. I knew when I hung up the telephone that Viola had already made up her mind not to accept the offer.

On the day before Thanksgiving, Viola took a train into Manhattan to attend a performance of the Jazz Tap Ensemble at the Joyce Theatre. She was good friends with the Artistic Director, Lynn Dally, and had followed Lynn's work for many years. Viola thought that the Jazz Tap Ensemble provided a perfect mixture of art and entertainment, and although she was not a huge fan of tap dancing, she thought that Lynn's choreography was a beautiful blend of tap and modern dance. Lynn Dally not only had studied modern dance, but had an MFA degree in dance from Ohio State University, and had had her own modern dance company, Lynn Dally and Dancers, for many years before going back to tap dancing.

Viola knew that she would have to dash to Grand Central Station immediately after the performance of the Ensemble. She wanted to deliver flowers to Lynn and to wish her good luck for the performance, so she found a way to get backstage. The two spoke only briefly, but Lynn remarked that how well Viola looked and how touched she was that Viola had come to the performance.

During intermission, Viola ran into one of her former Bennington students, Joanne Robinson Hill, who was now on the staff of the Joyce Theatre. The two chatted, and during the course of their conversation Joanne asked Viola how she was spending Thanksgiving. Viola told her that she was spending it right there in the theater. Joanne knew that the theater had not scheduled any event in the theater and tried to tell

Viola this, but Viola insisted that she was attending a "gathering" in the Joyce Theatre on Thanksgiving Day. Joanne decided to drop the subject, but said later that this really caused her great alarm and great concern about Viola's mental state.

After the Jazz Tap Ensemble performance, Viola went back to Bronxville and went to bed. The following morning, Thanksgiving Day, she awoke with one of the worst headaches she had ever had. She had always suffered from migraines, but this was different. She was invited to three different Thanksgiving parties, but did not know whether she was going to be able to attend any of them. She had had such a good time the night before and could not understand why she was feeling so ill.

I called her to wish her a happy Thanksgiving. I was in bed with a serious back injury, but wanted to ask how she was doing. When she answered the telephone, I knew immediately that she was not feeling well. Our conversation went like this:

"Are you ok, Dos?" I asked.

"No," she answered. "I have a terrible headache."

"A migraine?"

"No, worse!" she said

"Is there anything I can do for you?" I asked, getting concerned because of her recent history of dizziness.

"No," Viola said at first, and then with a laugh she added, "Well, you could come over and walk my dog."

I laughed, but was somewhat confused as Viola did not own, nor had she ever owned, a dog. I told her to feel better and that I would call her back the next day to find out whether she was feeling better.

Viola did not attend any of the parties that day, but spent much of the day in bed. I tried to reach the few people in Bronxville for whom I had phone numbers to ask whether anyone could go and check on Viola, but since it was a holiday, no one was home. I felt helpless and hoped that, if she was really ill enough, Viola herself would call someone.

Around one o'clock the next morning, Viola was seen sitting outside her apartment building on the back patio stairs. The person who saw her was concerned because of the late hour and asked her whether she was all right. Viola said that she was, and the person assumed that she was perhaps doing her laundry, because the laundry room was located on that floor, just inside the back entrance to the building.

I learned much later about the events that followed. Around eight a.m. the day after Thanksgiving, November 28, 1998, Mary Gibney was on her way to work. Mary lived in the apartment building directly behind Viola's. As she drove out of her building's garage, she first noticed what a beautiful, warm and sunny day it was, and thought that it was very warm for a late November morning. Perhaps it was Indian summer. Then Mary noticed an older woman popping up from a pile of leaves on the grounds in front of her. She recognized the woman as someone with whom she had spoken to several times, but did not know the woman's name. She had spoken to the woman while she was walking her dogs, but they had never exchanged names, and Mary did not even know in which apartment building the woman lived.

Mary stopped her car and ran over to see whether she could help the woman get up from the ground. When she got there, the woman was smiling and rolling around in the pile of leaves, but Mary sensed that something was wrong. When she asked the woman whether she was ok, the woman responded, "Yes, I'm fine," but Mary was dubious and suggested that she should try to stand up.

"Yes, perhaps I should get up," the woman answered, but she was unable to stand on her own. Mary knew a policeman who lived in one of the nearby apartment buildings. She propped the woman up against a tree and ran over to find out whether he was at home. The policeman answered his telephone and told Mary that he would call an ambulance, and that he would come right down to see if he could help.

When the off duty policeman arrived, he asked the woman whether she knew what her name was.

"Viola," she answered.

"Well, Viola," he went on. "What year is this?"

"Why, 63, of course!" Viola answered, looking at the policeman as if he had lost his mind. Mary did not know whether Viola meant that it was 1963 or that she was 63 years old. In any case, of course neither answer was correct. The ambulance soon arrived, and Viola was taken to Lawrence Hospital in Bronxville. One of the nurses in the emergency room recognized Viola from the time when she was a cancer patient there several years before, and she called Dr. Anne Galloway.

Nothing is known about what Viola did between one a.m. and when Mary Gibney found her at 8 a.m., but it was quickly determined that Viola had suffered a cerebral hemorrhage and that she needed surgery immediately to remove the blood clot and relieve the pressure on the brain. Dr. Galloway contacted Sarah Lawrence College, and before long several of Viola's colleagues arrived at the hospital's waiting room.

I received a telephone call from Donald Mahler. I was happy to hear from him, but also surprised that he had called me, because I had not heard from him in years. Then I heard in his voice that something was wrong. He told me what had happened to Viola and that she was in Lawrence Hospital, but he was not certain of the details and did not know exactly what condition she was in. The only thing that Donald could tell me was that he thought Viola had suffered a stroke.

I hung up the telephone and immediately called Viola's two sisters, Irene and Elisabeth, and let them know what was going on. They said that they would call the hospital and let me know what, if anything, they could find out. Hours passed before the telephone rang again.

Finally, that afternoon, Elisabeth called me from Chicago to let me know that she had found out that Viola had suffered a cerebral hemorrhage, but that she still could not find out any details of her condition. She had been told that Viola was conscious and could recognize people, but that she was not speaking except to say yes or no. The doctors had told Elisabeth that Viola would answer questions appropriately sometimes, but not always. They were not sure at that time how much brain damage the hemorrhage had caused.

The next day Viola was taken to surgery, and a very large blood clot was removed from the left frontal lobe of her brain. She came through that operation fairly well and was conscious and speaking a little. Karen Levey later told me that she would smile, but that she did not open her eyes very much. Physically, Viola could still move and was doing so quite actively. On the following Thursday, the telephone rang and I was told by Karen that Viola had suffered another cerebral hemorrhage in the right frontal lobe, that she was now paralyzed on the entire left side of her body, and that she was unconscious. I called my doctor, ordered him to send me a back brace, and made plane reservations for New York. Back injury or not, I needed to be with Viola.

Before leaving Long Beach, I called Jasper Johns to let him know what was going on. He was very upset, of course, as he and Viola had been close friends since the early 1950s. He told me to call him at his home when my plane landed in New York, and that he would meet me at Viola's apartment in Bronxville. I assured him that I would phone.

I arrived at Newark Airport at 5:30 a.m. the next day and called Jasper's home. He was surprisingly awake and said that he was leaving for Viola's place immediately. I took a taxi and went directly to the home of Mary LaChapelle to pick up a key to Viola's apartment.

Mary, a writing professor at Sarah Lawrence, who lived nearby, had become a good friend of Viola's and often looked after Viola's apartment when she was away. I let myself into Viola's place and began to weep uncontrollably. Her apartment was neat, but very dirty. Her laundry was lying there, separated into white and colored clothing, and a pile of quarters was lying on the hall table. She had obviously been planning to do her laundry that morning before wandering outside and falling into the pile of leaves where Mary Gibney found her.

Jasper arrived, and we had a quick look around the apartment. Before we headed out, he handed me an envelope and asked me to open it later. He said that it was something to help Viola during this time. I put the envelope down on her dining room table, and we left for the hospital, which was located only a few blocks away. I knew it well from the time in 1991 when Viola was there for her chemotherapy in 1991.

We found out from the information desk that Viola was in the Intensive Care Unit. As long as I live, I will never be able to forget my first impression of seeing Viola lying in the hospital bed as we walked into the ICU, nor will I ever forget the expression of sadness in Jasper's eyes when he saw Viola for the first time that day.

Viola lay on her back with her eyes closed, her mouth slightly open. There was a large white bandage around her head, a tube coming out of her head, and IVs were attached to both arms. There were machines everywhere monitoring her vital signs. The expression on her face was one of anguish, not pain. Her entire left arm was swollen to twice its normal size, and her feet, which protruded from the sheets at the foot of the bed, were also quite swollen. An instrument which monitored her temperature was attached to her right index finger, and Viola was waving her right arm around gently in the air, seemingly trying to remove it from her finger. She was in what the nurses called a semi-coma. However, she was obviously aware enough to hate the thing that was stuck to her finger like a clothespin to a clothesline.

Jasper sat down in the chair next to Viola's bed, and I went and took her right hand.

"Hi, Dos." I whispered.

She did not respond, nor did she open her eyes, but her hand grasped mine with a grip of such strength that I knew immediately that she knew I was there. I could not help beginning to cry, but tried not to let her know that I was doing so - - why, I don't know. When I looked at Jasper, I could see the sadness in his heart and thought that it was breaking. We both loved this woman very much. Her life had not been easy, and neither of us felt that she deserved to be in this situation. Had she not suffered enough? Had she not been through enough? "Why this, Baba?" Is all I could think.

A nurse brought me a chair, and I sat holding Viola's hand while talking to her and Jasper. We had been there about half an hour when Viola suddenly opened her eyes, looked directly into mine, and said the only words that I was to hear her say for the next three weeks. Those two words were "Oh, Dimt." I wept. The love that we had for each other had fought its way through Viola's coma and allowed her mind for one brief moment to surface long enough so that she could utter my nickname. She continued to stare at me for a few minutes while I talked to her, kissed her, and told her that I was there to help her get through this. She never said another word, but kept her gaze on me until the pressure on her brain won and she lapsed back into her coma.

As the day went on, several friends and colleagues of Viola's came and went. Karen Levey was there most of the time, as was John Yannelli. When visiting hours were over, I lingered in the ICU until the nurses finally told me that I had to leave and get some rest. I walked to Viola's apartment, and I sat down to make a few calls. As I was about to dial,

I remembered the envelope that Jasper had given me that morning. When I opened it, inside was a very large amount of money in one hundred dollar bills, and a note from Jasper saying simply, "You will need this! Love, Jasper." I was totally astonished. I knew that Jasper had helped out Viola financially when she had her cancer and her hip replacement, but I had not expected this. It was very clear how much Jasper loved Viola. He was right; I used every bit of that money to pay Viola's rent, as well as other bills that arrived while she was in the hospital. I am forever thankful to Jasper. He is not only an incredible artist, but one of the finest human beings I know.

Viola was wearing a pendant around her neck with a picture of Baba, and although she was in a coma, her right hand always found that pendant. She either simply held it, or at times she rubbed it between two fingers. Again, her love of and belief in Baba managed to fight its way from deep inside her subconscious. If the pendant slipped behind her neck and she could not find it, she became very restless, and her face took on an expression of distress. During these times I, or one of her friends, straightened the pendant so that Viola could find it, and she settled down.

Some time during the next three weeks, Viola's sister, Elisabeth, along with her husband, Lawrence, flew in from Chicago for a few days, and Elisabeth had long talks with Viola's doctors and surgeons. The outlook was not good, but no one was willing to give up hope.

When I arrived in Bronxville, the stories of how Viola had ended up in the hospital, the time of day she was found, and other details were unclear to me. I was hearing several versions of the chronology when and where Viola became ill, and I wanted to find out what really occurred. After talking to several hospital staff and faculty members at Sarah Lawrence College, I was able to track down the name of Mary Gibney, the woman who had found Viola in the pile of leaves. I was able to look up her telephone number and decided to call her. She proceeded to tell me in detail how, when, and where she discovered Viola, and then she went on to tell me something that made me weep.

Mary Gibney is a very religious woman who belongs to St. Joseph's Catholic Church in Bronxville. She told me that, after she had found Viola, that she shared her story with other members of her church and with her priest. Prayers were being said and candles had been lit for Viola daily ever since Mary had found her. Mary said that among many of the congregation at St. Joseph's who knew the story, Viola was now known as "Our Lady of the Leaves."

Viola was never alone for very long during these next difficult weeks. Karen Levey, who had known Viola since she had studied with her at Adelphi University in the early 1960s, was there for many hours every day, as was Ginny Sadowsky, another good friend. Emmy Devine, John Yannelli, Annie-Claude Dobbs, and Pauline Watts, all colleagues of Viola's, were also at the hospital every day, and all of these wonderful people helped me through that difficult period, and afterwards. Viola's sister, Irene, also came to see Viola. This was a great sacrifice for her because her husband, Bob, was being treated for prostrate cancer. Although her visit was short, Irene gave me much strength to continue.

Of course, the hospital had strict rules about the number of visitors who were allowed in the ICU at a time. Often, however, the nurses simply looked the other way when we, Viola's friends and family, broke these rules. Like us, the nurses loved Viola and hoped that we could somehow reach and pull her out of her coma. We took turns sitting beside Viola's bed talking to her and hoping desperately that she would hear us, open her eyes, and speak. This loving and inspiring woman had touched every one of us, and none of us wanted to let her go.

After three weeks, Viola was pronounced brain dead. The surgeon came to me and asked whether I wanted to keep Viola on life support or to remove it and let her die. He said that if she was kept on life support, she could possibly live for years in a vegetative state, only being turned over by nurses twice a day. I knew that Viola would not want that to happen, but because I was no longer married to her, I did not feel that I could make that decision on my own. I called Elisabeth in Chicago and asked her what the family wanted. She told me that she would discuss it with her sister Irene and get back to me. It was not long before Elisabeth called back with the decision to take Viola off life support. It was one of the hardest decisions in which I have ever had to participate.

Once off life support, Viola was moved to a semi-private room on the top floor of the hospital. Sarah Lawrence College faculty and students, who had not been allowed into the ICU to visit Viola, were finally permitted to come and say good-bye. The line of visitors was constant for two solid days, extending from her bedside to the elevator, which was a long way away from her room. I, and Viola's family, will forever be indebted to the doctors, nurses, and staff at Lawrence Hospital for their care, for their love, and for the way they allowed the horde of visitors to continue to see Viola during non-visiting hours.

One night, Merce Cunningham walked into Viola's room. I had not expected him to come, but there he was. The look of sadness on his face was heart-breaking. Viola and Merce had a loving friendship that had lasted long after she left his company. Merce's first words were, "That jaw is still there!" I looked and knew exactly what he meant. When Viola was determined to get what she wanted, she would set her jaw firm with her lips clamped tight. Her mouth was open now, but her jaw was still thrust forward in determination. I said hello to Merce and then let him sit with Viola alone for about ten minutes before re-entering the room. When I came back, he was sitting in the chair looking lovingly at Viola's face. That is an image forever imprinted in my mind.

Before I left the hospital on the night of December 23, I took Viola's hand in mine and began talking to her. I told her that she had once made me promise her that if the time came for her to stop performing, I would tell her. I told her that night in the hospital that the time had come for her to stop. I had no idea whether she could hear me. All I knew was that when one walked into her room, one could feel her presence; not in her body. It was clear that when I touched her, that she was not in that body any longer, and yet she was very much in the room. I was worried that she was holding on to life for me or for all the loving friends that surrounded her bedside day after day. I told her that it was time for her to go to Baba, and to let Him put his arms around her and welcome her home.

The next day, Christmas Eve, Dr. Galloway came into Viola's room to check up on her. She told me that she could not get a pulse and that Viola's temperature was, and had been for two days, 105 degrees. She said that I should go and get something to eat, that this was going to be a very difficult day for me, because she did not think that Viola would live more than twelve hours.

Karen Levey was there, as were Emmy, Annie-Claude, and Pauline. Karen said that she would go with me, and we went across the street to a small café and had lunch. We were not gone more than a half an hour when I told Karen that I needed to get back to the hospital. I simply did not want to be away from Viola's bedside. As we entered the hospital, I decided to call Viola's sister Elisabeth, and to tell her what the doctor had said. As I was talking to her, Emmy ran up to me with tears running down her face. I knew from her expression that Viola had died. Emmy read my thoughts and nodded. I then had to tell Elisabeth that her youngest sister, Viola, had passed away. It was the hardest thing that I had ever had to say out loud. Somehow, speaking the words made the actuality of it all the more real.

The doctor's report listed Viola's death as heart failure, and that she had died at 2 p.m. on December 24, 1998. The nurses let me sit alone with Viola's body for a few minutes. I broke down and cried, even though I knew that she was much better off. I wept for my own loss. I wept because I would no longer be able to call her up and talk for hours about everything and anything. I would no longer be able to hold her hand while walking down the street. I would no longer be able to dance with her, to tease her, or to argue with her. My dearest, closest friend was gone.

The nurses finally came into the room, and I stood there as they put Viola's body into an awful black plastic bag. As they were doing so, her hospital gown fell open, and there was the beautiful body that had given so many people joy as she danced. All of the swelling was gone, and her face had a wonderful peaceful look; the anguish was no more. Before the nurses were finished, I remembered the pendant, and quickly took it from around Viola's neck. She did not need it anymore, for she was now with the real Baba, not just a picture.

I found Dr. Galloway and signed all the necessary papers for Viola's body to be sent for an autopsy, and then to a funeral home where I had made arrangements when the doctors told me that it was only for a brief time that Viola could live without the life support system. Then I went back to her apartment and began making telephone calls to let friends know what had happened. I did not have to make many calls, as everyone that I spoke to volunteered to call others. Everyone was in shock, and some people whose telephone numbers I found in Viola's address book had not even been aware that she had been ill. It was very difficult to listen to the silence on the other end of the phone when I explained what had happened.

Once again, Karen Levey, John Yannelli, Pauline Watts, Annie-Claude Dobbs and Emmy Devine came to my rescue by offering to help me pack up all of Viola's belongings. I had paid Viola's rent for the month of January, but had to get rid of everything by the end of that month. Another long-time friend of Viola's, Tex Hightower, came from New York several times and helped me pack.

Then, of course, there was the matter of Viola's will. I had found the will shortly after I had arrived. Viola must have known that she would not be alive much longer, because she had put it where it could be found very easily. It was on the floor of her bedroom next to her television set, along with a stack of other important legal papers. The Will had been written, however, in 1981 the law firm that had handled it for Viola had gone out of business, and the lawyer who had drawn it up had died. Curtis was listed as executor of Viola's estate, a fact that did not please Viola's sisters at all. Fortunately, when I called Curtis in France, where he was then living, he told me that he really did not want to fly to New York simply to handle Viola's estate. I hired a lawyer in Bronxville, and he drew up papers for Curtis and Viola's sisters to sign, turning over the task of executor to me.

With the help of all my friends in Bronxville, I was able to pack up all of Viola's belongings that I was going to keep, items that I donated to Sarah Lawrence College were moved there, and the items that Viola had left to certain people were shipped off to them. We did all this before January 27th, when I had to be back in Long Beach to begin teaching. Viola's body was cremated, and Tex Hightower agreed to keep Viola's ashes with him until we decided where to put them. Viola's will was not specific about this fact, but I knew that she would want them taken to India if at all possible and buried near Baba's tomb. That required a lot of legal procedures, however, and we were not certain whether we would be able to accomplish it.

Chapter Eight

Tributes

THE STORY OF VIOLA FARBER did not end with her death. Before I left Bronxville, I made arrangements with the dean of Sarah Lawrence College and with the dance department to have the memorial for Viola tentatively set for March 8, 1999. I knew that we would have to have a memorial service in New York as well, and I wanted to coordinate the two events because I and members of Viola's family would have to fly in from other parts of the country. It was not long before I managed, with the help of Joanne Robinson Hill and choreographer Trisha Brown, for Viola's memorial in New York to be held at the Joyce Theatre on March 11th. I also contacted the Cunningham Foundation to find out whether Merce Cunningham would want to be part of the Joyce Theatre memorial. Then, together with Karen Levey, we came up with the idea to contact as many of the dancers from Viola's company as possible to see whether they wanted to join us onstage at the memorial to perform excerpts from dances choreographed by Viola. It would take some planning, but we thought that this would be a wonderful tribute to Viola.

Soon there were five memorials planned for the year of 1999. The first was held on March 1, 1999, at Sarah Lawrence College in the dance department's performance space. It was titled *Remembering Viola*, and there was a lovely drawing of Viola on the program by Shirley Kaplan, a faculty member of the college's theatre department. The service opened with a performance by dance students and the Chamber Improvisation Ensemble under the direction of John Yannelli. Music was played by Ed Niemann and Marjorie Landsmark-DeLewis. Speakers included Barbara Kaplan, dean of Sarah Lawrence College, and faculty members Pauline Watts, Michael Rengers, Karen Levey, and Shirley Kaplan, and a former student, Jessica Powers.

Students also performed a dance that they had choreographed titled *You're the Top*, which was first performed for Viola on her birthday on February 25, 1998, a dance which Viola loved very much. The beautiful video tape titled *Remembering Viola* by Donna Faye Burchfield was shown, and the service concluded with another student-choreographed work by Sophie Ernst, class of 2000, titled *Night Fragments*.

I also spoke, and during my talk I saw Dr. Anne Galloway in the audience. I was very touched that she attended the memorial. Viola had been fond of Dr. Galloway, as was I, and Viola must also have made an impression on her doctor.

Karen Levey brought everyone to tears at the service with her words, including a beautiful poem by Mary Oliver. With Karen's permission, I have included both.

> The first time I met Viola I was struck by her beauty. She was a creature - a force. To be in the presence of such an extraordinary woman was profound for me. I learned to work harder than I ever knew I could. Viola inspired me to work towards a kind of completion I had never known.
>
> She has been a part of my life for almost 40 years. But

no matter how sustained or brief or intimate or removed our acquaintances have been - we have all been touched - in some way - by Viola.

One Tuesday night shortly after we returned from break - many students and faculty met to express our feelings of loss and share thoughts and memories. It was very moving to hear the students reveal the effects Viola had on them and I was not surprised when their stories reminded me of my own.

Viola's legacy is in the careers of all artists and students and the first time I met Viola I was struck by her beauty. She was a creature - a force.

In the storytelling tradition - we all pass on meaningful moments by word of mouth or body to body.

When students ask me "What was it like when you studied and later danced with Viola?," I tell them - it was the same - she was demanding and fierce and loving. She believed in us and in what we could experience and achieve as dancers - as people.

Viola gave everything she knew to the dance and to her deep spiritual life.

That was her love - her work.

She committed herself to teaching - to taking responsibility for training her students and dancers. She taught us to focus on the work rather than on ourselves.

In her own life, she took risks, went against the grain, took the chance and lived the moment.

She worked to a completion that was never finished - always open - at risk - vulnerable - this left her exploring. Thus her work had incredible strength and yet was always fragile.

With this spirit and integrity she reduced things to their essence and then took them to their limits.

I was inspired to reach for the extremes of possibilities and the mysteries of experience, the fleeting moments and the rough edges.

Viola never gave up the struggle - either in her personal life or profession.

Viola never stopped working - she had jobs planned through next summer.

She was a contemporary artist in the truest sense. She lived the moment, expected the unexpected, and sought the unpredictable. She loved it that dancing had no debris and was gone in a flash. She inspired us, as students and faculty, to explore unknown territories, grow as thinkers, creators and performers. She demanded change. She never led us to believe doing the work would be comfortable, easy or safe.

If you went to Viola with two ideas

1) being practical - within reach, and the other, 2) being complicated, difficult, challenging, perhaps a fantasy, she would always encourage you to follow the dream, take the risk - go for it.

She loved beautiful dancing and devoted her life to making that happen.

Viola's commitment to Sarah Lawrence and the dance department was enormous. She loved her students. I know because I ate dinner with her almost 3 nights a week for 8 years, and heard her relive those remarkable moments in class where we all learned art has no boundaries. Where we learned to work with an intensity we had never known and where the reward is perhaps only in the doing.

I applaud Viola for her outstanding lifetime achievements and her leadership as director of our department, and for the energy and time spent here in the pursuit of excellence.

I plan on celebrating Viola's life by continuing to teach and dance with spirit, love and hard work.

After our elegant dinners at one of the many Bronxville trendy cafes I would drive Viola home - we would hang out in the car - exhausted - in front of her apartment house - until finally - with a sigh - she would open the door - get out - look back and say, "onward and upward."

Viola died on December 24th just before Christmas Eve. I would like to close with a poem by Mary Oliver entitled

DECEMBER, from her book *White Pine*.

Then the deer stepped from the woods.
It walked from the shadows under the trees
into a clear space. Antlers sprang from its
brow, each with five or six tines. From the
antlers, from each tine, green leaves were
growing, as if from the branches of a tree.

The deer stood without moving, brutish and
graceful as deer alive in the daylight, except
that its heavy, elaborate head was carrying,
upon the usual curvatures of horn, these
branches, this fountain of leaves.

Then it turned and vanished. In shyness,
perhaps, or simply because we get no more
than such dreamy chances to look upon the
real world. The great door opens a crack,
a hint of the truth is given - so bright it is
almost a death, a joy we can't bear - and
then it is gone.

The second memorial service was planned for March 11, 1999, at the Joyce Theatre. Between March 1st and March 11th , a great deal of work had to be done. The Joyce Theatre had been reserved on a Monday because the theater was dark that night. I and Joanne Robinson Hill, who had agreed to have the programs printed, had been in contact beginning right after Viola's death. Merce Cunningham had agreed to speak at the memorial and to have one of his dances performed. Ralph Lemon agreed to perform a solo from the duet he and Viola had performed in 1995, and Trisha Brown was presenting a solo from her company's repertory.

The essence of Viola's work materialized with the gathering of former members of her company. We all met at Larry Clark's loft on West 18th Street in Manhattan two or three days before the memorial service, and began to piece together different phrases that we could remember from the Farber company repertory. The dancers who assembled that day came from all over the United States, and from France and Venezuela. They were (in alphabetical order) Mirjam Berns, Jumay Chu, Larry Clark, Didier Deschamps, Willie Feuer, June Finch, Anne Koren, Joël Leucht, Karen Levey, Susan Matheke, Andé Peck and I.

We had only two rehearsals before performing at the memorial service, one at Larry's loft and one onstage just before the audience came into the theatre. We each chose to do a phrase or parts of duets that we remembered, while also dancing a long, slow section from Viola's work titled *Dinosaur Parts*. Anne Koren remembered that many sections in Viola's works had to do with diagonals across the stage, and so we decided to make the dance travel on a diagonal from upstage right to downstage left. The dance would end as we exited the space. Because I knew that it was some of Viola's favorite music, we selected David Tudor's score by the same title, *Dinosaur Parts*. This, of course, meant that I had to contact the David Tudor Estate and get permission for us to perform to his music. Luckily, with the help of Jean Rigg, there was no problem in our getting that permission.

Viola's sister Irene and her nephew Eric Lanzl flew to New York the day before the memorial, and both had agreed to speak. Viola's other sister, Elisabeth, could not attend because her husband was battling cancer. Didier Deschamps, who was working for the Ministry of Culture in France, was to present Viola's award, the *Officier de l'Ordre des Arts et des Lettres*, and Merce Cunningham had agreed to speak. I, too, was to give a talk. Many dancers thought that Viola and I were still married, because they often saw Viola and me holding hands in public as late as 1998. We did so out of a great love for each other. We were, in some strange way, soul mates.

On March 11th, the Joyce Theatre was filled to capacity with friends, relatives, dancers, musicians, and other artists who had come to pay tribute to Viola Farber. Jasper Johns was in the audience as well as were Trisha Brown, members of the Merce Cunningham Dance Company, the Trisha Brown Dance Company, the Ralph Lemon Dance Company, the Twyla Tharp Dance Company, the Martha Graham Dance Company, the Paul Taylor Dance Company, the Dan Wagoner Dance Company, and others. The audience members also included people who had grown to know Viola through her talks at Meher Baba gatherings, including her friends Tex Hightower; musician, Moshe

Goldberg; massage therapist, Joan Witkowski, and many, many others. The theater overflowed with people whom Viola had touched in some way through her teaching, her art, and her love for Baba.

Here is a listing of the program:

A Celebration of the Life in Dance

Of

Viola Farber

February 25, 1931 - December 24, 1998

Remembering Viola

Video tape by Donna Faye Burchfield

DANCE FOR VIOLA

Choreography and Performance: Former members of the Viola Farber Dance Company; Mirjam Berns, Jumay Chu, Larry Clark, Didier Deschamps, Willi Feuer, June Finch, Anne Koren, Joël Leucht, Karen Levey, Susan Matheke, Andé Peck, Jeff Slayton
Music: David Tudor

Speakers

Irene Aikin and Eric Lanzl, Didier Deschamps, Merce Cunningham, Jeff Slayton

----

The Prickly Rose

Ralph Lemon
Solo from *Threestep (Shipwreck)* 1994
Choreography: Viola Farber, Ralph Lemon
Music: *Bach Prelude from Unaccompanied cello Suite #4, in E-flat Major*
Cellist: Marie-Volcy Pelletier

Excerpt from Monteverdi's opera *L'ORFEO*
Choreography: Trisha Brown
Kathleen Fisher dances the role of "Messageria" - the messenger, who tells Orfeo the tragic news that his beloved wife is dead.

CROSS CURRENTS

Choreography: Merce Cunningham
Music: Music for Piano No 52-56 (1956-57 by John Cage, performed by David Tudor. *First performance*: Sadler Wells Theater, London 31 July 1964)
Original Dancers: Carolyn Brown, Merce Cunningham, Viola Farber.
Dancers: Jean Freebury, Koji Minato, Banu Ogan.

Tall, with a head of hair cropped shorter than any man's on that crowded downtown Broadway local rushing into the Village in the late 1960's, she stood out without seeming conscious of any oddity and, even stranger, no one seemed to notice her. A few hours later, there was the woman again, suddenly alone on the stage of The New School auditorium. This time she looked even odder and even more serenely attuned to herself and her surroundings, dressed in a slightly tatty bit of chiffon shift, a baseball catcher's mitt on one hand at the end of a long lean elegantly supple arm.

The first time one saw Viola Farber, whether on stage or off, tended to be an event, that quiet sensation of surprise diminishing only a little with repetition. She would have had her place in dance history by virtue of the fact that she was a founding member of the Merce Cunningham Dance Company, who clearly inspired the choreographer herself, with her look of being "two persons, another just ahead or behind the first," as he put it.

She was also a choreographer herself, with an eye for dancers with something of her individuality. She was an icon of French modern dance. But always she was that woman with the mitt, in her 1968 solo "Legacy": unbending, off-kilter, lyrical, dreaming, witty and unassuming. A mystery as plain as a catcher's mitt in an uneasy puzzling world.

-Jennifer Dunning

Do not worry. I am with you. --- Meher Baba

Family and friends thank The Joyce Theater
Foundation
Photo: Jack Mitchell
Support: Foundation for Contemporary Performance
Arts,
Trisha Brown, Merce Cunningham, Joanne Robinson
Hill.

It is important to mention that the Foundation for Contemporary Performance Arts was founded by Jasper Johns. Here again, Jasper gave generously to a woman and a friend whom he loved and admired. For many years, Viola had served on that foundation's panel of artists who selected artists to be awarded funding grants. It was a panel on which she thoroughly enjoyed serving, not just because it gave money to up-and-coming artists from many art media, but because it gave her a chance to see her friends Jasper Johns, Carolyn Brown, and others.

While the dancers from the Farber company were performing, I looked into each person's eyes and saw tears. It was very difficult for each one of us to dance these beautiful movements knowing that we would never again look on the face of our mentor, or laugh with our dear friend Viola.

During his speech, Didier Deschamps mentioned how sad all the dancers, musicians, visual artists, and set designers were, as was everyone who had come in contact with Viola during her three years as Director of the CNDC in Angers, France. He described how several of the dancers who had studied and/or worked with Viola during that time had gone on to become well-known choreographers and performers in France, among them Mathilde Monnier and Jean-François Duroure. He also presented to me the French award about which Viola knew before her death. The award that the French Government had sent was accompanied by a large emerald-colored stone lined with small white stones, hanging from a green and white ribbon. It looks like a medal that would have been pinned on the uniform of a French general in the 17th or 18th century.

Didier Deschamps noted during his speech that the dancers at the CNDC who had worked with Viola often say, "Viola, if you ever get bored up there, fly down and land in the arms of one of the dancers for a brief moment, and they will know what it is to feel light enough to soar."

Irene spoke beautifully about her sister, and how the family always knew, from the moment Viola was born, that she was someone special. Irene then sang, in German, a very brief song that she had written for Viola. The audience was quite moved by this gesture of love. Eric Lanzl then spoke, representing his mother Elisabeth. He told of how much Viola would be missed and to thank the entire dance community of New York for the wonderful tribute to his aunt.

Another very moving moment of that memorial occurred when Merce Cunningham walked up to the podium and opened his talk with the words, "I loved Viola."

The third memorial was a tribute to Viola at the American Dance Festival in Durham, North Carolina. The video tape *Remembering Viola*, was shown, and speakers included Martha Myers, Donna Faye Burchfield, and myself. Douglas Nielsen then performed a solo that Viola had choreographed for him in 1989, titled *Last Call*. Martha Myers' talk included the fact that Viola was to receive the 1999 Balasaraswati/ Joy Ann Dewey Beinecke Endowed Chair for Distinguished Teaching Award, but that everyone was now gathered for a much sadder occasion. The ceremony was brief, but it was seen by a group of dancers attending the festival who were too young to have studied with Viola, or to have seen her work. However, there were in the audience several dancers who had studied with her in New York during the 1970s.

I then traveled to Paris, France, to attend the fourth memorial, which was held at the Cinémathique Française and had been organized by the Cinémathique de la Danse. Again, a video was shown which highlighted moments of Viola performing with the Cunningham company and with her own company. The video was edited by Patrick Bensard, Director of the Cinémathique de la Danse. It included excerpts from Merce Cunningham's *Crises, Story, Winterbranch,* and *Antic Meet,* and Viola's works *Tendency, Double Walk,* and *January.* Speakers included Patrick Bensard; Mathilde Monnier, former member of the Farber company at the CNDC in Angers; Didier Deschamps; Merce Cunningham and myself.

Also on the program was a video showing an excerpt of the last solo that Viola had choreographed for herself while working in France in 1992. It was a solo which appeared within the work titled *Ainsi de Suite.* The footage was shot during a rehearsal, and it showed a very tired and vulnerable Viola, who had recently recovered from her battle with cancer, and who was struggling with arthritis in her left hip. The camera is not kind to Viola. She was not wearing make-up, and it includes several close-up shots of her face where we see the age lines that demonstrate all too clearly her history of suffering.

I was amazed that Merce Cunningham delivered his entire speech in French. I knew that he had once studied Russian, but had no idea that he also spoke French. I had to have a translator during my speech, and was told later by a person in the audience who spoke both languages that it lost a lot in the translation.

The final and, to this author, the most moving memorial, was held on November 9, 1999, in Angers, in one of the studios of the CNDC, which had recently been re-named the Centre National de Danse

Contemporaine d'Angers L'Esquisse with a change in directorship. Speakers included myself, Joelle Bouvier, Directrice Artistique of the CNDC, and Dominique Orvoine, Director of Communication and Outreach Work in Angers. What made this stand out from the other memorials were two things: That the people from the town of Angers were present, and that everyone was allowed a chance to get up and speak, or to tell stories about Viola. Very few of the speakers read from their notes, but they spoke candidly and openly about their love and respect for Viola, not only as a teacher, choreographer, or co-worker, but as a woman and friend. The audience was included in a way that had not happened at any of the other memorials, and the make-up of the audience was quite different.

One other significant element in this last memorial was the performance of the last dance that Viola had choreographed at the CNDC while she was the director. The dance was titled *Etudes*, and it was performed by 17 of the students who were currently studying there, none of whom had ever seen or studied with Viola. To them, she was a myth, a legend.

Etudes was originally choreographed for five dancers. Anne Koren was brought in to teach and coach the dancers, who had to learn most of the choreography from a videotape. Anne did an amazing job of setting this dance for these young dancers, and they performed it with the kind of energy, vitality, and risk that would have pleased Viola very much. I told the dancers afterwards that "Viola is smiling down on you right now!" The turnout was so great that night in Angers that there was a repeat performance of *Etudes* and of the videotape from the Cinémathique de la Danse on the night of November 10th.

Viola had a great influence on modern dance in France. Here is an article that appeared in the French newspaper Le Monde, on January

2, 1999, that conveys how much people in that country admired her work.

Viola Farber

A Spirit of Quick-Silver

Viola Farber, dancer and American choreographer, died during the day of December 24, 1998, near New York City following a brain hemorrhage. She was 67 years old.

Viola Farber had style to spare, with her air of severity and her straight, gray mane. Modest as well, and completely devoted to dance. Up until the end of her life, despite a bout with cancer from which she recovered, despite fatigue, she continued teaching at chic Sarah Lawrence College until death struck - a last onslaught which she was unable to ward off, because she did not see it coming. Agile herself, Viola Farber was ever skillful in the dances she invented at introducing a sense of fun, of structure, and of playfulness. Not an easy thing to capture. And yet...

Discipline of Body

There can be no doubt that she had good schooling, with Merce Cunningham of whom she was one of his first confidants from 1953 to 1965. Following that, Viola Farber founded her own company and became a choreographer in the American postmodern tradition: body discipline, composition, precise work in space, and collaboration with visual artists.

She was well-known in France. In 1981 she

succeeded her compatriot Alwin Nikolais as head of the National Center of Contemporary Dance in Angers. Finally a teaching style of dance which was not based on or inspired by classical dance was seen in our country. We recall, among dozens of works that were created during this time, "Villa Nuage" (Cloud Villa) or the curious "Oiseaux-Pierres" (Stone Birds). The beautiful and talented Mathilde Monnier, who today directs the Choreographic Center of Montpellier, danced in her company.

Always attentive to helping new talent, Viola Farber asked François Verret for a piece for her dancers. The impertinent "La Latérale de Charlie" (Charlie's Lateral) lives in our memory. Angelin Pereljocaj followed her teaching while still a teenager. We see the role that the choreographer played at the beginning of the 80's, accompanying the development of young dance, disciplining its rough edges, all the while understanding the expressionist roots of its new choreographers: she was born in Heidelberg on February 25, 1931. She lived in Germany until 1938, the year when her parents left to settle in the United States. Viola Farber was granted American citizenship in 1944.

Mathilde Monnier never severed the connection with her dance teacher; indeed they became friends. Viola Farber, once again at "Montpellier-Danse 1998" came to bring the light of her teaching, the simple beauty of her movement. The two choreographers were preparing to bring to a conclusion an exchange agreement between Sarah Lawrence College, where

Viola Farber directed the dance program since 1988, and the Choreographic Center of Languedoc-Roussillon.

So, Viola Farber had died, taking with her much of that quick-silver which is the possession of the founders of American contemporary dance.

Dominique Fretard, *Le Monde*

(Translated into English by Paul Lewis, June 21, 1999.)

Viola's brother-in-law, Lawrence Lanzl, came across an article that was written back in the mid 1970s for a University of Chicago student newspaper. What is amazing is that the author of the article only knew Viola for a few hours, but managed to capture the essence of Viola Farber, the person and the artist, in the opening paragraph of her article. She was writing about the Farber company's residency at the university, and I thought it appropriate to end this chapter with her words.

"Ask her what she makes dances about and she'll say, 'Movement, doing movement.' Try to write about her and your verbs go on strike. I have listened to her breathe, to the soft soprano of her voice, have seen her legs snap space into throbbing obedience, and still I cannot tell you what she is about. Both dancer and woman are the dance - a simple equation of intriguing implications."

Nancy G. Moore, circa 1978

Former members of the Viola Farber Dance Company outside the Joyce Theatre in New York City following the memorial for Viola Farber, 1999.

Left to right: Seated: Mirjam Berns, Larry Clark. Front row: June Finch, Karen Levey, Susan Matheke with son Louis Feuer, Jeff Slayton. Middle row: Anne Koren, Jumay Chu, Didier Deschamps, Willi Feuer. Back row: Joël Leucht, Andé Peck. Photographer: Teresa King

LE CONSEILLER
CULTUREL
№ 30

972 FIFTH AVENUE
NEW YORK, N.Y. 10021
212-439-1400

New York, January 6, 1999

Mr. Jeff Slayton
3565 Linden Avenue - # 266
Long Beach, CA 90807

Dear Mr. Slayton:

It is with profound sorrow that the country of France has learned of the passing of Viola Farber. We had engaged in a longstanding cultural dialogue with her and were privileged to encounter therein the power, lyricism, and individualism which distinguished her as a great figure in modern dance. In her dance, choreography, artistic direction, and teaching, she has left a rich legacy.

This past year, the French Minister of Culture officially recognized the work of Ms. Farber by naming her to the *Ordre des Arts et des Lettres*. I am grateful and consoled that through this award she was reminded of France's appreciation of her talent and work.

On behalf of the country of France, please accept my sincere condolences at the loss of a cherished artist and friend.

Sincerely,

Pierre Buhler

. Letter of condolence from the Ambassador de France, January 6, 1999.

Chapter Nine

Teaching Methodology

"A teacher needs to have the ability to teach technique without forgetting that it is about dancing, and that it isn't just about being in the right place at the right time, but that technique is in the service of dancing."

Viola Farber, quote taken from <u>The Art of Teaching Dance Technique</u> by Joan Schlaich and Betty DuPont, 1993.

VIOLA FARBER WAS CONSIDERED BY many to be one of the finest master teachers of modern dance in the United States and Europe. Although Viola would not have liked it, it is for her teaching more than for her choreography that she is most remembered and was sought after. For this reason, her teaching is one of the most important subjects to be written about here. There was a magic to her teaching that was as mysterious, and as difficult to pinpoint, as was her performing.

Viola was a guest teacher at many dance departments and dance festivals throughout the United States, as well as in Europe and other parts of the world. Without exception, all of the members of her company had been her students. She never held auditions for her company, but hired dancers who had studied with her for a length of time. It was important to her that the dancers in her company understood her style of movement and her philosophy of dancing before they performed in her company.

Karen Levey and I first studied with Viola at Adelphi University, Anne Koren at Vassar and the New York studio, Larry Clark at Ohio State University, Susan Matheke at New York University, June Finch and Margaret Jenkins at the Cunningham studio, and Andé Peck at Bennington College. Except for the French dancers who studied with Viola at the CNDC in Angers, the members of Viola's company came out of her studio in New York.

Many young dancers who studied with Viola for the first time were in awe of her, and if they were like the rest of us, they were probably totally lost in her classes for the first week or so. They watched how her arms flew around her body and marveled at the way her long legs sliced through space and seemed to move with incredible ease. She seemed to be in several places at once, but at the same time her movement was crystal clear. These young dancers were accustomed to the movement in class being very frontally orientated, but here was an amazingly beautiful dancer constantly changing direction at lighting speed, and the movement did not have the usual front, the mirror or the front of the studio, except at the beginning and end of the movement combinations. Even then, Viola would sometimes begin and end a combination facing on the diagonal or the back of the studio. Viola counted out the measures of the music as she demonstrated, but it was often difficult to find an exact movement that she was executing on any specific count. Because Viola was so beautiful to watch, dancers often forgot that they were supposed to be learning a movement or phrase. Overcome, these dancers knew that they could dance, but often found that their feet were frozen to the studio floor. As Viola put it to her students, "Go for it. Try it. Otherwise you'll never do anything except what you already can do."

She was usually very patient with young and inexperienced dancers, and if they managed to stay on with her, they were forever indebted to her for what they learned from her teaching. Viola taught her students that dancing was about movement, musicality, and expression. She was a great believer in the fact that the warm-up of a technique class should relate directly to the main center combination and the across-the-floor work. For Viola, dancing was the most important element in her technique class. She insisted that the student put the art of dancing first in her classes and leave their egos outside the studio, along with your personal problems. There was no room for anything except dancing in Viola's classes. Her classes were wonderfully choreographed and made the dancers feel as if they were performing in one of her works. She demanded technical excellence as she guided her students through and beyond their limits.

In an interview with Joan Schlaich and Betty DuPont, who wrote the titled The Art of Teaching Dance Technique, Viola commented on the subject of music for dancers and musicality in their dancing. Viola said that while in class, or while performing in a dance choreographed to music, a dancer should listen to the music and "think of yourself as another instrument. Add your part to the fabric or texture of the music."

When possible, Viola arrived at the studio at least an hour before the students in order to give herself a thorough warm-up, so that she was physically ready to demonstrate movements to her class. It was that kind of discipline that enabled her to dance as long and as beautifully as she did. She also used this time to plan her class. She often planned the warm-up exercises for the class during her own warm-up, but she choreographed the center phrase and across-the-floor movement on the spot while teaching. She was able to do this only after years of teaching, of course, and she admitted that, during the first ten years of her teaching career, she had planned almost every step before entering a class. Later, however, she could use movements from the warm-up part of her class, along with what she knew the students needed to work on technically. She could put together movement phrases right in front of the students without making them wait around while she did so. Most of the dancers in her classes never knew that she was choreographing the movement "on the spot," but assumed that she had planned all of it beforehand.

At other times, she choreograph part of a combination first and then made up, on the spot, the warm-up to prepare the class for the combination. Viola often used this method when she was choreographing a new dance for her company and wanted to see how the movement looked on her dancers, or how she could further develop a movement idea. Although it is normal for a choreographer who teaches to use the class time to work out choreographic ideas, Viola never let the choreography of a new dance come before her students.

Viola thought about her students' needs while she planned a class. During class, if she saw that she needed to drop what she had planned and do something totally different, she did so. She tried always to direct her teaching to the majority of the students, not just to the best in the class. She put it this way: "I don't plan a whole class ahead much because I like to be able to deal with whatever is happening at the moment, and I can't if I have a rigid idea about what I'm going to do. I have an idea of the kind of thing I'm going to do, but I don't really plan a whole class from beginning to end."

Viola went on to say, "If I see there is something that the class ought to be working on, I stop and I make something that just deals with that.

So I have to stay alert as well as the students. Even after years and years of teaching, sometimes I make something I think will be fun and it turns out to be terribly difficult for everybody. Something else I think will be difficult, everybody gets in a snap."

She choreographed her classes in order to make them appropriate for learning. If there was a difficult turn in one of her combinations, she always prepared the dancers beforehand by putting elements for performing that turn in different movement exercises. Thus, when the turn came, the dancers were better prepared to attempt it. She taught dancers how to use rhythm to accomplish difficult technical movements. It was how one used the rhythm of the movement along with one's technique that not only made it work, but made it exciting to watch.

Viola began class with a series of back exercises, curving movements designed to warm up the upper back muscles. One set of back exercises began from the top of the spine and slowly curved forward and then back up again. These exercises were followed by a foot warm-up movement, then by pliés, and then a very simple phrase that moved through space. Each day, however, Viola changed the foot warm-up exercise slightly, and changed the arms for the plié sequence, and the easy phrase that moved around would be a different from the day before. Sometimes she demonstrated a phrase differently the second time through, but the students learned to make a decision about which version to do, and to dance it with authority. If a wrong choice was made, Viola was the last one to care; it was the attempt that mattered most to her. What made Viola angry was when dancers got lazy and did not work, or when they let their egos get in the way of the dancing. Her temper could be quick, but she had lots of patience.

Viola taught her students how to learn movement. With the advanced class, she demonstrated a movement only twice or, on rare occasions, a third time. Then she walked to the side of the classroom and said the magic word "And" to have the dancers and the musician to get started. She let the class struggle through the first time, then gave corrections and had them repeat the movement phrase until she was satisfied with their work.

In the interview with Joan Schlaich and Betty DuPont, Viola said, "I realized that I often showed things about four times, and I discovered that people did not really watch until the last time. I started showing something only once so they would learn to pick up quickly. They have to do what is given, but not try to imitate, so they learn to do things from the inside out rather than some kind of superficial 'copying' thing."

Most dance studios have mirrors for the dancers to use as aids to learning. These mirrors can become a crutch; however, Viola liked to have mirrors in her studio most of the time. If the class was large, the mirrors helped the students to see her better and for her to see them. She did not like it when dancers stared at their own faces rather than concentrating on the work, and she thought that it was not a good idea to rely on mirrors in order to know what they were doing.

June Finch put it this way: "Every class was like a dance and completely challenging. It had the same rigor as I remember loving in Merce's (Cunningham) teaching, but it felt more connected to who I was. She allowed us to be people." Finch added, "If boring has an opposite that was it. Each class was unique, and the more you learned, the more you found there was to learn."

As it is to any good dance teacher, it was very important to Viola that she warm up a dancer's entire body during a class. She expected the dancers to arrive at the studio ahead of time and stretch out, but she did not expect them to be fully warmed up before class. Part of the stretching-out period for a dancer provides time to clear his or her mind of outside concerns, and to get mentally ready for class. A dancer who dashes in at the last second and directly into the class often is not truly prepared mentally. The later a dancer arrives, the harder it is for him or her to gain the full benefit from the class. This dancer often does not get properly warmed up and is "catching up" during the whole remainder of the class. For this reason, Viola rarely allowed a student to come into her class late unless she knew in advance that the he or she had a very good reason. This rule applied not only to students, but to the members of her company as well.

Viola disliked having to cheer dancers on in order to make them dance. She once said that she expected the dancers to work hard in her classes, but it was much more important that they <u>wanted</u> to do it. Hopefully the dancers in her classes would give themselves totally to the work to be done.

Many dancers who studied with Viola remember her talking little during class, but they never felt that she was not helping or teaching them. Her instructions and corrections were short, direct, and thorough. It was not so much what she said, but how she said it and the look in her eyes while she was speaking got her point across. That look, more than her words, sometimes showed her displeasure, as well as encouraged the students to excel.

Sylvain Richard, who danced with the company in France, said this of Viola's teaching: "She taught as an artist. She taught technique but more accurately she taught her art and how to *live* the dance, not just how to do it. She was always very passionate and drove us hard. In doing so, she built our confidence and strength."

Viola's demonstrations were so beautifully executed that one learned much about dancing by watching her. She did not depend on her demonstrations, however, but structured her classes for better training of her students. Phrasing, that is, how a dancer uses rhythm and music, was a very important element in Viola's teaching. She taught that the way movement was phrased brought about the ability to execute a movement, and that phrasing brought out the artistry, the expression in the movement. She taught dancers how to prepare for a difficult movement and how to end it. She taught that it was not simply a turn or a leap that was important, but how the dancer got into and out of that turn or leap was what would make the movement work best, and would help make it dancing.

Her way of teaching was not effective for everyone. Some dancers felt that her combinations were too intellectual or "heady," and that their bodies did not feel warmed up to dance extremely difficult movements. Often it is simply someone's body type that makes some particular technique style difficult. Many dancers who worked well in the Farber or Cunningham technique could not physically handle the Graham technique, because their hip sockets or knee joints could not withstand the strain they received while doing Graham's grueling floor exercises. It is important to note, however, that while Viola had her studio in New York (1969 to 1981), many dancers from the Merce Cunningham, Paul Taylor, Dan Wagoner, Alwin Nicholais, Trisha Brown, Twyla Tharp, and Lucinda Childs' companies took classes with her. The Farber technique seemed to be effective for the dancers in executing the style that was required of them in those companies. I think that this was because Viola had combined what she had learned from Cunningham and from studying ballet with Margaret Craske. She stressed good body alignment and worked within a dancer's own limitations, not trying to force a dancer into some ideal, but unrealistic position. This is not to say that Viola did not challenge or try to improve a dancer's body structure. Like most good dance teachers, Viola was always trying to have dancers improve their turn out (rotation of their legs), the height of their jumps, or any other facets of their dancing. She had an excellent eye for a dancer's body structure; she knew just how far to push a dancer and when not to force him or her any further.

One word that did not exist for Viola while teaching or choreographing was "transition." When one student asked her what the transition was between two movement phrases, she responded, "There are no such things as transitions! It is like saying that Tuesday is a transition between Monday and Wednesday." Viola said this with a smile, but the dancers knew that she was serious. Mary Wigman, the famous German choreographer and teacher, would have disagreed; Wigman said that dancing was made up totally of transitions. Viola believed that if you thought about transitions between movements, you were choosing to make one thing more important than another. To her every movement was important.

She wanted dancers to risk falling down in class. She insisted that they constantly test their limits as dancers and as artists. They were never allowed simply to indicate or, in dancer terms, "mark" the movement in her classes or in her rehearsals. They were asked always to dance "full out" as they would onstage. This was sometimes exhausting, but it was always rewarding. It is this to which students of Viola owe their dancing knowledge and abilities.

Viola taught efficiency in her class. Irene Dowd, a noted authority on dance body science, remembers one statement by Viola in particular: "Don't prepare to do the movement, just do it." By this she was encouraging her students to use only the necessary movement and energy in order to accomplish the dance phrase or movement that she gave them. Also, she was trying to stop them from adding unnecessary movements that they had picked up as bad habits. For example, some dancers always make a preparation movement with the arms or a hop before beginning to move.

"She had such a unique way of working," Larry Clark said during my interview with him in New York. "Every class that she taught was different. She would never do twenty minutes of the same movement any one day. So, from the pure mental standpoint, if I want to isolate that, it was the most ultimate challenge. You never could be comfortable in her class. You had to be there, mentally, physically, and spiritually, to get through her class. You were always pushing yourself to keep up with her, and she was always way ahead of you.

"Physiologically, she challenged you so much you always thought you were getting to a certain plateau, only to realize you had another ten plateaus to go." Larry continued with great excitement, "Viola pulled out of you what nobody else could pull out of you physically in a class. It was not just movement, it was also musicality, it was spacing, and it was individual expression. She wouldn't really say what it was, you just knew it."

He also said that Viola's classes were not like any others that he had been in. He mentioned how one was always exhausted from her classes. For him it was almost a spiritual experience trying to attain what seemed unattainable. "The carrot was in front of you, but you could never get a bite of it," as Larry put it.

Many who studied with Viola said that Viola challenged her students both psychologically and emotionally. Some went as far as to say that her classes were better than any therapy session. Those students who had studied with her for many years were totally dedicated to her. They believed that what she was doing was unique and geared directly toward them personally, and not toward herself or her own body type.

Viola approached a beginning dance class much in the same way as she did an advanced class. The movement was simpler, of course, but she expected inexperienced dancers also to give one hundred percent to each class. She, of course, wanted her beginners to develop a strong basic technique, but she focused on cultivating a love of moving. She did not make certain that each movement was perfect, or that their bodies were absolutely in the correct alignment, before letting them attempt a combination or exercise. Viola gave the movement, made sure that the students understood the movement, and then allowed them to dance. Dancing is hard work, but Viola wanted the beginners to feel comfortable, secure, and risk free.

"One thing that is not different is that no matter what the level of the class, my expectations within what's given in the class are the same," Viola said. "Obviously the material is different. I don't have beginners stand around in one place for a long time because they haven't got the stamina to concentrate for so long on one thing. A beginning class is just as serious as an advanced class. There isn't any point in trying to do anything less than well."

Touching a student in class is, especially now, a sometimes delicate subject. Often, a dance teacher had to take a dancer's leg in hand and put it into the correct alignment, or place his or her hand on a dancer's back or shoulder. Asking a student first whether it is all right to touch him or her is always the safest procedure, and Viola was always respectful about this fact. Some dancers do not like to be touched because of some past personal trauma in their lives. Others appreciate being manipulated physically. Viola was always careful only to manipulate the dancers of whom she knew that they had some flexibility in their joints. Others she allowed to feel the motion on her own body. She never forced physical manipulation. Her verbal clarity was as strong as her demonstration skills.

If she stopped a class to give an individual correction to a student, she would often make that student repeat a movement until it was correct, and Viola expected every dancer in the class to pay close attention while she was doing so. One of her pet peeves was, after having made a personal correction on one student, or answered a question in class, to have another student immediately ask the same question. She used to quote Margaret Craske: "When I correct Susie, I am correcting all of you!"

Viola was quoted as saying, "But after a while I really stop that [saying something over and over again] because I feel if I'm more interested in the student getting something correct than the student is, it's a little bit pointless."

Viola also showed me the importance of pacing within a class. If a class gets bogged down in too many periods of the dancers standing around listening to a teacher talk, then their bodies get cold, injuries happen, and the dancers are bored. On the other hand, if a class moves too fast, the dancers are left behind and become frustrated. How a class is paced can be critical for a teacher.

After leaving the Cunningham Company, I took Viola's beginning classes. I not only learned a great deal about having developed some bad habits after being on tour almost non-stop for three years, but I also learned a lot about teaching. I learned to train my teacher's eye to see the alignment work a student needed, and how to pick which dancers in class needed more personal attention. Viola taught me how to see the entire class and, at the same time, to see the individual dancers. She had an incredible talent for doing this.

I, myself, while studying with Viola, learned methods of saying the same thing in many different ways. Sometimes a student does not hear a correction until he or she is ready to hear it, or sometimes it is simply the way in which a teacher states a response that will suddenly reach the student.

One might have thought that it was how beautifully Viola herself performed the movements in her classes that were the key to her teaching, for her demonstrations were flawless and remarkable to watch. In 1995 she had been through surgery to remove an entire lung and hip-replacement surgery. In 1995 she was no longer able to demonstrate in the same way that she had twenty, or even ten, years earlier, and would often use an advanced student to demonstrate for her technique classes. She was sixty-four years old and her body had suffered greatly from many years of illness, yet her students at Sarah Lawrence College learned how to dance without her being able to demonstrate the movement thoroughly. When I spoke to some of these Sarah Lawrence dance students in 1995, a few of them also said that it was not what Viola said, but sometimes what she did not say or the look that she gave them, that helped them the most.

Viola taught how to find the quality of a movement through timing: How a dancer used time within the counts of music, or the use of a slow movement accented with a sharp one to make a particular statement. She never simply taught "steps," and she never allowed dancers to give her back anything less than their best, as the art of dancing deserved.

Viola danced from the moment she entered the studio. She even looked as if she were dancing while standing still. Her full attention was on the dancing and the dancers in the room. Nothing else existed during the one-and-a-half-hour class period, and if one paid attention and followed her lead, it was impossible not to become absorbed in her discipline, dedication, and love of dancing. Those students who could not do this either stopped studying with Viola or struggled through until somehow they learned to reach that goal.

It was always astonishing to see the change in the way people danced after they had studied with Viola. For one now famous male dancer, Joe Goode, the entire way he moved was altered by her teaching. It was in New York, some time in the middle or late 1970s that Joe studied with Viola at her Bleeker Street studio. Joe is very tall, more than six feet, and Viola felt that he was not using his height and leg length to their fullest. After a few weeks of trying unsuccessfully to get him to "move out," to cover more space when he danced, she stood very close to Joe and said loud enough for all to hear, "You dance like a giant midget." From that moment on, Joe danced as Viola always knew he could. She may have embarrassed him, or even made him angry, but Joe learned to move!

One of the most delicate parts of teaching dance is how the instructor handles giving corrections to the student dancers. Dancing is a very personal and private activity, even when a room is filled with other dancers. The dancer is constantly looking inward to find the needed strength and motivation. The dancer is always striving to become better, and when the instructor gives a correction, it is difficult not to take it personally. "What makes a correction effective," Viola said, "is if students take it and then realize that they're able to accomplish something they hadn't been able to accomplish before."

Viola was patient with her students for the majority of the time. She allowed then to fail, and then encouraged them to try again. When a dancer reaches his or her next plateau of technical skill, Viola was the first to congratulate him or her on their achievement.

There were no gender expectations or limitations in Viola's teaching. She expected the women to jump like the men, and the men to be as quick as the women. She did, however, admit once that she preferred working with men while she was choreographing. Viola was taller than most female dancers of her time, standing a little over five feet seven inches. She enjoyed dancing with the men in her company, because she fed off their energy. In turn, the men in her company and in her classes enjoyed dancing with Viola because her strength and energy matched theirs.

Concerning how students worked in her classes, I remember an experience back in the late 1970s. After completing one of her more difficult combinations, Viola paused a long time before speaking. She was leaning against the mirrors in the front of the class, and by the expression on her face; we knew that she was not pleased. When she finally spoke, she said only one very short sentence, in the form of a question: "You call that dancing?" Those words cut straight through us, because we felt that we had accomplished the combination quite well, or that at least we deserved a little praise for just getting through the difficult movement. Viola had us repeat the combination, and by the end of it we all knew that she had been right in making us repeat it. We realized that what we had done the first time through had not been dancing, but that we had only been doing the steps. We had focused on getting through the challenging movement, not on really dancing it.

When asked whether she ever became angry at her students, Viola said, "I must say that I never do it on purpose, but I have a temper, and sometimes you can shock people into pulling themselves together." She went on to say, "For different types of students, different ways of dealing with them are effective. I think some people would just be incapacitated by having someone terribly angry at them. For other people, that works very well."

Viola taught many master classes during her lifetime, especially when her company was on tour. When asked how she planned the master classes, she said, "There is no way of planning when you don't know who will be there. It's absolutely hopeless to teach technique in one session. I just try to get students to move around, change directions, and change speeds. I enjoy master classes."

A list of the institutions where Viola taught part-time, or where she was invited for teaching residencies includes: Adelphi University; Bennington College; New York University; University of Wisconsin, Madison; University of Utah, Salt Lake City; George Washington University, St. Louis; University of Michigan, Ann Arbor; Sarah Lawrence College; The Place in London; the London Conservatory of Contemporary Dance; and the CNDC in Angers, France. When asked to compare teaching in academia with teaching in the professional dance world, Viola did not answer the question directly. She often said, however, that she preferred teaching in professional studios to teaching in the academic arena.

"It's hard to say," Viola said, trying to avoid answering the question. "Even before I went to Sarah Lawrence, my ideas about teaching changed because I went to France, for instance. Because it was such a different situation from the situation in New York; the conditions under which people took classes were so different. In New York they had to see for themselves how they managed to pay for classes and how they managed to afford that life. And in France the students were fortunate enough to get paid salaries for coming to class. In England they were not paid salaries, but they had their tuition paid. Unfortunately, there is a different kind of situation set up there now."

Viola found teaching in academic institutions difficult not so much because of the students, but because of the politics involved in departments and administrations. She once said that the politics in academe was more complicated and seemed more vicious than that on Capitol Hill in Washington, D.C. Also, she found that many students in academia too often focused more on their grades for a dance class than they did about learning how to dance well. Professional dancers are more worried about having money for rent and food, often spending money they do not have in order to take dance classes. For the professional or aspiring professional dancer, dancing is her or his life and work. Viola did said that she enjoyed teaching master classes in the academic environment, but I think it was because she did not, at that time, have to get involved in that department's politics. She walked in, taught the master class, collected her fee, and left.

In the academic world, teachers are evaluated by their students.

Many teachers throughout the United States have become afraid of these evaluations because a poor evaluation from one's students can mean the difference between being promoted or not, or getting a merit raise or not. The student evaluations are also reviewed by the administration when a faculty member is up for tenure. Therefore, Viola felt that some faculty members focused more on being liked by their students, than on making certain that the students were learning.

Especially while she was at Sarah Lawrence, Viola said that being nice sometimes means being honest. Being nice means teaching students whatever subject they are studying. In dance, it does not always mean telling them that their dancing is beautiful or that everything they do is wonderful. She was often accused by the administration at Sarah Lawrence of being a bit too tough on her students, or that she demanded too much of them. In reality, she received some of the highest scores within the college on her student evaluations.

Among Viola's personal belongings was a copy of a letter that she sent to Dean Kaplan at Sarah Lawrence upon her return from her semester sabbatical. Viola wrote quite beautifully about that semester and her accomplishments during her time away from being the chairperson of the dance department. Her letter demonstrates her continuing devotion to teaching and, even when she complained about having to teach all the time, how much she received back from her teaching:

October 28, 1996

Dear Dean Kaplan:

It had not been my intention to do so, but I taught dancing -- various aspects of it -- during my sabbatical semester.

In England and France, I taught dancers from many different cultural backgrounds who were either seriously training to enter the professional dance world or were already working in dance companies and continuing their professional training, as dancers always must in order simply to stay in shape as well as to find new powers and strengths as artists.

At the London Contemporary Dance School and within the resident company as well as at the Centre National de Danse Contemporaine in Angers, France, I found a vitality, high level of proficiency and curiosity, a matter-of-fact willingness to explore new and unfamiliar territory among my students that was very refreshing. One of the dancers in the London Contemporary Dance Company, who had also studied with me in the mid-eighties, subsequently was chosen by audition to work with the Twyla Tharp Company during its current tour. I saw his excellent performance in September at SUNY Purchase. In Angers, one of the students said to me "this is wonderful. You give phrases to do and we give them back to you. That's what's supposed to happen, isn't it?" I agreed happily. With that group we presented a performance of work they had made within two weeks.

To be, also, in an environment where the value of what everyone was doing was naturally pretty much accepted by everyone in the institution and for me to be able to concentrate all my energies upon the art of dancing with such receptive students, some already familiar to me from previous years and others entirely new, was a source of great pleasure, delight and even inspiration (a word of which I am wary.)

I feel that my sabbatical gave me the energy to continue working through the summer at the American Dance Festival, independently in New York and this semester at Sarah Lawrence with renewed vigor and enthusiasm.

Sincerely,

Viola Farber

One of the things most important to Viola when it came to dancing or learning how to dance was that the dancer should remain an individual. She put it this way: "I think in all dancing, no matter how precisely you do what someone else is doing, unless you put yourself into it, it's not very interesting. Yes, I want them to be on the right foot, to do things with the right rhythm, even to have whatever quality it is I've given them, but for every student that's going to be very different because we're all physically different, and in precision there still is a great deal of room for individuality."

This individuality extended into Viola's teaching of dance composition and choreography. During her entire tenure at Sarah Lawrence, Viola never choreographed a dance for her students. She strongly felt that they needed to learn how to choreograph dances that were their own. She also did not believe that one should teach them too many rules for making dances, but should give them studies that would guide them to learning how to put a dance together that worked. Viola taught her choreography students how to see dance, and hopefully to know if a choreographer's intent came across or not.

I remember watching Viola teach a choreography class at the American Dance Festival in Durham, North Carolina in 1987. She first had the dancers make up short movement phrases using everyday gestures, such as combing one's hair or brushing one's teeth. She then had them choreograph an eight-count movement phrase that traveled through the space, and one posed movement that remained stationary. When the dancers had finished making up their material, Viola had them start running on diagonals across the studio while incorporating the gesture phrases. She then told them that they could break out of the diagonal at any time and begin their movement phrases. She let the dancers do this for a while, and then had them stop. Next, she added that, while running, if they came near another dancer who was doing a movement phrase, they could mimic or copy what that dancer was doing. She then gave specific rules that the dancers could add to produce short duets or trios or larger group movements whenever they met.

Each time that Viola had the dancers begin this choreographic exercise, she added another rule, and by the end of the hour and a half class period, she had come up with a three minute section of a dance. The section was added to others that were produced that summer and performed at the end of the festival.

I came across Viola's class descriptions for that summer and add them to help the reader see how she viewed her classes. I was impressed especially by the last sentence in her Composition/Repertory Workshop course description, which was the class that I observed.

COMPOSITION/REPERTORY WORKSHOP
Movement, phrases, and situations made by students and instructor will be arranged to make a dance which can be performed at one or several specific sites. The

work will require some physical rigor and skill as well as
the usual mental lucidity and sense of adventure.

That last sentence describes very clearly what was required of dancers
who wanted to be in Viola's company.

In the next description, she lists the requirements of dancers for her
composition course. Again, very few words describe beautifully the
structure of her own dances.

COMPOSITION

Exploration, invention, finding movement materials -
structuring them in solo or group forms which may
be open and indeterminate as well as fixed and highly
controlled.

One thing that always impressed me about Viola's teaching whether
it is dance technique, composition, choreography, or repertory, was that
she always directly taught the individuals who were in her classes. She
never taught a "formula" class. If a class of dancers needed something
different on a particular day than what she had planned, she discarded
her plan and taught them what she thought they needed to learn. This
is the trait of a master teacher of any subject or art form, and Viola was
definitely a masterful teacher of dance.

Class at the Viola Farber Dance Studio, White Street, New York, NY, 1970.
Photographer: Babette Mangolte

Viola Farber teaching a technique class, location and photographer unknown.

Chapter Ten

On Choreography

"I'm very interested in the diversity of things and people in the world. But as far as movement is concerned, I don't deal in every day movements. I'm very interested in my dancers doing things that are technically difficult, in going beyond what is natural and easy."
Article by Patty Moore, <u>The Dallas Morning News</u>, December 20, 1976

DIFFERENT CHOREOGRAPHERS BEGIN TO PLAN a dance differently. There are no any set rules or formulas that dictate how a choreographer must work. Some choreographers are inspired by a piece of music. Others begin with a story line or emotion, choreograph the dance and then either apply an original score, or they search out existing music that suits their idea. Choreographers like Merce Cunningham create their dances quite separately and independently of the music that is eventually used, letting the dance and the music share the time and space, but having each as an entity by itself.

Viola did not adhere to a set formula when choreographing a new work. She sometimes had a movement idea that she followed, and other times a dance was inspired by an event that took place in her life. She worked differently on each dance, as probably many choreographers do. She even got some of her ideas from the movements that she came up with while teaching. She once told me that she got the idea for one of her dances after viewing a painting of two women in a museum in London. She did not tell me which artist or which painting it was. I sometimes noticed her observing a person in the street and the next day saw some of that person's mannerisms included in the movement phrases in her technique class.

One critic called Viola "a true modernist," and I suppose that title applied to many of her dances. A modernist is one who uses the elements of experimentation, unrealism, and individualism and who usually stresses the cerebral rather than the emotive aspects of his or her work. Viola did all that in many of her works, for example in *Survey*, *Co-Op*, *Spare Change*, and *Willi I*. Such dances were built, as was the catch phrase of the 1970s, on "pure movement." These dances strictly consisted of movement for movement's sake, and were void of emotional content or a story line. In other works, however, such as in *Poor Eddie*, *Legacy*, and *Mildred*, there were definite emotional overtones. *Poor Eddie* was about irritation and conflict between people. *Legacy* and *Mildred* were inspired by the death of her parents and the emotions that their dying created in her. She constantly explored new ideas for her work. I agree with several critics who wrote that her artistry always moved into new directions. This did, however, make it next to impossible for the majority of critics to pigeonhole her in a single category.

Viola's company performed in all kinds of venues, including the outside lobby of a bookstore on the Avenue of the Americas in midtown Manhattan, the lobby of the Staten Island Ferry station, the Brooklyn

Academy of Music, small, dirty theaters in New York, as well as some of the best theaters in France. She used a wide range of music or no music at all, even within a single program. Her company was made up of dancers with many different body types, heights, and personalities. Viola enjoyed these differences, and often paired dancers of very different heights in order to see what happened, and how it affected the movement.

"In my dances I am interested in a kind of quickness - and I don't mean just of foot! I like to work with people who don't let themselves remain comfortable with what they can do, but who are constantly trying to do things that aren't perhaps easy to do. I haven't got a set formula for making dances, and the things that engage my attention change off and on. When you've done something for a certain amount of time, you learn how to do it, and that can be very disappointing, so I try then to set myself up to do something that I don't know how to do.

"I don't think that I would describe my style. One isn't a person who drinks Perrier and coffee here and an artist there; or somebody who sits and talks to you here and then somebody else when he does his work elsewhere. We're all different kinds of people. We all have things in common, but we all have our own store of information that we've accumulated in our lives, and that comes out in our work intentionally or unintentionally. I am interested in a kind of virtuosity; I suppose you could call it a technical proficiency, that doesn't submerge the person executing it."

Viola did not use the chance method of choreographing as did Merce Cunningham with his I Ching or flipping of coins to determine which dancer did what movement, or which movement followed which. Nor did she use graphs or write down her work except for a few sentences that meant something only to her.

Many of the dances that Viola choreographed between 1968 and 1974 were performed in silence. They included solos, duets, and group dances. These dances, which she choreographed for her company, were *Seconds* (1965), *Timeout* (1968), *Legacy* (1968), *Excerpt* (1968), *Duet For Mirjam And Jeff* (1969), *Passage* (1969), *Standby* (1969), *Tendency* (1970), *Area Code* (1970), *Curriculum* (1970), *Co-Op* (1970), *Patience* (1971), *Survey* (1971), *Default* (1972), *Some of the Symptoms* (1974), and *Houseguest* (1974). By 1975, Viola had begun using music with her dances, the exception being *Solo*, which she choreographed in 1977.

Dances for which Viola used music as her inspiration included *Dinosaur Parts* (1974) to music by David Tudor with the same title; *Night Shade* (1975) to Beethoven's *Opus 27, No. 2*; *Turf* (1978) to Poulenc's *Organ Concerto in G minor*; and *Bequest* (1981) to Mendelssohn's *Trio in D Minor No. 1, Opus 49*. Many of her dances were choreographed first and the music was added later, or she collaborated with a composer, as she did with Alvin Lucier. The works performed to Lucier's music included *Dune* (1972), *Poor Eddie* (1972), *Soup* (1973), *Spare Change* (1973), *Willi I* (1974), *No Super, No Boiler* (1974), *Motorcycle/Boat* (1975), *Duet for Willi and Susan* (1975), *Five Works for Sneakers* (1975), and *Sunday Afternoon* (1976). Lucier composed the score for *Houseguest* which included the slamming of doors during the performance, but later dropped the idea when audience members complained about the noise.

Viola expected the audience be actively involved in viewing her work. She rarely choreographed specifically for the audience, but made dances that reflected what she saw in the world. Former company member Larry Clark said about Viola's work, "She choreographed because she was interested in making dances for herself. Consequently, what was for her was for you."

Many of her early works were filled with sections where the dancers in her company were allowed to rearrange, or improvise on, a very set movement phrase. She set definite rules or limits for them so that they were not free to do just anything they wanted.

Here is one example how a section of a dance was constructed: Viola would teach the dancers a thirty-two-measure phrase in rehearsal. They would practice this in unison, with Viola sitting at the front of the rehearsal space counting out the numbers. When she was satisfied that everyone knew the phrase, she asked them to learn the same phrase starting to the left side. After a while, the dancers were given a set of rules as to what to do with this phrase. Sometimes they were told to change the tempo of the phrase, but to keep it in the original order. Then Viola would add another possibility such as allowing the dancers to change the directions of the phrase, taking it anywhere in the space that we chose. Then she might ask them to jump a movement that was not originally designed to be jumped, or to do the movement on the floor when it was originally choreographed standing up. The dancers might be allowed to rearrange the order of movements in a phrase. Then Viola sat back and watched them experiment with the phrase. Sometimes she let this go on for five or ten minutes before stopping the dancers. She did this in order to allow them to find as many possibilities as they could. She enjoyed watching this type of rehearsal and often was heard to say that she could sit for hours and watch the dancers experimenting with just one phrase.

While her company had its home in Angers, France (1981-1983), she was quoted as saying,

> "I've been dancing now for 30 years, and I am very conscious of the fact that no matter how intense the preparation, what happens on the stage is always unpredictable and in a certain measure out of any

control.   When I choreograph a dance, I generally include sections where I leave the dancers the freedom to choose what they will do with the given elements. Therefore the pieces are structured in such a way that each event is an obvious manifestation of the newness of that very moment, and of the possibilities of change within us. I like to imagine that in my ballets music is a landscape where movements are produced as a dialogue between the movements of sound and bodies."

Article by Marcelle Michel, <u>CNAC Magazine</u>, circa 1982.

She also choreographed many sections in each dance where movements were set and where there were no freedoms whatsoever. For the dancers to go from one section to the next, a cue was given, such as a visual cue, a movement cue, or a sound cue. One example of a sound cue being used is when June Finch ran from dancer to dancer quietly saying "ready." When she had reached everyone, the dancers went into the next part of the dance. Often the cue to change sections would be a movement cue taken from one of the dancers onstage, or from a dancer entering the space who had not been onstage during a particular section. If the dance had internal or set musical cues, the dancers changed sections as choreographed with the music.

Over the years, Viola used less of the "indeterminacy" in her work, but some of it was always there. For want of a better phrase, I like to think of those earlier works of Viola's as "very organized chaos. " It is true that her early dances gave the audience the feeling that one gets from watching to a three ring circus. The audience had to make decisions as to which dancers to watch and which to ignore. Viola thought of this like a part of life. One has to make decisions all day, every day, about what to watch and what not to ignore.

One dancer in her company, Anne Koren, thought that Viola's work would have been much stronger and more accessible to the general public if she had edited her work more carefully, using fewer of the sections where the dancers were free to improvise on movements. Others, including me, believed that Viola edited her work as she choreographed it, and they saw nothing in any dance that needed to be taken away. If certain sections were weak, perhaps it was the dancers who were to blame; this may be why Viola got further and further away from this kind of formula, and thus was able to make it easier for the audience members to see what she wanted them to see.

Viola enjoyed having her dancers take risks with a movement, or taking the movement "to the edge." To her, this was the life's blood of her dances. She also wanted the dancers to be part of the making of her dances. "I think that was very important to me. I found it very strange initially to tell people what to do. I thought that it was an odd position to be in. So that was one way of trying not to do that," Viola said in an interview I had with her. "I also was very aware of the limitations of one person…me…perceiving what somebody could do and what they couldn't do, and what they should do and what they shouldn't do. Although, God knows, I have a strong leaning in that direction," she laughed.

She did not want to assume that a dancer could not jump in a particular way. She choreographed a movement, gave the rules, and let the dancer discover her/his limitations. It was Viola's way of not letting the dancers be limited by her perception of them.

When told that the dancers had felt that they had a part in producing what the audience saw of her work, she smiled and said, "They did. And that was only possible because of the kind of dancers they were."

But, it wasn't totally because of who they were, or what type of dancers they were. Yes, her dancers were strong and very willing to do anything Viola asked of them, and that was because Viola had an enormous part in training the dancers how to do her work and allowing them to feel secure in taking on that responsibility.

Viola was always inspired by particular while choreographing a work. Even if the dance was one purely of movement, its seed came from some event in Viola's life, or something that she had read or seen. It could be the illness of a family member, as in *Legacy* (1968), or a something that might happened on a trip, such as in *Route 6* (1972) and *Motorcycle/Boat* (1975). It may have been influenced by an event or relationship in her personal life, such as in *Solo* (1977) or *Private Relations* (1978). The audience members may not have gone home with the same experience as what inspired Viola to choreograph a dance, but they went home with a feeling that they had experienced some part of the way that she looked at the world.

In a 1972 article in a Philadelphia newspaper, Viola is quoted about influences on her choreography:

> "I danced in the Merce Cunningham company for more than 12 years. I began to know myself as a dancer in that context. I admire his work, his dance art. I don't try to do what he does so well. I have also studied music, played piano, taken many ballet classes, worked by myself, taught lots of students, gone horseback riding in the West, spent time at the ocean, read some books, gone canoeing, worked with my own and other companies, I live in New York, travel, I admire tap dancers, skiers, parachutists, and many other people. Influences - the dancers with whom I have worked,

what I see, how I've seen it, how I see it. Nothing stops."
Article by Alexandra Grilikhes, <u>The Drummer</u>, Philadelphia, 1972.

In an article in *Dancemagazine*, Viola gives her views on dancing. The article also gives a hint into why she made dances the way that she did, and her views on keeping old works alive. In the second paragraph of this excerpt from the *Dancemagazine* article, she gives us a hint as to why her work has not been preserved any better than it has since she disbanded her company and since her death. Viola often said that she was not interested in having her work survive after her.

"Dancing is movement, movement is change, life. I am interested in the relationships of people and things and the variety of forms in the world. I think art demands the expenditure of energy on the part of the viewer, as well as the doer - an active participation. I am interested in the relationship of people and things in the world. Dance is anything one wants to have it be. I think dance is mainly about moving. I like making some dances that are performed a few times, for specific situations, then dropped, forgotten - absolutely no litter."

Article by Carol Egan, <u>Dancemagazine</u>, 1977.

".......dropped, forgotten - absolutely no litter." Viola said to me on more than one occasion that what she loved most about dance was the fact that, when it was not being performed, that it did not exist. This, of course, is also why it does not bring in as much money as do some of the other arts such as music or painting; one can not buy a dance and take it home to own. One can buy a video of a dance, but the art form does not always translate very well to video, unless the dance is made specifically for that medium.

In a letter regarding the above interview with Carol Egan, Viola wrote the following.

"In a world where money is the accepted medium for rewarding work, it is difficult not to be able to pay the dancers in my company and the administrators adequately. The competence, sometimes artistry, skill, integrity, givingness, hard work, concern for the work of the dancers in my company is amazing to me. It is sometimes difficult for me to be worthy of all this. In my lucid moments, however, I realize that no one has forced any of us into doing what we do. And there are many rewards, no matter how ephemeral their nature.

"Art and what I do - I am convinced that my dances deal with situations we experience and see daily, with my vision of the continuing dramas of everyday life. We turn right instead of left, turning right we meet X, turning left 2 minutes later we would have seen Y.

"I love the variety in creation. Clearly there is no equality, and what equals what? I have a philosophical commitment and an involuntary one to my own time. I feel uncomfortable in my own time often, but there is no choice. I would like to welcome it. I use contemporary music mostly for my dances, made by someone living in this time with me, producing sound in a way not possible in the past. I have also used Beethoven, Czerny, Chopin, blue-grass music, no music. I am working on a dance now where the dancers make sounds and someone plays jazz piano. Are these aberrations? No. I still love melody, harmony, and rhythm.

"I know that when I've written this and sent it away to be fixed, deathless, in print, in some form, I will wish that I had said things I didn't say and not said things I did. I am trying to learn discretion in my life, and would like more and more to put it aside in my art."

One critic, who lived in Minneapolis and who had seen Viola's company perform many times between 1971 and 1979, wrote the following about her choreography:

"Farber's choreography is not easy stuff; it's passionate, violent, energetic and as dangerous as a napped power line shooting and spitting sparks at anyone within reach. Its beauty (and there is plenty of beauty in her work these days) doesn't come from prettiness, but from something much more primal.

There is such an overriding will to survive, to beat the odds and come out on top-screaming-that Farber's work sometimes literally takes your breath away."

Allen Robertson, Minnesota Daily, February 2, 1979.

In her journals and notes, the following was written while Viola was the director at the CNDC in Angers. This would date the writing some time between 1981 and 1983.

"One of the aspects of dance that I love is that it takes place at the moment of action. The dancers create each dance every time they perform it, no matter how fixed the choreography may be. When the dancers are not dancing a dance, that dance does not exist anywhere - it is not an object in our world. All attempts to preserve the movements of action - video taping, film, written descriptions or directions do not capture the moment, they simply make objects out of action, which then become themselves, but do not duplicate the vitality and immediacy of the dancers moving, giving and receiving energy from each other."

"To conserve is not that interesting - of course, you need some notations to work with, to check back on, but there is video for that. Why rework something. Everything changes all the time, and so do I," Viola told me in a 1995 interview.

There is a beautiful quote of Viola's that appeared in a *New York Times* article about her and her company. The quote again shows the way in which life influenced Viola and her art. Although Viola did not write often, she most certainly had a very poetic way of putting words together.

"My dances report what I see. They are my response to the way everything is mixed up together in this world - people and microbes and elephants and cassowary birds. Not only do we live in a mixed-up world of shapes and sizes, the ways in which we relate to each other are mixed up as well."
Article by Jack Anderson, <u>New York Times</u>, 1978.

Viola's choreography was considered not to be accessible. Audiences had to work at seeing and understanding her dances. As many hated her work as there were those who loved it. In 1979, Viola and five other choreographers were interviewed for an article in the *New York Guide*. The following are Viola's views on considering the audience while choreographing.

> "I never know who that audience is. An audience is many people who come to see something, bringing what they are, what they've experienced that day - maybe they slipped down the aisle or have the hiccups. I find it presumptuous to make too many decisions about this collection of individuals or what kind of baggage they bring with them.
>
> "When I start to work on something, I don't bring the audience into the studio with me. It's an unknown quantity. If I were to try and please them, I don't know whom I would have to try and please, or excite, or depress, or whatever I wanted to do to them."
>
> Article by Brett Raphael and Tullia Bohen, <u>New York Guide</u>, 1979.

In an article that appeared in Lyon, France, around 1980, Viola stated that she was not a minimalist, and that minimalists would not accept her as a member. She continued to state that her work could not be described as having any one style that she could not and did not want to be "pigeonholed" into any category. However, in the same article she continues by saying,

"I don't belong to anything, but then I am not very much interested in tradition, but maybe I am a classicist after all. Yes, that's it, I am a classicist. I don't care for decoration, ostentation. Dancing, for me, is the only way to give something. One never dances for oneself alone. But what is surrendered must be authentic; it is also possible to dance, give what we don't have - I don't like that, because there is nothing within then, just something phony, a form that is moving about. Dancing does not cheat because it involves an immediate inner disclosure."

She went on to say that she was sometimes "obsessed with movement," but that mostly her choreography evolved out of scenes that struck her, that took place in, or came from different periods of her life.

"I was working with the Ballet Theatre Français in Nancy. I was somewhat lonely and cold, and it was the gray month of November. Just to do something, I went to the museum where I looked at paintings; they were not particularly good, but I found them moving. So, in my head, I composed *Private Relations* (1978), and created it the moment I was back in New York."

When I asked Viola about choreographing for advanced dancers as opposed to less experienced dancers or performers, her response was this:

> "I always had the idea that people were advanced dancers, or professional dancers, or whatever, and people who were learning, and knew that they had a long way to go, had something to offer each other, and there was something valuable that could come out of working with each other, and that the people who were more recent in the activity had a kind of enthusiasm and freshness that people who were good at it perhaps had lost. And you know, that worked very beautifully

at the American Dance Festival the year that I was there (1987), because I had people who had danced professionally and it hasn't even so much to do with the facility or the skill, but simply with the experience of doing it, which gives you a kind of authority with what you do. Then there were people who were really students in college who hadn't had a lot of experience, and the combination of working with those people together was wonderful! It also had to do with the fact that the people who were real dancers were very nice people."

Viola's last dance that included many of the members of her company was *January*, made in England for British television in 1985. The order for the dance was found scribbled in pencil inside one of her journals. It is, for her, a rare example of choreographic notes. Often she wrote down the internal order of a dance and threw the notebook away once the dance was finished. After reading the following, you will see that her notes meant very little to anyone but herself. She did not intend them for anyone else to read or understand.

London, 1984
1. Parallel and turned out waltz
2. Parallel and turned out Paris and Jeff combination
3. Running, touch, touch turn
   To the floor
   Touch close, chin (to floor)
4. Slow walking, stopping, shifting, dropping - alone, together
5. Walking from back - arms wiping

6. Turns

Arabesque into parallel

Bouree (dip turn)

Pas de chat phrase

7. Reading portions (long, lunge)

(to floor, moving on floor)

8. Talking arms

(3 versions)

Violent and large, nervous, smooth

8b. [8. RR arms with walking 8]

9. Instruction partnering

10. Tap dance rhythm hops

11. Small self-indicated jumps

12. Little lifts form walking

[13.] Occasional waltz - 10?

14. Running to partner (who is in place)

Grabbing - then up and down

14b. Start big

15. Parallel walking duet

16. Parallel hanging

17. Little 6's with arms open and closed

Also found among Viola's personal belongings were journal after journal related to her private thoughts, but very few that related to her work. Notes taken in rehearsal that were corrections for dancers, or things that she wanted to change, were included, but only one example for the order of a dance was among Viola's archives. It was for a dance titled *POP. 11*, which was choreographed in 1971 for dancers at New York University. In the title, the word POP. stood for population, meaning in this case that there were eleven dancers populating the dance or performance space. One of the performers in this dance, Susan Matheke, later became a member of Viola's company.

Here is what Viola wrote about the first section of *POP. 11*. It is not clear whether the dance actually was performed in this order. At times Viola's handwriting was illegible, and I left places blank instead of making a perhaps incorrect "educated" guess.

POP. 11

Phrases - 5 minutes

10 minutes - walking

Foot jabbing front and back

Turn toward back foot

Foot j. across to 2nd

Onto parallel arabesque

Each person jump

Circle - slow, sustained, stamping, running, etc.

Changing places, crawling very fast or continuous

Men can pick up women

Women can move a part of men

Everyone up in parallel into air fall

Up into first

Start jumping steps

4 end facing back

Rest front

Repeat jumping step with alteration - original back group ends

Front - fr. gr. Back

Byron in back joins front group

(jumps to 8 hold 9, 10 while B runs to front)

All jump 11, 12 - repeat

Circles

Paul slows down - goes to everyone - cue for changing tempo

Three women - two men stay and do quintet.

Three people enter, st. 12.

One on man's back [picture drawn here of someone sitting on another's shoulders] doing slow gr. Battement, other woman [stick figure drawing] to [stick figure drawing] two beats in closed pos. Diagonal then str. Downstage.

Two people - man and woman enter stage. 1. Doing parts of 2 phrases - man in back of woman (while on ramp) slow and continuous.

Continue diagonally to just left of outer stage.

Quintet people face each other doing slow gr. B. (grand battement) and releve - changing facing

Repeat legs. Do arching arms and top - Jung Ja falls backward, is caught by 4 others, [stick figure drawing] arches back onto floor on back, change to back up crouch - Byron does somersault, jumps - jumps over.

St. Right three get into pos. & change.

St. Left woman does [stick figure drawing]

Extend and down very fast

Man runs after her, picks her up and puts her down.

Stage r. and quintet group change places and people

From the Viola Farber Archives, 1971

Another typical example of the kind of notes that Viola kept on her choreography was found buried in an old manila envelope in her closet. It is a list of sections of her dance *Dinosaur Parts*. Only one page long and it is the only page in the entire legal-sized note pad that has anything written on it. The numbers underneath certain notes tell me that Viola was keeping track of the length of time that the dance was taking. She stopped listing the time length after section number six. Either she forgot to check her stopwatch, or she was not sure that she wanted to keep the remaining sections exactly like they were on that day, and so she did not bother to time them.

DINOSAUR PARTS

1. Arms & leg fling - staggering

1'45"

2. Old adagio - others

3. Flying jumps

4. Cauliflower -> Jeff and Larry   ending with W. &

V. *[Willi Feuer and Viola)*

4'45"

5. Anne - steeple, June - arm fling turns

6. Willi & Viola end of cauliflower

9'30"

7. June & Larry pushing, Jeff leg ->

Viola parallel foot shove -> rack

Others anything (S&W finger turns) *[Susan Matheke*

and Willi Feuer]

8. Hovering with alerts

9. Loose and tight -> kneeling & bending

10. Peel off

11. Head duet

Steeple

Pointing

Peter's hip - into bent frogs

Leg - grab opp. Same leg - walk

list

Parallel turns - picking up legs

Linda Smith, the artistic director of the Repertory Dance Theatre in Salt Lake City, was kind enough to give me notes written by one of the company members that related to *Passengers*, which Viola choreographed for that company in 1970. I have included an excerpt from those notes.

PASSENGERS (1970)

Choreographer: Viola Farber   Music: Silence

Passengers shows dancers dancing. Ms. Farber utilizes many of the revolutionary choreographic concepts developed by the avant-garde choreographer, Merce Cunningham, to formulate a compositional structure that allows for chance relationships and spontaneous manipulations of movement material.

Movement sections using individual steps, duets and group work are the basis for a score which may be "rewritten" for every performance. The length and order of the sections is variable and many creative choices are offered to the performers. The work is performed without music. The result is a fresh and inventive experience for the dancers as well as the audience.

Passengers was choreographed in 1970 through collaboration between Repertory Dance Theatre and

Viola Farber's notes on Dinosaur Parts (1974);
from Viola Farber's personal archives.

the Department of Modern Dance at the University of Utah. The piece was set on 12 RDT dancers as well as a larger group of 23 dance students in the dance department who performed their version on a concert April 16, 17, 18, 1970 in Kingsbury Hall under the title of *Intransit*.

RDT continued to perform and tour Passengers for many years and revived the work in 1997, just before Viola died. *Passengers* was very adaptable and could be performed in a variety of spaces and situations.

FACTS:
There are 30 different sections or components
11 dancers have their own "individual" steps or phrases that the dancers may vary.
7 duets
2 trios
10 group sections

For each performance a score is created designating what, where, who, how long. That is, someone may decide how many sections are to be performed, who is to dance in each section, which part of the stage space should be used, how long the sections are to be danced, who will be performing and who will cue the beginning of the sections.
Some sections may occur simultaneously.
Two stopwatches keep track of the time. Dancers on

each side of the stage start the timers.

A dancer may exit to check the time during the performance

The piece should be at least 15-20 minutes long.

PASSENGERS SECTIONS
GROUP sections

Group walk (slow walk)

Men's section

Girl's dance

Run and Fall

Tangle Trio

Lean and Leave

Long Positions

Arm Flips

Point and Swoon

5's and 10's

DUETS

Bill and Joan

Manzell and Linda

Linda Smith and Eric Newton "leg" duet

Rich and Ruth

Tim and Kay

Greg and Lynne

Rick and Kathy

TRIOS

Floppy Trio: (Linda, Bill, others)

It seems appropriate to end this chapter on Viola's choreography with notes from one of her lectures that I found among her personal belongings. It appears in notes from Viola journals and is written in her own hand, on yellow lined legal notebook paper. It is what Viola prepared for one of the many lecture demonstrations in which her company performed while on tour. The notes were not dated, and it is only my guess that it was written in or around 1974, shortly before the completion of her work titled *Dinosaur Parts*, with music by David Tudor. The paper was discovered folded and stuffed inside a notebook that was literally falling apart.

I know from experience that Viola would read from these quickly written notes while onstage during the performance, standing at the podium dressed in her leotard and tights, and barefoot. She usually wrote these lecture/demonstration notes during the early morning hours when she could not sleep. She disliked talking publicly, and she always kept the lecture part of these events at a minimum.

It is certain that there was more to this lecture than is given here. Viola would have gone on to list the other works being performed that day, and she would have introduced each dancer as he or she appeared onstage.

> "In the past when we've done lecture demonstrations we've performed dances and taken care of the lecture part by answering questions after the dancing. My feeling has been that the best thing we could do was our work, which is dancing. I have felt and still do feel that what I say about our work and what we do are two - at least two - different things. I'm also very well aware of the fact that what I say may obscure someone's perception of the thing seen. Still, I've been

thinking about what I do and I have some things I'd like to say about it as long as you realize that what I say is not the whole truth, that what I say is what I say today and to be taken about as seriously as anything you have eaten today.

Dancing does not exist when it's not being done. There is no byproduct, no waste. Each time a dance happens it has a new and different life. We are not the same people now that we were this morning. In all of our works there are sections where the dancers are free to use given material in different ways - by changing sequence, timing, and space, so that what happens from performance to performance in these sections is made, to a large extent, by the dancers who execute it - no matter how set the dance is. Dancers are people - so if my works are about anything they are certainly about people. We are people who spend a great deal of time learning our craft, and our craft or art is one that has no limits - we can never get to the end of what dancing might be. We are individuals of different physical characteristics and we come together from different places, and what has accumulated in our heads, hearts and spirits is obviously different. When we work at dancing we can try to grow into the demands of familiar and new situations, by risking what is safe, what is comfortable, what is secure, nudging at our limitations as individuals and becoming more ourselves. We each go as far as we can go and that can keep us busy forever.

My dances don't have to do with stories, or

with symbols. They do have to do with situations, with people alone and people together - with someone arriving, someone leaving, and someone staying for a while.

I could have all the ideas for dances in the world, but without the dancers who make them happen I'd have nothing. I'm extremely grateful to them all and respect the life each gives to his and her work."

Appendix

<u>A. _Merce Cunningham Dance Company premieres_</u>
<u>_with Viola Farber_</u>

1953 - Banjo, _Dime A Dance, Septet_

1954 - _Minutiae_

1955 - _Springweather and People_

1956 - _Suite For Five, Nocturnes, Galaxy_

1957 - _Labyrinthian Dances, Picnic Polka_

1958 - _Summerspace, Antic Meet_

1959 - _From the Poems of White Stone, Gambit for Dancers and Orchestra, Rune_

1960 - _Crises_

1961 - _Aeon_

1962 - _The Construction of Boston_ (a play)

1963 - _Field Dances, Story_

1964 - _Winterbranch, Cross Currents, Paired_

B. The Viola Farber Dance Company

All Works Choreographed by Viola Farber.

Her archives were incomplete. Some of the information was filled in when dancers in the company provided copies of concert programs. Very often when there is no costume designer listed, it meant that the costumes were designed by Farber herself and constructed by the dancers in the company.

EXCERPT (1968)

Costumes:Albert Hamowy

Dancers: Margaret Jenkins, Dan Wagoner

(Later performed by Anne Koren and Larry Clark)

DUET FOR MIRJAM AND JEFF (1969)

Costumes:Albert Hamowy

Dancers:Mirjam Berns, Jeff Slayton

QUOTA (1969)

Music:Blue Grass

Costumes:Albert Hamowy

Dancers:Margaret Jenkins, June Finch, Viola Farber

PASSAGE (1969)

Costumes:Albert Hamowy

Dancers:Larry Clark, Viola Farber, June Finch, Anne Koren, Andé Peck, Jeff Slayton

STANDBY (1969)

Choreographed and performed by: Viola Farber

TENDENCY (1970)

Costumes: Albert Hamowy

Dancers:Viola Farber, Jeff Slayton

AREA CODE (1970)

Costumes:Albert Hamowy

Dancers:June Finch, Andé Peck

CURRICULUM (1970)

Dancers:Viola Farber, June Finch, Andé Peck

CO-OP (1970)

Timer:Viola Farber

Dancers:Larry Clark, June Finch, Anne Koren, Rosalind Newman, Andé Peck, Jeff Slayton

SURVEY (1971)

Costumes:Albert Hamowy

Dancers:Larry Clark, June Finch, Anne Koren, Rosalind Newman, Andé Peck, Jeff Slayton

PATIENCE (1971)

Dancers:Larry Clark, Viola Farber, June Finch, Anne Koren, Rosalind Newman, Andé Peck, Jeff Slayton

MILDRED (1970)

Music:Carl Czerny

Costume:Albert Hamowy

Dancer:Viola Farber

DEFAULT (1972)

Dancers:Viola Farber, Jeff Slayton

ROUTE 6 (1972)

Music:Longines Radio Favorites

Costumes:Albert Hamowy

Dancers:Viola Farber, Andé Peck, Jeff Slayton

DUNE (1972)

Music:Alvin Lucier: *I Am Sitting In A Room*

Costumes:Albert Hamowy

Dancers:Larry Clark, Viola Farber, June Finch, Anne Koren,
Susan Matheke, Andé Peck, Jeff Slayton

POOR EDDIE (1972)

Music:Alvin Lucier: *World Music System 1 For Bowed Stringed Instruments*
(1972)

Costumes:Albert Hamowy

Dancers:Viola Farber, Anne Koren, Andé Peck, Jeff Slayton

SOUP (1973)

Music:Alvin Lucier

Dancers:Larry Clark, Viola Farber, June Finch, Anne Koren,

Susan Matheke, Andé Peck, Jeff Slayton

SPARE CHANGE (1973)

Music:Alvin Lucier: *North American Time Capsule* (1967)

Costumes:Viola Farber

Dancers:Larry Clark, June Finch, Anne Koren, Susan Matheke, Andé Peck, Jeff Slayton

WILLI I (1974)

Music:Alvin Lucier: *The Fires In The Minds Of The Dancers*

Costumes:Sally Hess

Dancers:Larry Clark, Viola Farber, Willi Feuer, June Finch, Anne Koren, Susan Matheke, Andé Peck, Jeff Slayton

SOME OF THE SYMPTOMS (1974)

Choreographed and performed by: Viola Farber

DINOSAUR PARTS (1974)

Music:David Tudor: Dinosaur Parts (1974)

Dancers:Larry Clark, Viola Farber, Willi Feuer, June Finch, Anne Koren, Susan Matheke, Andé Peck, Jeff Slayton

NO SUPER, NO BOILER (1974)

Music:Alvin Lucier, Pat Richter

Dancers and Performers: Larry Clark, John Conlon, Viola Farber, Willi Feuer,

June Finch, Anne Koren, Susan Matheke, Andé Peck,

Jeff Slayton

357

DEFENDANT (1974)

Choreographed and performed by: Viola Farber

HOUSEGUEST (1974)

Sound:Alvin Lucier (Beginning in 1975, Houseguest was performed in silence.)

Dancer:Jeff Slayton

MOTORCYCLE/BOAT (1975)

Music: Alvin Lucier

Costumes:Michael Watson

Dancers:Larry Clark, Viola Farber, Willi Feuer, June Finch, Anne Koren, Susan Matheke, Andé Peck, Jeff Slayton

NIGHT SHADE (1975)

Music:Ludwig van Beethoven, *Opus 27, No. 2*

Costumes:Viola Farber

Dancers:Larry Clark, Viola Farber, Willi Feuer, June Finch, Anne Koren, Susan Matheke, Andé Peck, Jeff Slayton

DUET FOR WILLI AND SUSAN (1975)

Music:Alvin Lucier

Costumes:Viola Farber

Dancers:Susan Matheke, Willi Feuer

FIVE WORKS FOR SNEAKERS (1976)

Costumes:Viola Farber

Dancers:Jumay Chu, Larry Clark, Viola Farber, Willi Feuer, Anne Koren, Susan Matheke, Andé Peck, Jeff Slayton

SOME THINGS I CAN REMEMBER (1976)

Music: Pat Richter

Dancer:Viola Farber

SUNDAY AFTERNOON (1976)

Music:Alvin Lucier: *Vespers*

Costumes:Viola Farber

Dancers:Jumay Chu, Larry Clark, Viola Farber, Willi Feuer, Anne Koren, Susan Matheke, Andé Peck, Jeff Slayton

BRAZOS RIVER - Video for Dance (1977)

Music:David Tudor, Alvin Lucier

Costumes:Robert Rauschenberg

Director:Dan Parr

Dancers:Jumay Chu, Larry Clark, Viola Farber, Willi Feuer, Anne Koren, Susan Matheke, Andé Peck, Jeff Slayton

LEAD US NOT INTO PENN STATION (1977)

Music:Alvin Lucier

Dancers:Jumay Chu, Larry Clark, Viola Farber, Willi Feuer, Anne Koren, Susan Matheke, Andé Peck, Jeff Slayton

SOLO (1977)

Choreographed and performed by: Viola Farber

TURF (1978)

Music:Poulenc: *Organ Concerto in G Minor*

Dancers:Larry Clark, Viola Farber, Willi Feuer, Andé Peck, Jeff Slayton

DOUBLEWALK (1978)

Music: Traditional Country and Western

Costumes: Viola Farber and Jeff Slayton

Dancers:Viola Farber, Jeff Slayton

PRIVATE RELATIONS (1978)

Music:Tapiola Children's Choir

Dancers:Jumay Chu, Michael Cichetti, Larry Clark, Viola Farber, Anne Koren, Ed Henry, Susan Matheke, Andé Peck

DANDELION (1978)

Costumes: Robert Rauschenberg

Dancers:Michael Cichetti, Larry Clark, Viola Farber, Anne Koren, Ed Henry, Susan Matheke

LOCAL (1978)

Music:Alan Evans

Dancers:Michael Cichetti, Larry Clark, Anne Koren, Karen Levey, Joël Leucht

DUET (1979)

Costumes:John Daygar

Dancers:Jumay Chu, Anne Koren

LEDGE (1979)

Music:Jean-Pierre Drouet

Costumes:Lois Long

Dancers:Michael Cichetti, Robert Foltz, Anne Koren, Karen Levey, Joël Leucht

TIDE (1979)

Costumes:Lois Long

Dancers:Michael Cichetti, Viola Farber, Robert Foltz, Anne Koren, Karen Levey, Joël Leucht

TRACKS (1980)

Costumes:Robert Rauschenberg

Dancers:Michael Cichetti, Viola Farber, Robert Foltz, Anne Koren, Karen Levey, Joël Leucht

FREEHOLD (1980)

Dancers:Michael Cichetti, Viola Farber, Robert Foltz, Anne Koren, Karen Levey, Joël Leucht

BRIGHT STREAM (1980)

Music: Alan Evans

Costumes:Denise Mitchell

Dancers:Michael Cichetti, Robert Foltz, Mary Good, Anne Koren, Karen Levey, Joël Leucht

BEQUEST (1981)

Music:Felix Mendelssohn, *Trio in D Minor No.1, Opus 49*

Costumes:Denise Mitchell

Dancers:Michael Cichetti, Viola Farber, Robert Foltz, Mary Good, Anne Koren, Karen Levey, Joël Leucht

CINQ POUR DIX (1981)

Music:Michel Portal, Henri Texier

Lighting:Claude Noel

Costumes:François Garotte

Dancers:Anne Koren, Michael Cichetti, Didier Deschamps, Robert Foltz, Chantal de Launay, Joël Leucht, Nadège Macleay, Mathilde Monnier, Sylvain Richard, Claire Verlet

ATTENTE (1981)

Music:Villa-Lobos, *Bachianas Brasileiras No. 1 and No. 5*

Lighting:Claude Noel

Costumes and Sets:Francois Garotte, Bernard Prigent

Dancers:Anne Koren, Michael Cichetti, Didier Deschamps, Robert Foltz, Chantal de Launay, Joël Leucht, Nadège Macleay, Mathilde Monnier, Sylvain Richard, Claire Verlet

VILLA-DUAGE (1981)

Music:Michel Portal

Lighting:Claude Noel

Costumes:François Garotte

Dancers:Anne Koren, Michael Cichetti, Didier Deschamps, Robert Foltz, Chantal de Launay, Joël Leucht, Nadège Macleay, Mathilde Monnier, Sylvain Richard, Claire Verlet

ETUDES (1982)

Music:Dominique Lofficial on piano

Costumes:Claude Noel

Dancers:Anne Koren, Michael Cichetti, Didier Deschamps, Robert Foltz, Chantal de Launay, Joël Leucht, Nadège Macleay,

Mathilde Monnier, Sylvain Richard, Claire Verlet

ECHANGES (1982)

Music:David Tudor

Costumes:Claude Noel

Dancers:Anne Koren, Michael Cichetti, Didier Deschamps, Robert Foltz, Chantal de Launay, Joël Leucht, Nadège Macleay,

Mathilde Monnier, Sylvain Richard, Claire Verlet

ÉCRITURES SUR L'EAU (1983)

Music:Dominique Lofficial

Musicians:Merzack Moutana, percussions

François Mechali, contrebasse

Dominique Lofficial, piano

Lighting:Fritz Reinhart

Rehearsal Director: Karen Levey

Dancers:Anne Koren, Assistante - Rehearsal Director

Chantal de Launay, Didier Deschamps, Jean-François Duroure,

David Liebart, Joël Leucht, Nadège Macleay, Mathilde Monnier,

Sylvain Richard, Claire Verlet

C. Other Works by Viola Farber

TITLE	COMPANY	DATE
Seconds	Viola Farber	1965
Notebook	June Finch, Margaret Jenkins, Dan Wagoner, Rosalind Newman	1966
Time Out	Viola Farber	1968
Legacy	Viola Farber	1968
Tristan and Iseult	Viola Farber, Don Redlich (Collaboration)	1969
The Music of Conlon Nancarrow	Viola Farber, Peter Saul	1969
Passengers	Repertory Dance Theater	1970
Pop. 18	Ohio State University, Columbus	1971
Pop. 11	NYU Performing Arts, New York City	1971
Five In The Morning	Repertory Dance Theater	1971
Window	Ruth Currier Dance Company	1972
Untitled Work	University of Michigan, Ann Arbor	1973
Minnesota Mash	University of Minnesota, Minneapolis	1975
Untitled Work	Margaret Jenkins Workshop San Francisco	1976

TITLE	COMPANY	DATE
Temporary Site	Nancy Hauser Dance Company	1976
Autumn Fields	Ballet Theatre Contemporaine, Angers	1977
Untitled Work	Viola Farber Workshop, New York City	1977
Transfer	Nancy Hauser Dance Company	1977
Jeux Choréographique	Ballet Theatre Français and Larry Clark, Lyon	1979
Clearing	Ze'eva Cohen	1979
Untitled Work	Janet Gillespie and Present Co.	1980
Just Correspondence	Viola Farber, Jeff Slayton (Collaboration)	1980
Tea For Three	Viola Farber, Sarah Stackhouse	1981
Untitled Work	Susannah Payton-Newman	1981
Untitled Work	Viola Farber Workshop, New York City	1981
Meanwhile Back In The City	Long Beach Summer School of Dance	1982
Untitled Work	Viola Farber, Jeff Slayton (Collaboration)	1983
Last Waltz	Viola Farber, Jeff Slayton (Collaboration)	1984
Day's Return	Long Beach Summer School of Dance	1984

TITLE	COMPANY	DATE
Venom and Antidotes	London Contemporary Dance School	1984
Autumn Edge	London Contemporary Dance School	1984
January	Television South West, London	1985
Bank Holiday	London Contemporary Dance School	1987
Passing	London Contemporary Dance School	1987
Winter Rumors	Extemporary Dance Theatre, London	1987
Take-Away	Extemporary Dance Theatre, London	1987
Preludes	National Youth Dance Company, London	1987
Preludes	New Dance Ensemble	1988
Last Call	Douglas Nielsen	1989
Ainsi de Suite	Viola Farber, Mathilde Monnier (Collaboration)	1992
Threestep (Shipwreck)	Viola Farber, Ralph Lemon (Collaboration)	1994
Dreams of Wind and Dust	CE DE CE, Setubal, Portugal	1996
It's Been A While	Viola Farber, Jeff Slayton (Collaboration)	1996

List of Photographs

1. Dora Farber, family photograph, Germany, April 1919.
2. Left to right: Viola's sister Irene, Viola at age 6 months, Dora Farber, Elisabeth; family photograph, Heidelberg, Germany, 1931.
3. Left to right: Eduard Farber, Dora Farber, Anna (Nanny), Irene, and Elisabeth on a family walk, Germany, 1934.
4. Viola at age 2 (center) with her sisters Elisabeth and Irene; family photograph, Heidelberg, Germany, 1933.
5. Left to right: Elisabeth, Viola, Irene; family photograph, Heidelberg, Germany, circa 1935.
6. Left to right: Irene, Elisabeth, Viola at age 4, Eduard Farber; family photograph, Ziegelhausen, Germany, Spring 1935.
7. Left to right: Elisabeth, Eduard, Viola, Irene; family photograph, Heidelberg,Germany, 1937.
8. Farber family boarding the ship Europa to sail to America. Left to right: unknownWoman, Irene, Elisabeth, Eduard, Viola, Dora; family photograph, Brennerhaven,Germany, July 19, 1938.
9. Farber family at dinner aboard the passenger ship *Europa* while sailing to America; family photograph, July 24, 1938.
10. Viola at age 12; family photograph, New Haven, Conn., 1943.
11. Viola at age 20; family photograph, Washington, D.C., 1951.
12. Viola in Washington, D.C.; family photograph, 1952.
13. *Septet* (1953). Left to right: Merce Cunningham, Viola Farber,

Steve Paxton. Photographer unknown. Copyright: Cunningham Dance Foundation.

14. Dora Farber; family photograph, 1955.

15. Eduard Farber at work; photographer unknown. Washington, D.C., circa 1955.

16. *Nocturnes* (1956), Left to right: Viola Farber, Bruce King, Remy Charlip,Carolyn Brown, Merce Cunningham. Photographer: Louis A. Stevenson, Jr.

17. Viola with her father, Washington, D.C., 1957, family photograph.

18. *Nocturnes* (1956), Merce Cunningham and Viola Farber, Photographer: Louis A. Stevenson, Jr.

19. *Nocturnes* (1956), Merce Cunningham and Viola Farber, Photographer: Richard Rutledge.

20. Viola Farber in Merce Cunningham's *Summerspace* (1958), Photographer: Richard Rutledge.

21. Viola and Susan Rossin horseback riding in Helmville, Montana on the Rossin's ranch. Photograph by Alfred Rossin, circa 1958.

22. Viola with dancer friends at the Meher Baba Center in Myrtle Beach, South Carolina, 1959. Photograph property of the Viola Farber Archives.

23. Viola Farber and Merce Cunningham in *Crises*, 1960. Photographer: Harry Shunk.

24. Viola Farber and Merce Cunningham in *Crises*, 1960. Photographer: Harry Shunk.

25. Viola Farber and Merce Cunningham in *Crises*, 1960. Photographer: John Wulp

26. Heidelberg, Germany; family photograph.

27. Painting by Jasper Johns titled *Portrait – Viola Farber* (1961-1962),

with window closed. Photograph by Rudolph Burckhardt. Art ©
Jasper Johns/Licensed by VAGA, New York, NY

28. Painting by Jasper Johns titled *Portrait – Viola Farber* (1961-1962),
with window open. Photograph by Rudolph Burckhardt. Art ©
Jasper Johns/Licensed by VAGA, New York, NY

29. *Aeon*, Merce Cunningham Dance Company. Left to right: Steve
Paxton, Carolyn Brown, Judith Dunn, Marilyn Wood, Viola Farber,
Shareen Blair (on floor). Photographer: Robert Rauschenberg

30. Left to right: Viola Farber, Merce Cunningham, Carolyn Brown
in *Story*, 1963, Photographer: Marvin Silver

31. Viola at the American Dance Festival, Connecticut College, New
Haven, CT., 1964, Photographer: Remy Charlip

32. Barbara Lloyd and Viola in Tokyo, Japan during the World Tour
with the Cunningham company, 1964. Photographer unknown.

33. Viola and Merce Cunningham in *Paired*, 1964. Photographer:
Sig T. Karlsson.

34. Meher Baba; photograph curiosity of the Meher Spiritual Center,
Inc.

35. Viola in *Legacy*, 1968. Photographer: Teresa King

36. Left to right: Viola Farber, Andé Peck, June Finch in Viola's
Curriculum, 1970. Photographer: Teresa King

37. Viola Farber and Jeff Slayton in *Tendency*, 1970. Photographer:
Teresa King

38. Viola Farber in *Tendency*, 1970. Photographer: Teresa King

39. Class at the Viola Farber Dance Studio, White Street, New York,
NY, 1970. Photographer: Babette Mangolte

40. Viola Farber and June Finch in rehearsal for *Curriculum*, 1970.
Photographer: Mark Lancaster

41. Left to right: Andé Peck, June Finch, Anne Koren, Larry Clark,

Rosalind Newman in Farber's *Survey*, 1971. Photographer: Teresa King

42. Viola Farber in *Mildred*, 1971. Photographer: Jack Mitchell

43. Viola Farber and Jeff Slayton, circa 1972. Photographer: Terry Stevenson

44. Andé Peck, Viola Farber and Jeff Slayton in rehearsal for *Route 6*, 1972. Photographer: Mark Lancaster

45. Jeff Slayton and Viola Farber in *Route 6*, 1972. Photographer: Mary Lucier

46. Left to right: Jeff Slayton, Viola Farber, Andé Peck, Anne Koren in Farber's *Poor Eddie*, 1972. Photographer: Mary Lucier

47. Left to right: Viola Farber, John Conlon (actor), June Finch, and Alvin Lucier (musician/composer) in Farber's *No Super, No Boiler*, 1974. Photographer: Mary Lucier

48. Alvin Lucier, 1974. Photographer: Mary Lucier

49. Viola Farber, *Sneakers, Dances In Public Places*, 1974, IDS Building lobby in Minneapolis, MN. Photographer: B. Hagen

50. Viola Farber Dance Company in *Sneakers, Dances In Public Places*, 1974, IDS Building lobby in Minneapolis, MN. , 1974, IDS Building lobby in Minneapolis, MN. Left to Right: Viola Farber, Anne Koren, Andé Peck. Photographer: B. Hagen

51. Viola Farber Dance Company in *Sneakers, Dances In Public Places*, 1974, at the Staten Island Ferry Terminal Building, Staten Island, NJ. Left to Right: Viola Farber, Susan Matheke, Jeff Slayton, Willi Feuer, Anne Koren, Andé Peck. Photographer: David Schmidlapp

52. Left to right: Viola Farber, Jeff Slayton (front), June Finch, Willi Feuer in Farber's *Willi I*, 1974. Photographer: Johan Elbers

53. Left to right: Jeff Slayton, Andé Peck, Anne Koren, Viola Farber, Willi Feuer in Farber's *Willi I*, 1974. Photographer: Johan Elbers

54. Viola Farber's notes on *Dinosaur Parts* (1974); from Viola Farber's personal archives.

55. Left to right: Viola Farber (at the piano), Willi Feuer, June Finch, Susan Matheke, Andé Peck in Farber's *Night Shade*, 1975. Photographer:

56. Jeff Slayton, Viola Farber in *Night Shade*, 1975. Photographer: Susan Cook

57. Viola Farber watching company rehearsal, circa 1976. Photographer: Susan Cook.

58. Farber company in rehearsal, Broadway/Bleeker studio, circa 1976. Left to right: Viola Farber (seated), Larry Clark, Anne Koren, June Finch, Willi Feuer, Jeff Slayton, Susan Matheke, and Andé Peck. Photographer: Chuck Osgood

59. Composer/musician David Tudor preparing his sound equipment for *Brazos River*, Fort Worth Museum of Contemporary Art, Fort Worth, TX., 1976.Photographer: David Wharton

60. Robert Rauschenberg with Director Dan Parr on the set of *Brazos River*, Fort Worth Museum of Contemporary Art, Fort Worth, TX. 1976. Photographer: David Wharton

61. Larry Clark, Ande Peck, Jeff Slayton on the set of *Brazos River*, Fort Worth Museum of Contemporary Art, Fort Worth, TX., 1976. Photographer: David Wharton

62. Farber company in *Lead Us Not Into Penn Station*, 1977. Left to Right: Anne Koren, Willi Feuer, Susan Matheke, Larry Clark, Andé Peck, Jumay Chu, Jeff Slayton. Photographer: Johan Elbers

63. Farber company in *Turf*, 1978. Left to right: Viola Farber, Andé Peck (on floor), Larry Clark, Jeff Slayton. Photographer: Johan Elbers

64. Left to right: Jeff Slayton, Viola Farber, Irene and Bob Aikin (Viola's sister and husband), Elisabeth and Lawrence Lanzl (Viola's

eldest sister and husband), 1978, at the Aiken's home in Woodside, CA. Family photograph.

65. Viola Farber, Jeff Slayton, 1978, Woodside, CA. Family photograph.

66. Michael Cichetti and Viola Farber in Farber's *Bright Stream*, 1980. Photographer: Susan Cook

67. Farber's *Untitled*, 1980. Left to right: Joël Leucht, Larry Clark, Jumay Chu, Andé Peck, Anne Koren, Michael Cichetti, Karen Levey. Photographer: Unknown

68. Jeff Slayton and Viola Farber in rehearsal at the Abbaye de Pont a Mousson, France. Circa 1980. Photographer: Unknown.

69. Viola Farber teaching a technique class, location and photographer unknown.

70. Viola Farber in *Bequest*, 1981. Photographer: Lois Greenfield

71. Company rehearsing *Attente* at the Centre National de Danse Contemporaine d'Angers, 1981. Photographer: Pierre Petitjean

72. Viola (center) with her two sisters Irene Aiken and Elisabeth Lanzl, Cannon Beach, OR. 1988. Family photograph.

73. Viola (center) with her two sisters Irene Aiken and Elisabeth Lanzl clowning around at Cannon Beach, OR., 1988; family photograph.

74. Viola Scheffler, Viola's Godmother, 1988.

75. Viola Farber, shortly after her battle with cancer, with Mathilde Monnier in Montpellier, France, 1992. Photographer: Brian Ashley

76. Viola Farber at Sarah Lawrence College, Bronxville, NY, 1995, Photographer: Brian Ashley

77. Viola Farber, Ralph Lemon in Threestep (Shipwreck) at the Joyce Theatre in New York, 1995, Photographer: Sara Krulwich

78. Former members of the Viola Farber Dance Company outside the

Joyce Theatre in New York City following the memorial for Viola Farber, 1999. <u>Left to right</u>: Seated: Mirjam Berns, Larry Clark. Front row: June Finch, Karen Levey, Susan Matheke with son Louis Feuer, Jeff Slayton. Middle row: Anne Koren, Jumay Chu, Didier Deschamps, Willi Feuer. Back row: Joël Leucht, Andé Peck. Photographer: Teresa King

79. Letter of condolence from the Ambassador de France, January 6, 1999.

80. Susan Matheke, Larry Clark in *Spare Change* (1973), choreography: Viola Farber. Photographer: Mary Lucier

Bibliography

Viola Farber Dance Company Archives, 3137 San Francisco Avenue, Long Beach, CA. 90806. Includes company concert programs; promotional materials; booking and other business related materials; photographs; Viola Farber's personal journals and notes; personal letters. Pg. 63-65, 77-78, 81-82, 179-182, 192-195, 200-202, 210-216, 279-280, 282, 284, 295-296, 299-303, 306-307

The Cunningham Dance Foundation Archives, 1995, 55 Bethune Street, New York, NY, 10014. Reviews, articles, and photographs.

Merce Cunningham: Fifty Years, David Vaughan, copyright 1997, published by Aperture, 20 East 23rd Street, New York, NY. Pg. 40, 57

Oral History: Viola Farber, Rose Ann Thom, 1991, New York Public Library for the Performing Arts, New York, NY.

The Dance of Love: My Life With Meher Baba, Margaret Craske, Copyright 1980, Sheriar Press, 801 13th Street, Myrtle Beach, SC. 29582. Pg. 49

The Village Voice, New York, NY, February 24, 1960, Dance review of the Merce Cunningham Dance Company by Jill Johnston. Pg. 57

Dance and Dancers, London, July 19, 1964, Dance review of the Merce Cunningham Dance Company by Clive Barnes. Pg. 60

The Village Voice, New York, April 9, 1964, *Paired*, Dance review of the Merce Cunningham Dance Company by Jill Johnston. Pg. 57

Dancemagazine, New York, April 1965, Dance review of the Merce Cunningham Dance Company by Marcia Marks. Pg. 58

Le Combat, Paris, France, June 18, 1964, Dance review of the Merce Cunningham Dance Company by Dinah Maggie. Pg. 53

The Times of India, Bombay, October 16, 1964, Dance review of the Merce Cunningham Dance Company, author unknown. Pg. 54

The Times of India, Bombay, October 17, 1964, Dance review of the Merce Cunningham Dance Company, author unknown. Pg. 54

Ode 4 Viola, poem by Steve Paxton, circa 1962, from the Viola Farber Dance Company Archives, 3137 San Francisco Avenue, Long Beach, CA. 90806. Pg. 63-65

The Village Voice, New York, November 12, 1970, review by dance critic Deborah Jowitt. Pg. 334

Dance and Dancers, Vol. 23: No. 1: Issue 265, January, 1972, review by John Percival, Paris performance of the Viola Farber Dance Company. Pg. 92

The Drummer, Philadelphia, PA., 1972, newspaper article by Alexandra Grilikhes. Pg. 293

<u>Reader</u>, Chicago, IL, October 11, 1974, article by Sally Banes and Ellen Mazer. Pg. 129

<u>The Village Voice</u>, New York, NY, December 1, 1975, review by dance critic Deborah Jowitt. Pg. 126

<u>Soho Weekly News</u>, New York, NY, November 20, 1975, review by Robert J. Pierce. Pg. 290

<u>The Dallas Morning News</u>, Dallas TX,, December 20, 1976, article by Patty Moore. Pg. 327

<u>Dancemagazine</u>, New York, NY, February 1976, review by Robb Baker. Pg. 146, 290

<u>Dancemagazine</u>, New York, NY, April 1977, article by Carol Egan. Pg. 293

<u>New York Times</u>, New York, NY, February 26, 1978, review by Jack Anderson. Pg. 132

<u>New York Guide</u>, New York, NY, 1979, article by Brett Raphael and Tullia Bohen. Pg. 297

<u>Minnesota Daily</u>, Minneapolis, MN, February 2, 1979, review by Allen Robertson. Pg. 295

<u>Cityside</u>, Milwaukee, WI, 1979, interview with Viola Farber by Angela LaMaster. Pg. 151, 337

<u>Cityside</u>, Milwaukee, WI, 1979, interview with Viola Farber by Angela LaMaster. Pg. 151-152

<u>The New Yorker</u>, New York, NY, April 20, 1981, review by Arlene Croce. Pg. 189

<u>CNAC</u>, France, 1982, magazine article by Marcelle Michel. Pg. 289

<u>Passion</u>, London, England, 1983, review by . Pg. 169

Video tape <u>Interview with Viola Farber</u>, Hollins College, Roanoke, VA, 1993, by DonnaFaye Burchfield. Pg. 223-224

<u>New York Times</u>, New York, NY, October 3, 1995, article Jennifer Dunning. Pg. 255

<u>New York Times</u>, New York, NY, October 5, 1995, review by Anna Kisselgoff. Pg. 219

<u>New York Times</u>, New York, NY, October 1995, review by Tobi Tobias. Pg. 219

<u>New York Times</u>, New York, NY, December 31, 1998, Viola Farber obituary by Jennifer Dunning. Pg. 255

<u>Centre National de Danse Contemporaine Archives</u>, Angers, France, April 1999. Concert programs and promotional materials. Pg. 319-321

<u>Repertory Dance Theatre Archives</u>, Salt Lake City, UT, 2003 and 2004. Company archival materials relating to the cast of *Passengers* supplied by RDT company management. Pg. 303-305

Interview with Viola Farber by Jeff Slayton, 1995 in Bronxville, NY. Throughout entire book.

Interview with Larry Clark, 1995, New York, NY. Pg. 73-75, 88-89, 120, 271, 287

Interview with June Finch, 1995, New York, NY. Pg. 69, 79, 92-93

Interview with Sylvain Richard, 2004. Pg. 164-166, 171, 174, 176, 268

Interview with Elisabeth Lanzl (Farber's sister), 1995, Chicago, IL. Pg. 12, 14, 16, 37, 78

Interview with Irene Aikin (Farber's sister), 1996, Hood River, OR. Pg. 14, 16, 18, 26-28, 37

Letters from Viola Farber to Jeff Slayton. Pg. 69-71, 155-157, 159-162, 172, 176-177

Index

Printed in the United States
92618LV00004B/20/A